Blackstone's
Police Q& A

Crime 2009

Blackstone's
Police Q&A
Crime 2009

Seventh edition

Huw Smart and John Watson

OXFORD
UNIVERSITY PRESS

OXFORD
UNIVERSITY PRESS

Great Clarendon Street, Oxford OX2 6DP

Oxford University Press is a department of the University of Oxford.
It furthers the University's objective of excellence in research, scholarship,
and education by publishing worldwide in

Oxford New York

Auckland Cape Town Dar es Salaam Hong Kong Karachi
Kuala Lumpur Madrid Melbourne Mexico City Nairobi
New Delhi Shanghai Taipei Toronto

With offices in

Argentina Austria Brazil Chile Czech Republic France Greece
Guatemala Hungary Italy Japan Poland Portugal Singapore
South Korea Switzerland Thailand Turkey Ukraine Vietnam

Published in the United States
by Oxford University Press Inc., New York

British Library Cataloguing in Publication Data

Data available

Library of Congress Cataloging in Publication Data

Data available

Typeset by Laserwords Private Limited, Chennai, India
Printed in Great Britain
on acid-free paper by
Ashford Colour Press Limited, Gosport, Hampshire

ISBN 978-0-19-954767-8

10 9 8 7 6 5 4 3 2 1

Contents

Contents

Introduction

Before you get into the detail of this book, there are two myths about multiple-choice questions (MCQs) that we need to get out of the way right at the start:

1. that they are easy to answer;
2. that they are easy to write.

Take one look at a professionally designed and properly developed exam paper such as those used by the Police Promotion Examinations Board or the National Board of Medical Examiners in the US and the first myth collapses straight away. Contrary to what some people believe, MCQs are not an easy solution for examiners and not a 'multiple-guess' soft option for examinees.

That is not to say that *all* MCQs are taxing, or even testing — in the psychometric sense. If MCQs are to have any real value at all, they need to be carefully designed and follow some agreed basic rules.

And this leads us to myth number 2.

It is widely assumed by many people and educational organisations that anyone with the knowledge of a subject can write MCQs. You need only look at how few MCQ writing courses are offered by training providers in the UK to see just how far this myth is believed. Similarly, you need only to have a go at a few badly designed MCQs to realise that it is a myth nonetheless. Writing bad MCQs is easy; writing good ones is no easier than answering them!

As with many things, the design of MCQs benefits considerably from time, training and experience. Many MCQ writers fall easily and often unwittingly into the trap of making their questions too hard, too easy or too obscure, or completely different from the type of question that you will eventually encounter in your own particular exam. Others seem to use the MCQ as a way to catch people out or to show how smart they, the authors, are (or think they are).

There are several purposes for which MCQs are very useful. The first is in producing a reliable, valid and fair test of knowledge and understanding across a wide range of subject matter. Another is an aid to study, preparation and revision for such examinations and tests. The differences in objective mean that there are slight differences in the rules that the MCQ writers follow. Whereas the design of fully validated MCQs to be used in high stakes examinations which will effectively determine who passes and who fails have very strict guidelines as to construction, content and style, less stringent rules apply to MCQs that are being used for teaching and revision. For that reason, there may be types of MCQ that are appropriate in the latter setting which would not be used in the former. However, in developing the MCQs for this book, the authors have tried to follow the fundamental rules of MCQ design but they would not claim to have replicated the level of psychometric rigour that is — and has to be — adopted by the type of examining bodies referred to above.

These MCQs are designed to reinforce your knowledge and understanding, to highlight any gaps or weaknesses in that knowledge and understanding and to help focus your revision of the relevant topics.

I hope that we have achieved that aim.

Good luck!

Blackstone's Police Q&As — Special Features

References to Blackstone's Police Manuals

Every answer is followed by a paragraph reference to Blackstone's Police Manuals. This means that once you have attempted a question and looked at an answer, the Manual can immediately be referred to for help and clarification.

Unique numbers for each question

Each question and answer has the same unique number. This should ensure that there is no confusion as to which question is linked to which answer. For example, Question 2.1 is linked to Answer 2.1.

Checklists

The checklists are designed to help you keep track of your progress when answering the multiple choice questions. If you fill in the checklist after attempting a question, you will be able to check how many you got right on the first attempt and will know immediately which questions need to be revisited a second time. Please visit www.blackstonespolicemanuals.com and click through to the Blackstone's Police Q&As 2009 page. You will then find electronic versions of the checklists to download and print out. Email any queries or comments on the book to: police.uk@oup.com

Acknowledgements

This book has been written as an accompaniment to Blackstone's Police Manuals, and will test the knowledge you have accrued through reading that series. It is of the essence that full study of the relevant chapters in each Police Manual is completed prior to attempting the Questions and Answers. As qualified police trainers we recognise that students tend to answer questions incorrectly either because they don't read the question properly, or because one of the 'distracters' has done its work. The distracter is one of the three incorrect answers in a multiple-choice question (MCQ), and is designed to distract you from the correct answer and in this way discriminate between candidates: the better-prepared candidate not being 'distracted'.

So particular attention should be paid to the *Answers* sections, and students should ask themselves 'Why did I get that question wrong?' and, just as importantly, 'Why did I get that question right?' Combining the information gained in the *Answers* section together with re-reading the chapter in the Police Manuals should lead to greater understanding of the subject matter.

The authors wish to thank all the staff at Oxford University Press who have helped put this publication together. We would also like to show appreciation to Alistair MacQueen for his vision and support, without which this project would never have been started; also Fraser Sampson, consultant editor of Blackstone's Police Manuals, whose influence on these Q&As is appreciated.

Huw would like to thank Caroline for her constant love, support and understanding over the past year — and her ability to withstand the pressures of being the partner to a workaholic! Special thanks to Lawrence and Maddie — two perfect young adults. Last but not least, love and special affection to Haf and Nia, two beautiful young girls.

John would like to thank Sue, David, Catherine and Andrew for their continued support, and understanding that 'deadline' means 'deadline'.

1 | State of Mind

STUDY PREPARATION

This chapter looks at the 'recipe ingredients' that make the offence cake, in other words what has to be present for the offence to be made out.

One of the most important ingredients is *mens rea*, a person's awareness of the fact that his or her conduct is criminal, and is the mental element. Your knowledge of this is tested together with other important states of mind like intent, negligence and recklessness, and even 'strict liability' which requires no fault element.

The chapter goes on to test how some states of mind can be 'transferred'.

When answering questions in this chapter you should remember that although they are based on substantive offences committed, they are testing the general principles of criminal law.

QUESTIONS

Question 1.1

GULLIVER hates his wife and plans to kill her. He intends to cut her throat on Tuesday morning whilst she is still asleep. On Monday, GULLIVER picks his wife up from work and is driving home; he is deep in thought about the following day's planned action. Owing to his inattentiveness, GULLIVER drives through a red light, and his car is struck on his wife's side. She dies as a result of the accident.

   Could GULLIVER be guilty of murder in these circumstances?

A Yes, as he has achieved his desired outcome.

B Yes, as he was thinking about the murder at the time of the accident.

C No, he cannot be guilty of murder in these circumstances.

D No, but he could be guilty of manslaughter.

Question 1.2

SULLIVAN had been lawfully arrested by an officer for being in possession of counterfeit currency. Due to SULLIVAN'S violent conduct, the officer had placed handcuffs on SULLIVAN and still had the counterfeit currency in his hand. SULLIVAN saw her opportunity to destroy the evidence and tried to snatch the note out the officer's hand using her mouth and teeth. During this action she bit the officer on the hand, drawing blood.

Considering the concept of 'recklessness' has SULLIVAN committed an assault on the police officer?

A Yes, as there was an obvious risk of contact with the officer's hand and the defendant took that risk.

B Yes, as the defendant was reckless as to the extent of injury she might have inflicted on the officer.

C No, the assault was committed accidentally; there was no intention to injure the officer.

D No, the defendant was not reckless as to whether she injured the officer; she was reckless as to whether she would destroy the evidence.

Question 1.3

A few, relatively rare offences can be committed by 'negligence'. However there are offences that do, in effect, often impose liability for negligence but that also demand a mental element.

In relation to this, which of the following is correct in relation to that 'mental element'?

A The prosecution would have to prove that the defendant had a particular state of mind.

B The prosecution must show that the defendant was aware of a risk yet still took it.

C It is what the reasonable man in the circumstances would have believed that is important.

D It is what the accused believed in the actual circumstances that is important.

Question 1.4

GLADWIN was in a crowded pub and was larking about with her friends. She decided to throw a pint of beer over her friend, WITHERALL. Unfortunately the glass slipped out of her hand and smashed in WITHERALL's face, causing cuts which required stitches.

In relation to assault occasioning actual bodily harm, what must be proved?

A Intention to commit any type of assault.

B Intention to cause the harm actually caused.

C Recklessness as to the assault itself.

D Recklessness as to the injury actually caused.

Question 1.5

JEFFRIES is a bit of a risk taker. In front of him are 100 chocolates, one of which he knows contains sufficient arsenic to kill someone should they eat it. He takes 25 of the chocolates and puts them in a bag and offers them out to friends, he also eats some himself. JEFFRIES has no way of knowing whether the chocolates in the bag contain the poisoned one or not, and because of that he does not foresee a real risk in what he does.

In relation to the legal notion of recklessness as outlined in *R v G and R* [2003] 3 WLR 1060, which of the following best describes why JEFFRIES' actions were reckless or not reckless as the case may be?

A It is obvious to anyone that there was a risk, no matter how small and JEFFRIES took it.

B Even though JEFFRIES did not believe there to be a real risk, it is obvious there is a risk and JEFFRIES took it.

C JEFFRIES is aware that a poisoned chocolate may be in the bag, and yet chose to take the risk.

D JEFFRIES believes the risk to be reasonable, and as he has taken the risk himself he cannot be reckless.

Question 1.6

Some criminal offences are said to be offences of 'strict liability'. Consider an offence where it is illegal to take a person aged 16 years or under on a rollercoaster (note this is a fictitious offence!).

Assuming this offence is one of 'strict liability' which of the following is correct in relation to this 'strict liability'?

A You only have to show the child was taken on the rollercoaster.

B You only have to show the person taken on to the rollercoaster was aged 16 years or under.

C You have to show the child was taken on the rollercoaster and that they were aged 16 years or under.

D You have to show that the accused knew or should have been aware that the person taken on to the rollercoaster was aged 16 years or under.

Question 1.7

MUSTAQ lives with his partner, who is 6 months' pregnant. They have frequent rows and in the past MUSTAQ has been violent towards her. During a blazing row MUSTAQ takes a knife, stabbing his partner in the upper arm and slashing her face. She is hospitalised and requires extensive treatment, but does not die from her injuries. However the shock of the incident causes her to go into early labour, and the child is born, but dies about an hour after birth. When interviewed MUSTAQ admits he intended to cause grievous bodily harm to his partner, but did not intend to kill her, although he states 'she had it coming'. He also states he had no intentions at all to harm the baby and deeply regrets the death of the child.

Considering only the doctrine of transferred malice, which of the following is correct in relation to the death of the child?

A MUSTAQ is guilty of murder as his intention was to cause grievous bodily harm to his partner, and this malice can be transferred to the child.

B MUSTAQ is guilty of murder as he was reckless as to whether he would kill his partner or not, even though that was not his intention and this malice can be transferred to the child.

C MUSTAQ would not be guilty of murder as the malice cannot be transferred, but he may well be guilty of manslaughter of the child.

D MUSTAQ would not be guilty of murder or manslaughter, as the malice cannot be transferred in relation to either offence.

Question 1.8

Various mental states discussed in considering criminal conduct undeniably present courts and juries with difficult practical problems since even when one is clear about the precise meaning of the mental state to be proved, it is not easy to be sure whether that corresponds to what actually went on in the accused's mind. Even in apparently clear cases, the accused's denial may raise a doubt in the minds of the jury. Section 8 of the Criminal Justice Act 1967 gives guidance as to what a court or jury, in determining whether a person has committed an offence, should consider.

Which of the following statements best outlines what s. 8 states?

A The accused anticipated that the outcome of his actions was expected and likely.

B The accused anticipated that the outcome of his actions was likely.

C The more likely the prospect of an outcome, the more likely it is that the accused anticipated that outcome.

D The accused intended an outcome of their conduct because it was practically certain to happen that way.

Question 1.9

SMITHSON has been charged with wilful neglect of a child under s. 1 of the Children and Young Persons Act 1933. SMITHSON's 3-year-old daughter was found to be suffering from severe malnutrition and the prosecution alleges that SMITHSON failed to provide adequate food and medical aid for her.

In relation to the term 'wilful', what must the prosecution show in respect of SMITHSON's state of mind, in order to prove this offence?

A That SMITHSON intended the child to be ill as a result of not feeding her, or providing medical aid.

B That SMITHSON intended the child to be ill as a result of not feeding her, or providing medical aid, or at least foresaw that this would happen.

C That SMITHSON had considered the consequences of not feeding her, or providing medical aid and intended those consequences to happen.

D That SMITHSON was aware of the risk but took it anyway due to not caring whether the child's health was at risk or not.

ANSWERS

Answer 1.1

Answer **C** — Murder is a crime of specific intent, and requires a specific *mens rea*, i.e. an intention to kill or seriously injure. To be guilty of a criminal offence requiring *mens rea*, an accused must possess that *mens rea* when performing the act or omission in question, and it must relate to that particular act or omission. If, for example, a man accidentally kills his wife in a car crash on Monday, the fact that he was planning to cut her throat on Tuesday does not make him guilty of her murder (which makes answer A wrong), even if he was thinking about the planned murder at the time of the accident (making answer B incorrect), and even if he is subsequently delighted to find that his wife has died. Similarly, he could not be guilty of manslaughter (answer D) which also requires a specific *mens rea*.

Crime, para. 1.1.3.1

Answer 1.2

Answer **A** — Consider the statutory expressions that exist in English law; the more common expressions are:

- intent
- recklessness
- wilfully
- dishonestly

Looking at the differences between intent and recklessness then an advantage of recklessness over intention is that the former is easier to prove by the attendant circumstances; a disadvantage is the different elements attributed to the word 'reckless' by different courts considering different offences.

An example of this dilemma occurs in *D v DPP* [2005] Crim LR 962. A police officer attended a domestic incident involving a dispute as to the defendant's access to his newborn daughter. The defendant was outside the property. He was arrested to prevent a breach of the peace. When he had calmed down he was allowed to see his daughter. He then ran away pursued by the officer to his home address. During a subsequent struggle the defendant bit the officer on the left hand. The defendant was arrested for assaulting a police constable. He was charged with an offence contrary to s. 89 of the Police Act 1996. The justices found that the defendant was guilty of assaulting the officer by biting him, on the basis that the defendant's actions were reckless. The defendant appealed, arguing that a bite could not be reckless; either it was deliberate or it was accidental.

The Divisional Court held, dismissing the appeal, the test of recklessness in an assault of this kind involved foresight of the risk that the complainant would be subjected to unlawful force and the taking of that risk, that state of mind being coincident with the act of biting. In this scenario the defendant would have realised that a reckless battery might be inflicted using teeth to try to snatch something from the hand of the officer restraining her, being aware that she might make contact with the officer's hand in the process. In these circumstances the defendant would be guilty of a 'reckless' assault and could not argue that it was accidental, or that the recklessness amounted only to whether they would snatch the evidence; answers C and D are therefore incorrect.

The courts have also held that assault occasioning actual bodily harm only requires proof of recklessness as to the assault and there is no need to show that the defendant was reckless as to the extent of the harm caused by his or her assault (see *R v Savage* [1992] 1 AC 699). In this scenario the case would be decided on the recklessness as the assault itself and not the recklessness as to the injury likely to be caused, and for this reason answer B is incorrect.

Crime, para. 1.1.4.2

Answer 1.3

Answer **C** — Some would exclude negligence from a discussion of *mens rea* on semantic grounds, i.e. on the basis that *mens rea* is concerned with states of mind and negligence is not a state of mind but is rather a failure to comply with the standards of the reasonable man; answer A is therefore incorrect. However, *mens rea* is here being used in the wider sense of the fault element required for liability, and although the required fault is, at least as regards the more serious offences, usually defined in terms of a state of mind, it is not exclusively so.

Despite the potential appeal of the compromise of negligence, offences are rarely defined expressly in terms of negligence. Manslaughter is the one exception at common law but here the negligence has to be 'gross'. Nor do statutory offences themselves normally expressly employ the words 'negligence' or 'negligently' but they do in effect often impose liability for negligence (i.e. for failure to comply with the standards of the reasonable man); an example of this would be in relation to standards of driving.

It matters not what the accused actually believes, it is what the reasonable man in the circumstances would have believed which counts and therefore the minimum basis of liability is negligence; answer D is therefore incorrect. The prosecution are not required to prove a state of mind (including an appreciation of risk), although the accused's knowledge of facts may be a relevant factor; answer B is therefore incorrect.

Crime, para. 1.1.3.3

Answer 1.4

Answer **C** — An assault or battery must be committed intentionally or recklessly, so the least you have to prove is recklessness, not necessarily actual intent (making answers A and B incorrect). If injury is caused, it need not even be proved that the injury was foreseeable. This is now clear from the decision of the House of Lords in *R* v *Savage* [1992] 1 AC 699, in which S aimed to throw the contents of a beer glass over B, but inadvertently allowed the glass to slip from her hand and break, with the result that B was injured by it. A conviction for an offence under s. 47 of the Offences Against the Person Act 1861 could be successful, because throwing beer over B was an intentional assault (indeed a battery) and that same assault had resulted in B's injury. Therefore recklessness as to the assault is all that is needed — not recklessness as to the extent of the harm likely to be caused (making answer D incorrect).

Crime, para. 1.1.4.2

Answer 1.5

Answer **C** — *R* v *G and R* [2003] 3 WLR 1060, stands as a benchmark to a particular form of 'recklessness'.

The relationship between intention and recklessness, and indeed the debate about the scope of recklessness itself, can be seen more clearly from the following list:

(a) Consequence desired: intention.
(b) Consequence foreseen as virtually certain: intention may be found.
(c) Consequence foreseen as probable: typically recklessness (subjective).
(d) Consequence foreseen as possible: typically recklessness (subjective).
(e) Consequence not foreseen but ought to have been: negligence (objective recklessness).
(f) Consequence even reasonable man would not foresee: strict liability.

The difference between (d) and (e) essentially represents the distinction between the narrower subjective *'Cunningham'* recklessness (*R* v *Cunningham* [1957] 2 QB 396) and the wider objective *'Caldwell'* recklessness (*Metropolitan Police Commissioner* v *Caldwell* [1982] AC 341) favoured for two decades by the House of Lords but now rejected by them, for criminal damage at least, in *G and R*.

But it is to *G and R* we have to turn to answer the question as it should be clear that both *Caldwell* and *Cunningham* recklessness are present in the question. *G and R* recklessness is defined by Lord Bingham:

A person acts recklessly ... with respect to —
(i) a circumstance when he is aware of a risk that it exists or will exist;
(ii) a result when he is aware of a risk that it will occur;
and it is, in the circumstances known to him, unreasonable to take the risk.

This effectively removes the *Caldwell* notion of what ought to have been known, and takes us to what is actually known; answers A and B are therefore incorrect. In the question JEFFRIES is aware that there is a risk, no matter how small, that the poisoned chocolate is in the bag. We now have to consider only whether the risk is unreasonable. Ask yourself, 'would I take a chocolate from JEFFRIES?' Assuming the answer to be yes(!) makes his actions unreasonable and he is reckless, even reckless with his own life; answer D is therefore incorrect.

Crime, para. 1.1.4.2

Answer 1.6

Answer **C** — The term 'strict liability' is sometimes loosely explained as meaning 'liability without fault' but this is misleading insofar as it suggests that no mental or fault element whatsoever is required. Strict liability offences are normally those where no fault element is required in relation to one (perhaps crucial) element of the *actus reus* but where *mens rea* is required in relation to other aspects.

In relation to our fictitious offence there is absolutely no mental element required, taking a person on a rollercoaster is an absolute offence which would be committed where:

- a person is aged 16 or under, and
- is taken on a rollercoaster.

Both elements would need to be shown however; answers A and B are therefore incorrect.

The wording of the statute leaves no room for manoeuvre for the accused, there would be no defence of 'I honestly thought he was 17'; answer D is therefore incorrect.

If the caveat of 'without the person's parents or legal guardian's permission' were added to the rollercoaster offence does add a mental element to it, however it would still be an offence of 'strict liability' in relation to the facts outlined above. It would in effect still be an offence of strict liability.

Crime, para. 1.1.2

Answer 1.7

Answer **C** — The state of mind required for one offence can, on occasions, be 'transferred' from the original target or victim to another. Known generally as the doctrine of 'transferred malice' because it originates from a case involving malicious wounding (see chapter 1.8), the doctrine only operates if the crime remains the same. For example, in the original case (*R v Latimer* (1886) 17 QBD 359) the defendant lashed out with his belt at one person but missed, striking a third party instead. As it was proved that the defendant had the required *mens rea* when he swung the belt, the court held that the same *mens rea* could support a charge of wounding against any other victim injured by the same act. The House of Lords has acknowledged that this doctrine is somewhat arbitrary and is an exception to the general principles of law (*Attorney-General's Reference (No. 3 of 1994)* [1998] AC 245).

If the nature of the offence changes, then the doctrine will not operate. Therefore if a defendant is shown to have thrown a rock at a crowd of people intending to injure one of them, the *mens rea* required for that offence cannot be 'transferred' to an offence of criminal damage if the rock misses them and breaks a window instead, although this is not exclusive to offences of an entirely different nature.

The defendant intended only to injure his partner, and although had she died this would have been enough to support a charge of murder, she did not die. Attempted murder requires intention to kill, which is absent here. As there is no intention of the defendant in relation to murder, this intention cannot be transferred; answers A and B are therefore incorrect.

There was, however, intention to harm, which can be transferred and therefore support a charge of manslaughter; answer D is therefore incorrect.

Crime, para. 1.1.5

Answer 1.8

Answer **C** — Section 8 of the Criminal Justice Act 1967 states:

A court or jury, in determining whether a person has committed an offence, —
(a) shall not be bound in law to infer that he intended or foresaw a result of his actions by reason only of its being a natural and probable consequence of those actions; but
(b) shall decide whether he did intend or foresee that result by reference to all the evidence, drawing such inferences from the evidence as appear proper in the circumstances.

There is also the body of case law which has developed around the area of 'probability', culminating in two cases in the House of Lords (*R* v *Moloney* [1985] AC 905 and *R* v *Hancock* [1986] AC 455). Following those cases it is now settled that foresight of the probability of a consequence *does not amount to an intention to bring that consequence about, but may be evidence of it*; answers A and B are therefore incorrect.

In other words, you cannot claim that a defendant *intended* a consequence of his or her behaviour simply because it was virtually certain to occur; answer D is therefore incorrect. What you can do is to put evidence of the defendant's foresight of that probability before a court who may infer an intention from it. In proving such a point the argument would go like this:

- at the time of the criminal act there was a *probability* of a consequence;
- the greater the probability, the more likely it is that the defendant *foresaw* that consequence;
- if the defendant foresaw that consequence, the more likely it is that the defendant *intended* it to happen.

Crime, para. 1.1.4.1

Answer 1.9

Answer **D** — The term 'wilfully' is *not* restricted to occasions where a defendant must be shown to have desired the consequences of his or her actions or at least to have foreseen or considered them (*subjective* recklessness). Answers A, B and C are therefore incorrect as they relate to a positive intent to bring about consequences.

The leading case is *R* v *Sheppard* [1981] AC 394, which found that the term will include *objective* recklessness (see the decision of the House of Lords in *R* v *G and R* [2003] 3 WLR 1060). In *Sheppard*, Lord Diplock provided a model direction as follows:

... on a charge of wilful neglect of a child under section 1 of the Children and Young Persons Act 1933 by failing to provide adequate medical aid...the jury must be satisfied (1) that the child did in fact need medical aid at the time at which the parent is charged with failing to provide it (the *actus reus*) and (2) either that the parent was aware at that time that the child's health might be at risk if it were not provided with medical aid, or that the parent's unawareness of this fact was due to his not caring whether his child's health were at risk or not (the *mens rea*).

Crime, para. 1.1.4.3

2 | Criminal Conduct

STUDY PREPARATION

This chapter goes on from the first chapter to look at how all the ingredients are physically put together to make the offence cake.

Where *mens rea* is the mental element, *actus reus* is the conduct or positive act by the accused. This chapter examines how the principle of 'an act does not make a person guilty unless (their) mind is also guilty' by examining the interface that *mens rea* has with *actus reus*.

Once this is established there are other factors to consider like voluntary acts, omissions, causal links and intervening acts.

You are also tested on how one offender can link with an accessory, and how 'acts' and 'states of mind' are affected in joint offending. Also 'the responsibility of the superior for the acts of their subordinate' is examined; how organisations can commit offences, as well as being responsible for the acts of their staff.

QUESTIONS

Question 2.1

GREEN was broke and anxious to inherit his mother's money. One night he put potassium cyanide in his mother's bedtime drink with the intention of killing her. In due course, the following morning, it was discovered that his mother had died. GREEN was arrested on suspicion of murder. In fact, GREEN's mother had drunk very little; certainly, nowhere near enough to kill her. She had died of natural causes.

In relation to this, which of the following is true?

A   GREEN is guilty of murder as there is a causal link between his actions and his mother's death.

B GREEN is not guilty of any offences as his mother died of natural causes.

C GREEN is guilty of attempted murder due to his intention.

D GREEN is guilty of attempted murder due to his actions, irrespective of his intentions.

Question 2.2

ALBARETTI worked for a major retail company on the night shift. The company, to save money, had unisex facilities including changing and toilet facilities. The night shift manager walks in on ALBARETTI whilst she is changing and is standing in her underwear. The manager walks over to her and takes his penis out inviting ALBARETTI to put it in her mouth, he then grabs her bra strap. The manager is charged with an offence under the Sexual Offences Act 2003.

What, if at any, is the company's corporate liability in relation to the activity of its manager?

A They would be liable as he is effectively their representative on night shift.

B They would be liable as they introduced unisex facilities, thus increasing the risk of this type of activity.

C They would not be liable at all for the actions of their employee in these circumstances.

D They could be liable as accessories or aiding and abetting the activity should relevant evidence exist.

Question 2.3

SCULTHWAITE is on his way to hospital to have his appendix removed. NIELSEN has long had a hatred of SCULTHWAITE and sees him just outside the hospital. NIELSEN punches SCULTHWAITE on the head, not that hard. SCULTHWAITE, however, has a very weak skull (NIELSEN has no knowledge of this), and as a result of the blow suffers a serious head injury. The head injury is not life threatening, but the doctors are unable to operate on him. SCULTHWAITE's appendix bursts due to this delay in operating, and as a result he dies.

In relation to causation, which of the following is true?

A NIELSEN has caused the death of SCULTHWAITE because of the punch he gave him.

B NIELSEN has caused the death of SCULTHWAITE because there was no intervening act.

C NIELSEN has not caused the death of SCULTHWAITE; there is no link between the punch and the death.

D NIELSEN has not caused the death of SCULTHWAITE, as he had no knowledge of his weak skull.

Question 2.4

BOTHA was employed to operate a level crossing on a railway whilst a fault with the automated system was repaired. While at work, BOTHA called his girlfriend on his mobile phone. He was so engrossed in the conversation that he forgot to close the crossing gates when a train was coming. A car was crossing at the time and the train hit it, killing the driver.

Is BOTHA criminally liable in the death of the driver of the car?

A No, there was no positive action by BOTHA to cause the accident.

B Yes, he had failed to carry out his duty and is criminally liable.

C No, BOTHA did not have the relevant *mens rea*.

D Yes, as there is a causal link between his actions and their consequences.

Question 2.5

MULLER intends to commit a burglary at a local electrical goods shop. He confides in BERGSTROM, who tells his wife who works in that shop. BERGSTROM's wife tells her husband that as far as she knows the security guard is always asleep at nights, but she does not tell him that the rear door alarm is currently broken. BERGSTROM tells MULLER to commit the offence at 4 am, which he does by entering through the back door.

What is the BERGSTROMS' liability, if any, for the burglary?

A Both husband and wife are guilty as counsellors of the offence.

B Both husband and wife are guilty as procurers of the offence.

C Only Mr. BERGSTROM is guilty as counsellor of the offence.

D Only Mr. BERGSTROM is guilty as procurer of the offence.

Question 2.6

STRAUSS intends to murder his wife's lover by shooting him. He goes to see XIAN, whom he knows to be an illegal gun supplier. STRAUSS tells XIAN what he intends to do, and asks him to supply a gun. XIAN is unconcerned whether the murder is successful or not, and is only interested in his profit from the deal. STRAUSS commits the murder, but is caught and tells the police about XIAN.

Is XIAN an accessory to the murder?

A No, he does not have the required *mens rea*.

B No, as he has no intention of aiding the actual shooting.

C Yes, he is reckless as to whether the shooting will happen or not.

D Yes, he is an accessory to the murder, as he knows the circumstances.

Question 2.7

MILLERSHIP is a soldier living in barracks. MILLERSHIP has a fight with PRETORIUS during which he stabs him twice in the stomach with a bayonet. Realising the seriousness of PRETORIUS' injuries, two other soldiers carry him to the nearby medical centre. PRETORIUS is a large man and, due to his heavy weight, the soldiers drop him 3 times on way to the medical centre. On one of those occasions, PRETORIUS hits his head very hard on the ground. On arrival at the centre, the overworked doctor fails to notice that PRETORIUS' lung has collapsed and the treatment he receives from the doctor is less than adequate. PRETORIUS dies from a culmination of all the injuries and the mistreatment he received.

Given the way PRETORIUS was treated after his injury, is MILLERSHIP criminally liable for PRETORIUS' death?

A Yes, the chain of causation is not broken.

B No, due to the intervening act of the other soldiers.

C No, due to the intervening act of the doctor.

D Yes, provided the stab wound was the major cause of death.

Question 2.8

BALDWIN is one of a gang of armed robbers who rob people in their own houses. They plan to go to GRAHAM's house and rob him. BALDWIN is aware that knives will be carried, although he will not carry one himself. BALDWIN is also aware that the knives may be used for violence, and that the rest of the gang is violent. During the robbery GRAHAM tries to fight back and is stabbed by one of the gang. GRAHAM dies as a result of his injuries.

In order to show that BALDWIN is guilty of murder through joint enterprise, what would have to be proved?

A BALDWIN agreed to kill, using the knives.

B BALDWIN agreed to cause really serious injury using the knives.

C BALDWIN agreed to use knives for any purpose.

D BALDWIN contemplated that the knife could be used to cause serious bodily injury.

Question 2.9

MALLOY wished to scare a business rival and recruited two persons to carry out his wishes using a loaded firearm. Unfortunately one of the hired men lost his nerve and shot the business rival they were only supposed to scare. The business rival died of his injuries.

As the secondary party to the killing, what would need to be shown for MALLOY to be liable for manslaughter as a 'joint enterprise'?

A That the secondary party had an agreement, even tacitly, that the primary party would do what he had done.

B That the secondary party had a clear agreement that the primary party would do what he had done.

C That the secondary party had foreseen the possibility that the primary party would do what he had done.

D That the secondary party could have *reasonably* foreseen the possibility that the primary party would do what he had done.

Question 2.10

INGHAM and PRYCE were in dispute over £40,000 drugs money owed to PRYCE. PRYCE intended sending out a message to the dealers in the area and decided to kill INGHAM. He approached his friend BRYCE, whom he knew owned a firearm. BRYCE loaned PRYCE a pistol, suspecting that he would use it to kill INGHAM.

If PRYCE were to carry out his plan, what else would the prosecution need to prove, in order to show that this was a joint venture between PRYCE and BRYCE?

A That BRYCE intended assisting PRYCE, and that his actions actually assisted in the commission of the crime.

B That BRYCE actually knew that PRYCE would kill INGHAM, and that he approved of the commission of the offence.

C Only that the act was committed by PRYCE, nothing further needs to be proved.

D Only that BRYCE intended to assist PRYCE in the act, regardless of whether his actions actually assisted in the commission of the crime.

Question 2.11

RODRICK is driving his car at night when he knocks over a pedestrian walking on the pavement. The pedestrian is not dead, but lies bleeding and severely injured in the road, on the carriageway itself. RODRICK gets out of his car, sees the pedestrian and then in panic, drives away. CARTER is also driving down the road, but is distracted as he is using his mobile phone. CARTER fails to see the pedestrian lying in the road and drives over his head killing him instantly.

Considering only a 'causal link', which of the following is correct in relation to causing death by dangerous driving?

A RODRICK could *only* be guilty if it was proved the pedestrian would ultimately have died from the injuries he received in the first collision.

B RODRICK could be guilty as, without his collision with the pedestrian, he would not have been lying in the road.

C RODRICK would not be guilty even if the injuries he caused would have killed the pedestrian, as there was an intervening act when CARTER hit the pedestrian.

D RODRICK would not be guilty, but only because of the inattentiveness of CARTER who may have seen the pedestrian had he not been on his phone.

Question 2.12

GOLD stabs KHAN in the leg, almost severing the femoral artery. KHAN is rushed to hospital and his life can be saved by blood transfusion. KHAN refuses as he is paranoid that the blood he will be given will contain the HIV virus. This is an unreasonable belief due to the screening process transfusion blood has to go through. In fact KHAN does not die of blood loss as the hospital staff work a small miracle without giving him a blood transfusion, however he contracts multiple antibiotic-resistant, Staphylococcus aureus (MRSA) and dies as a result of that disease.

How culpable is GOLD for the death of KHAN?

A He is fully cupable as the stab wound was the first injury KHAN received.

B He is partly culpable, as the stab wound was not the primary cause of death.

C He is not be culpable at all, as KHAN's blood loss did not cause his death.

D He is not culpable at all as there were two new intervening acts between his actions and the death of KHAN.

Question 2.13

GUNNERSON is homeless and enters a shop during opening hours and hides in the storeroom as it has been below freezing all week at night. During the night, the heating is off in the storeroom. Being a former electrician GUNNERSON rigs the heating system, however in doing so he leaves several live wires bare. In the morning he leaves the storeroom in the condition he made it. Later that day an assistant electrocutes herself on a wire that GUNNERSON had made bare.

Is GUNNERSON liable by omission for the assistant's injuries?

A Yes, as he was under an obligation to avert the danger he had caused.

B Yes, as he took it upon himself to assume responsibility for the electrical system in the storeroom.

C No, he is not under any statutory obligation to intervene before the assistant was injured.

D No, there was no proximity between him and the assistant at the time she was injured.

ANSWERS

Answer 2.1

Answer **C** — There are two primary factors to any crime: the *mens rea* and the *actus reus*. The mental element, or intention, is vital and there is a presumption that *mens rea* is required for a criminal offence unless Parliament clearly indicates otherwise (*B (A minor)* v *DPP* [2000] 2 WLR 452). Therefore, answer D is incorrect. The relevant *mens rea* for attempted murder is intention to kill. GREEN has also taken action by poisoning the drink. However, where *actus reus* is proved, you must show a causal link between that and the relevant consequences. Despite his best efforts she had died, coincidentally, of natural causes. GREEN's conduct had not in any sense contributed to this and he is not guilty of murder (*R* v *White* [1910] 2 KB 124). Therefore, answer A is incorrect. Had he waited just one more day, there would be no criminal liability upon him. However, his intentions together with his actions make him guilty of attempted murder; therefore, answer B is incorrect.

Crime, paras 1.2.2.2, 1.2.4

Answer 2.2

Answer **D** — This question addresses the issues of corporate liability. Companies have been successfully prosecuted for offences involving strict liability (*Alphacell Ltd* v *Woodward* [1972] AC 824) as well as offences which require *mens rea* (*Tesco Supermarkets Ltd* v *Nattrass* [1972] AC 153).

Liability is not limited to summary offences and companies can be liable for the actions of some of their employees as accessories under certain circumstances (*R* v *Robert Millar (Contractors) Ltd* [1970] 2 QB 54) making answer C incorrect.

Clearly there are some offences that would be conceptually impossible for a legal corporation to commit (e.g. some sexual offences) but, given that companies can be guilty as accessories they may well be capable of aiding and abetting such offences even though they could not commit the offence as a principal; answers A and B are therefore incorrect.

Crime, para. 1.2.7

Answer 2.3

Answer **A** — Although legal causation must be 'operative and substantial', it need not necessarily be a direct cause of the proscribed result. In *R* v *McKechnie* [1992]

Crim LR 194, a man inflicted serious head injuries on another man. These were not in themselves fatal, but they prevented doctors from operating on the injured man's duodenal ulcer, and he died when the ulcer burst. The perpetrator was held to have caused his death. There was a link, therefore answer C is incorrect. In what is known colloquially as the 'Eggshell Skull' rule, a person must ordinarily take his victim as he finds him. If, for example, the victim of an assault is unusually vulnerable to physical injury as a result of an existing medical condition or old age, the person responsible must accept liability for any unusually serious consequences which result. This is true particularly where a blow is struck; answer D is therefore incorrect. In relation to intervening acts, no such intervening act can break the chain of causation if it merely complements or aggravates the ongoing effects of the defendant's initial conduct. The chain of causation can be broken only where the effect of the intervening act is so overwhelming that any initial injuries are completely unconnected to the end result, therefore answer B is incorrect.

Crime, para. 1.2.4

Answer 2.4

Answer **B** — Most offences require a positive act, together with the requisite state of mind for the offence to be complete. However, some offences are brought about by a failure to act, and most of these arise from some sort of duty to act (this makes answers A and C incorrect). A person may in some cases incur criminal liability through failure to discharge his official duties or contractual obligations. A typical example is provided by *R v Pittwood* (1902) 19 TLR 37, in which P was employed to operate a level crossing on a railway but omitted to close the crossing gates when a train was signalled. P was convicted of gross negligence manslaughter. It is not a causal link which requires proof that the consequences would not have happened 'but for' the defendant's actions of omission; here, had the train been even one minute late, the accident would not have happened (answer D is also incorrect).

Crime, para. 1.2.3

Answer 2.5

Answer **A** — A principal offender must meet all the requirements of the particular offence, and for procurement there must be a causal link between his conduct and the offence. Counselling requires no causal link (*R v Calhaem* [1985] QB 808); all that is required is the principal offender's awareness of the counsellor's advice or encouragement — and this is true even if the principal would have committed the offence anyway (*Attorney General* v *Able* [1984] QB 795).

Generally, the state of mind (*mens rea*) which is needed to convict an accessory is: 'proof of intention to aid as well as of knowledge of the circumstances' (*National Coal Board* v *Gamble* [1959] 1 QB 11). The minimum state of mind required of an accessory to an offence is set out in *Johnson* v *Youden* [1950] 1 KB 544. In that case the court held that, before anyone can be convicted of aiding and abetting an offence, he or she must at least know the essential matters that constitute that offence. There must also be a further mental element, namely an intention to aid the principal, so in what way is there evidence against Mrs. BERGSTROM? None, in fact there is evidence to the contrary in that she did not indicate that the back door alarm was faulty. So only Mr. BERGSTROM is an accessory and at that a counsellor; answers B, C and D are therefore incorrect.

Crime, paras 1.2.6, 1.2.6.1

Answer 2.6

Answer **D** — One of the leading cases on the state of mind for accessories is *National Coal Board* v *Gamble* [1959] 1 QB 11, where Devlin J at p. 20 stated: '... aiding and abetting is a crime that requires proof of *mens rea*, that is to say, of intention to aid as well as of knowledge of the circumstances'. However, as Devlin J went on to point out, at p. 23, intention to aid does not require that the accused's purpose or motive must be that the principal offence should be committed:

> If one man deliberately sells to another a gun to be used for murdering a third, he may be indifferent about whether the third man lives or dies and interested only in the cash profit to be made out of the sale, but he can still be an aider and abettor. To hold otherwise would be to negative the rule that *mens rea* is a matter of intent only and does not depend on desire or motive.

There must also be an intention to aid the principal offender, and as such recklessness and negligence are not enough to convict an accessory. Thus, answers A, B and C are incorrect.

Crime, para. 1.2.6.1

Answer 2.7

Answer **A** — A defendant will not be regarded as having caused the consequence for which he stands accused if there was a new intervening act sufficient to break the chain of causation between his original action and the consequence in question — in this case the death of PRETORIUS. The chain of causation can be broken only where the effect of the intervening act is so overwhelming that any initial injuries are relegated to the status of mere historical background. In the leading case of *R* v *Smith* [1959] 2 QB 35, which broadly follows the circumstances outlined in the question, the Courts-Martial Appeals Court held:

> If at the time of death the original wound is still an operating cause and a substantial cause, then the death can properly be said to be the result of the wound, albeit that some other cause of death is also operating. Only if it can be said that the original wounding is merely the setting in which another cause operates can it be said that the death did not result from the wound. Putting it another way, only if the second cause is so overwhelming as to make the original wound merely part of the history can it be said that the death does not flow from the wound.

It follows that a conviction could still be secured. Answers B, C and D are incorrect.

Crime, para. 1.2.5

Answer 2.8

Answer **D** — The main features that will determine BALDWIN's liability as an accessory in a joint enterprise will be:

- The nature and extent of the agreed offence.
- Whether the accessory knew the principal had a knife.
- Whether a different knife was used.
- Whether the knife was used differently than agreed.

Proof of prior knowledge of the actual crime intended is not necessary if he contemplated the commission of one of a limited number of crimes by the principal, and intentionally assisted in their commission. For an accessory to be found guilty of murder as a joint enterprise it is not necessary for the prosecution to prove that the principal would kill; it is sufficient to prove that he might kill. The accessory, however, will not be guilty where the lethal act carried out by the principal is fundamentally different from the acts foreseen or intended by the accessory: *R* v *Powell* [1999] 1 AC 1.

It is therefore enough that BALDWIN contemplated that knives might be used, and that no actual agreement needs to be reached by the parties to the crime; therefore, answers A, B and C are incorrect.

Crime, para. 1.2.6.2

Answer 2.9

Answer **C** — This particular area of law is complicated by various factors, particularly when one party is not present at the scene of the crime so to speak. Enormous problems have been encountered where one person involved in a joint venture goes beyond that which was agreed or contemplated by the other(s).

Fortunately for students of the law the Court of Appeal has confirmed the law in relation to joint enterprise in *Attorney-General's Reference (No. 3 of 2004)* [2005] EWCA Crim 1882. It was alleged that the defendant had recruited two co-defendants to scare someone with a loaded firearm but one of the co-defendants subsequently went on to shoot the victim dead. The issue turned on whether the first defendant could be convicted of manslaughter on the facts. The primary question raised by the Attorney General was whether a secondary party to a joint enterprise was guilty of manslaughter if he had contemplated an unlawful act to frighten the victim and the principal carried out that act with the necessary intention for murder.

The Court held that the test was whether the secondary party had foreseen the possibility that the primary party would do what he had done. In this case the act done by the primary party (shooting the victim) was of a fundamentally different character from any act contemplated by the person who had recruited him — he had not foreseen the possibility of any harm to the victim, let alone any intentional harm. These principles were in accordance with *R v Powell* [1999] 1 AC 1 which was to be regarded as representing the law.

There is no need to have an agreement, tacitly or otherwise; answers A and B are therefore incorrect. And the secondary party's foresight does not have to be reasonable; answer D is therefore incorrect.

Crime, para. 1.2.6.2

Answer 2.10

Answer **A** — The issue of joint enterprise normally arises in circumstances, for example, when more than one person is present at the scene of the offence and one person commits an offence (the principal offender), and another is present at the scene, but does not physically take part (the accessory).

The issue is more complicated when the accessory is *not* present during the substantive offence. In *R v Bryce* [2004] 2 Cr App R 35, it was decided that in such cases, the prosecution will need to show *intentional assistance* by the accessory and in order to do this, they would need to prove:

• an act was done by the accessory;

- the act *in fact* assisted the later commission of the offence;
- that the accessory did the act deliberately, realising that it was capable of assisting the offence;
- that the accessory, at the time of doing the act, contemplated the commission of the offence by the principal offender (e.g. he or she foresaw it as a real or substantial risk or real possibility); *and*
- when doing the act the accessory *intended* assisting the principal offender.

Dealing with the answers above, the prosecution would not be required to show that BRYCE *knew* that PRYCE would kill INGHAM; merely that he *contemplated the commission of the offence*. Also, his *approval* is irrelevant according to the *Bryce* case. Answer B is therefore incorrect. Answer C is incorrect, because the prosecution would need to show more proof than the fact that a firearm was loaned by the accessory to the principal offender (although this would count as evidence in the case). Answer D is incorrect, because the prosecution must show that the accessory's actions actually assisted in the commission of the crime.

Crime, para. 1.2.6.2

Answer 2.11

Answer **B** — Once the *actus reus* of an offence has been proved, a causal link must then be shown between it and the relevant consequences. That is, it must be proven that the consequences would not have happened 'but for' the defendant's act or omission. The *actus reus* for this offence is that a collision caused a death of a person. So a causal link is required.

As far as CARTER is concerned there is a causal link, the pedestrian would not be dead but for his driving over his head!

With RODRICK it is more complicated, is there a causal link? Whilst evidence that the pedestrian would have died from his injuries had he not been hit for a second time would be good, and would almost certainly show a causal link, it would probably be very difficult to establish. In fact it is not needed as a *prima facie* causal link. This approach ignores the issue of RODRICK's foresight. Roads are, by their nature, used by vehicles and it is clearly foreseeable that a person left lying on the road is at risk of being further injured by an inattentive driver; answer A is therefore incorrect.

Hence, as RODRICK left the pedestrian on the road with knowledge of that risk and the foreseen event occurred, he remains the more proximate cause of the death. In other words 'but for' RODRICK hitting the pedestrian, and 'but for' RODRICK leaving him in a very vulnerable position on the road, he would not have died.

This is the case even had CARTER been paying full attention to the road and still not seen the pedestrian; answer D is therefore incorrect.

Although effectively there has been an intervening act, it was not enough to break the chain of causation that links RODRICK to the death. Had someone approached the pedestrian on the road and fatally stabbed him, then the chain would clearly be broken.

Although the pedestrian died of injuries caused by CARTER, as far as causation is concerned RODRICK is culpable in that death (whether he would be charged or not is questionable however); answer C is therefore incorrect.

Crime, para. 1.2.4

Answer 2.12

Answer **A** — A defendant will not be regarded as having caused the consequence for which it is sought to make him liable if there was a *novus actus interveniens* (or new intervening act) sufficient to break the chain of causation between his original action and the consequence in question.

However the chain of causation can be broken only where the effect of the intervening act is so overwhelming that any initial injuries are relegated to the status of mere historical background. So what caused KHAN's death? The answer is the stab wound because 'but for' it KHAN would not have been in hospital to contract MRSA, the fact he did not die of blood loss caused by the wound is irrelevant; answer C is therefore incorrect. No matter how many intervening acts there have been, the chain of causation in this case is unbroken; answer D is therefore incorrect.

GOLD is fully culpable, not partly culpable if you apply the 'but for' test; answer B is therefore incorrect.

Crime, paras 1.2.4, 1.2.5

Answer 2.13

Answer **A** — Most criminal offences require the defendant to carry out some positive act before liability can be imposed. There can ordinarily be no liability for failure (or omission) to act, unless the law specifically imposes such a duty upon a particular person. The general rule is illustrated by this example from Stephen's Digest of the Criminal Law (3rd ed., 1887):

> A sees B drowning and is able to save him by holding out his hand. A abstains from doing so in order that B may be drowned, and B is drowned. A has committed no offence.

Although A may have failed to save B, he did no positive act to cause B's death.

GUNNERSON certainly committed an act that led to the injuries, but how liable is he? Most of the occasions where failure or omission will attract liability are where a *duty to act* has been created. Such a duty can arise from a number of circumstances the main ones being:

D The creation of a **D**angerous situation by the defendant. See, for example, *R v Miller* [1983] 2 AC 161 where the defendant, having accidentally started a fire in a house, moved to another room taking no action to counteract the danger he had created.

U **U**nder statute, contract or a person's public 'office'. Examples would be where a police officer failed to intervene to prevent an assault (*R v Dytham* [1979] QB 722) or where a crossing keeper omitted to close the gates at a level crossing and a person was subsequently killed by a train (*R v Pittwood* (1902) 19 TLR 37).

T Where the defendant has **T**aken it upon himself or herself to carry out a duty and then fails to do so. Such a duty was taken up by the defendant in *R v Stone* [1977] QB 354 when she accepted a duty to care for her partner's mentally ill sister who subsequently died.

Y In circumstances where the defendant is in a parental relationship with a child or a **Y**oung person.

One of those occasions is the duty to avert a danger of one's own making. If a person creates a dangerous situation through his own fault, he may be under a duty to take reasonable steps to avert that danger, and may therefore incur criminal liability for failing to do so.

GUNNERSON had not 'assumed' responsibility for the electrical system, which still remains the shop's responsibility; answer B is therefore incorrect. Although he has no statutory duty as can be seen the almost moral duty he holds does not release him from his liability; answer C is therefore incorrect. Proximity to the victim may be compelling in a duty to protect someone from danger, but it is not a prerequisite; answer D is therefore incorrect.

Crime, para. 1.2.3

3 | Incomplete Offences and Police Investigations

STUDY PREPARATION

Having looked at the key building blocks of *mens rea* and *actus reus*, you now need to go on to consider specific criminal offences and their constituent parts. Before doing so, however, you need to get a few problematic situations out of the way.

The first of these deals with those occasions where the defendant, despite his or her best or worst endeavours, fails to do what he or she set out to do.

These are 'incomplete' offences. The second area deals with defences to criminal charges — these are addressed in the next chapter.

When dealing with incomplete offences there are two key things to remember: first, that the physical impossibility of actually achieving what the defendant set out to do will not absolve him or her from criminal liability (and why should it?); and secondly, that some offences — such as summary offences and some incomplete offences themselves — cannot be attempted.

Finally, in this chapter we deal with the related area of police operations, where the evidential and substantive issues often overlap with those of the incomplete offences involved.

QUESTIONS

Question 3.1

ROBINSON owned a failing jewellery shop and planned to defraud his insurance company. First he carried out a fake robbery and called the police. The police were

3. Incomplete Offences and Police Investigations

very thorough in their investigation and uncovered a letter from ROBINSON asking for a claim form to be sent for the robbery. The letter was dated 4 days before the fake robbery took place and was never posted.

Considering only the Criminal Attempts Act 1981, which of the following is correct in relation to an attempt to defraud the insurance company?

A As the letter pre-dates the robbery, the robbery itself will be preparatory to the claim and there will be an attempt to defraud.

B As the letter pre-dates the robbery, the letter will be preparatory to the claim and there will be an attempt to defraud.

C Neither the robbery nor the letter will be anything more than merely preparatory as the letter was never sent.

D The letter will only be merely preparatory even when posted, as only the completed claim form would actually be more than merely preparatory.

Question 3.2

WILLIAMS and MYERHOFF are employees of a major cinema company. They both agree to take the master copies of the latest blockbuster to a friend who will make pirate DVD copies of it to sell. This happens and the DVDs are sold through car boot sales, however the cinema attendances are not really down, and the company appears to make no real economic loss. WILLIAMS and MYERHOFF, however, make a large amount of money from their endeavours.

Would this constitute an offence of conspiracy to defraud (contrary to common law)?

A Yes, provided 'Ghosh' dishonesty is proven in the defendants.

B Yes, irrespective of the 'Ghosh' dishonesty test.

C No, there is no reduction in attendance at the cinema.

D No, there is no economic loss to the cinema.

Question 3.3

JANE and JOHN BRANDRICK are married. They plan for JOHN to defraud his insurance company over the reported theft of his car. They involve PEARD in their plan by asking him to hide JOHN's car in his garage until the insurance company pay out. However, a few hours before the plan is initiated, PEARD say he does not want to be involved and the BRANDRICKS give up the idea.

Who, if anyone, is guilty of conspiracy to defraud the insurance company?

A No one as the offence contemplated did not take place.

3. Incomplete Offences and Police Investigations

B No one as you cannot conspire with your spouse.

C JANE and JOHN only.

D All three of them.

Question 3.4

TIMPKINS is the licensee of the Masons Arms public house, which is wholly owned by a well-known major brewing company. He contacts his friend HOUSE, who makes a very potent real ale home brew. They agree to install a barrel of the real ale and sell it at the pub, contrary to the licence TIMPKINS holds which allows him to sell only the brewery's beers.

Would TIMPKINS and his friend be guilty of the offence of conspiracy, contrary to common law in these circumstances?

A Yes, but only if it can be shown that the customers were not aware that what they were drinking was not produced by the brewery.

B No, because TIMPKINS' friend is not employed by the brewery and it takes at least 2 persons to conspire to commit the offence.

C Yes, but only if it can be shown that the company actually lost business as a result of TIMPKINS and his friend's actions.

D Yes, both TIMPKINS and his friend would be guilty of the offence in these circumstances.

Question 3.5

Constable HAYWARD is standing in the forthcoming election for police federation representative. Having spoken to many of his colleagues Constable HAYWARD is confident of election as most have indicated they will vote for him. However, to avoid disappointment he makes an agreement with Constable MAPPS to ensure success. They agree to collect voting slips from a number of officers stating that there is a printing error and that another will be sent to them by the federation office. The officers take these forms and complete them in favour of Constable HAYWARD, falsely signing the forms themselves. The result of the election was overwhelming and Constable HAYWARD was elected achieving 90 per cent of the vote. In fact Constable HAYWARD would have won the vote without submitting any of the voting slips that he submitted himself.

In these circumstances have the two officers committed an offence under common law of conspiracy to defraud?

A Yes, the officers have signed the forms dishonestly and in doing so have committed this offence.

B Yes, the officers have deprived their colleagues of their right to vote for who they want and in doing so have committed this offence.

C No, there is no statutory offence of 'vote rigging' and as the end result of their action is not an offence they have not committed this offence.

D No, their actions did not affect the outcome of the vote, and as no one was deprived of their right to be elected they have not committed this offence.

Question 3.6

The offence of vehicle interference is laid out in s. 9 of the Criminal Attempts Act 1981.

Which of the following must the prosecution prove to make the offence of vehicle interference complete?

A An intention to commit one of the further offences mentioned.

B An intention to commit any of the further offences mentioned.

C An interference only; no intention is needed.

D An interference along with evidence that the vehicle is a motor vehicle.

Question 3.7

PRETTY wishes to kill his wife who will not grant him a divorce, and looks for a contract killer. The police, however, are aware of his plan and send an undercover officer to meet him. PRETTY and the officer agree that for £2,000 the officer, posing as a contract killer, will shoot and kill PRETTY's wife. Naturally the officer has no intention of committing the murder.

In relation to conspiracy, which of the following is true?

A As an agreement has been reached to carry out an offence, this is a statutory conspiracy.

B As an agreement has been reached to carry out an offence, this is a common law conspiracy.

C As the officer will not carry out the murder, the offence of conspiracy is not made out.

D Although the officer will not carry out the murder, PRETTY is still guilty of conspiracy.

Question 3.8

CUNLIFFE tries to persuade SCHALK to distribute leaflets in the street. Both persons are aware that the leaflets may stir up racial hatred, and both know it is an offence to distribute these leaflets. CUNLIFFE only uses persuasion and does not pressurise or intimidate SCHALK. Although SCHALK took the leaflets, he did not distribute them, he burned them.

In relation to the common law offence of incitement, which of the following is true?

A CUNLIFFE has incited SCHALK even although he only used persuasion.

B CUNLIFFE has incited SCHALK as SCHALK took the leaflets from CUNLIFFE.

C CUNLIFFE has not incited SCHALK as no pressure was put on SCHALK.

D CUNLIFFE has not incited SCHALK as no offence was committed by SHALK.

Question 3.9

DUBROWSKY decides he is going to commit an armed robbery at the local bank. He takes a lighter disguised as a self loading pistol and puts it in his pocket. He walks to the bank with the gun still in his pocket and stands outside the door intent on robbing the bank. He is pushed into the bank by an impatient customer and at this point he loses his nerve. He approaches the counter and takes out £5 from his own account and places it in the pocket containing the imitation firearm.

At what point, if any, does DUBROWSKY commit the offence of attempted robbery?

A At no point does he commit this offence.

B When he places the firearm in his pocket with the necessary intent.

C When he is standing outside the door of the bank with the necessary intent.

D When he actually enters the bank still in possession of the firearm.

Question 3.10

LARK is an undercover officer working on a drugs operation. The police are carrying out an operation on XHOSH, a known drug dealer. LARK is authorised (proper authorities for this operation have been obtained) to purchase drugs from XHOSH. He approaches XHOSH who offers to sell him a wrap of amphetamine. LARK hands over the money and takes the drugs. During the transaction LARK asks XHOSH if he can supply a firearm for a robbery he is planning. XHOSH agrees to this and plans a later meeting.

In relation to LARK's request, which of the following is true?

A   This is not entrapment as XHOSH is volunteering to get the firearm.

B   This is not entrapment as the undercover operation has been authorised.

C   This may be entrapment as LARK is no longer a passive observer.

D   This is entrapment as LARK was not authorised by the operation to buy firearms.

Question 3.11

PATTERSON was a carer for an elderly person, MORGAN. PATTERSON believed that MORGAN was wealthy and set out to discover if he had made a will and who would inherit his estate when he died. Over a period of 6 months, PATTERSON continually asked MORGAN questions in an attempt to gain this information, without success. Eventually, MORGAN became suspicious that PATTERSON had been stealing items from his house and reported her to the police. The police arrested PATTERSON and found the stolen items in her house, together with a will that she had written leaving MORGAN's entire estate to her. The will was dated 6 months previously and was unsigned. When interviewed, PATTERSON admitted that she was only going to use it if she found out that MORGAN had no relatives to inherit his estate.

In these circumstances, would PATTERSON commit the offence of attempting to make a false instrument, contrary to s. 1 of the Criminal Attempts Act 1981?

A   Yes, when she actually wrote the will.

B   No, as her intention to commit the offence was conditional on whether MORGAN had any other family.

C   No, as she had not committed an act which was more than merely preparatory.

D   Yes, when she attempted to find out details of MORGAN's family and whether or not he had made a will.

Question 3.12

DEEN was on holiday in Spain with his wife and while he was there, he became friendly with LAWRENSON. During a conversation one evening, DEEN told LAWRENSON that he was fed up with his wife and wished she were dead. LAWRENSON told DEEN that for a fee, he would see if could locate someone who would do the job. They then discussed how they would meet again in the UK at a later time together with the person LAWRENSON knew would kill the wife. Unknown to them, their conversation was overheard by PAINTING, an off-duty police officer. Upon returning from holiday, PAINTING made a witness statement regarding the conversation to the local Crown Prosecution Service.

Could DEEN and LAWRENSON be prosecuted for an offence of conspiracy to commit murder in these circumstances?

A Yes, provided they return to this country to commit the substantive offence.

B Yes, whether or not they return to this country to commit the substantive offence.

C No, as neither DEEN nor LAWRENSON would actually carry out the offence.

D No, a person may only be guilty of conspiring in this country to commit an offence abroad.

Question 3.13

BOW, GREENE and BURGESS agree to be drug dealers for SCIMITER. They collaborate to ensure that the drugs SCIMITER supplies to them are then further supplied to drug users. They each select a particular area of the town they live in to be their 'turf', that is, the area for which they will be the main supplier of drugs. At the moment though, no actual drugs have been supplied to them by SCIMITER.

Are any of these persons guilty of statutory conspiracy to supply controlled drugs contrary to s. 1 of the Criminal Law Act 1977?

A All four are guilty, as each of them is aware of the overall common purpose to which they all attach themselves.

B BOW, GREENE and BURGESS are guilty as they are the ones with the joint agreement.

C SCIMITER only is guilty, as although there is a joint agreement only he will actually supply the drugs that are subject to the agreement.

D None of them is guilty as the intended recipient of the drugs to be supplied was the conspirators themselves.

ANSWERS

Answer 3.1

Answer **C** — Section 1(1) of the Criminal Attempts Act 1981 requires the accused to have committed an act which is 'more than merely preparatory' to the offence attempted. A mere omission cannot suffice, even where accompanied by the requisite *mens rea*.

A defendant's actions must be shown to have gone beyond mere preparation towards the commission of the substantive offence. Whether the defendant did or did not go beyond that point will be a question of fact for the jury or magistrate(s). So what is the offence here that may be being attempted? It is one of fraud against the insurance company, so although this is always a question of fact for a jury or a magistrate, as a starting point, the insurance company would at least have to be aware of a claim. In this scenario the letter is unsent; the insurance company was ignorant of any false claim against it. Until they are aware there can be no attempt to commit the substantive offence as all other actions will be more than merely preparatory; answers A and B are therefore incorrect.

However posting the letter would probably be the start of the actual claims process not when a claims form is completed; answer D is therefore incorrect.

Crime, para. 1.3.4

Answer 3.2

Answer **A** — Common law conspiracy to defraud involves:

> ... an agreement by two or more [persons] by dishonesty to deprive a person of something which is his or to which he is or would or might be entitled [or] an agreement by two or more by dishonesty to injure some proprietary right [of the victim]...

(*Scott* v *Metropolitan Police Commissioner* [1975] AC 819: *Crime*, para. 1.3.3.2)

Intent to defraud a victim must be shown (*R* v *Hollinshead* [1985] AC 975).

It must also be shown that a defendant was dishonest as set out in *R* v *Ghosh* [1982] QB 1053; answer B is therefore incorrect.

There is no need to show proprietary loss in anyway; answers C and D are therefore incorrect.

Crime, para. 1.3.3.2

Answer 3.3

Answer **D** — One of the exclusions to conspiracies is that husband and wife cannot conspire, but this is when they agree together as the sole conspirators. If, however, a husband and wife conspire with a third person who is not a child under 10 or the intended victim, all three may be liable to conviction (*R* v *Chrastny* [1991] 1 WLR 1381 confirmed in *R* v *Lovick* [1993] Crim LR 890), and therefore answers B and C are incorrect. Conspiracy does occur even though the offence intended never occurs and therefore answer A is incorrect. Once the agreement is made the offence is complete.

Crime, para. 1.3.3.1

Answer 3.4

Answer **D** — The common law offence of conspiracy to defraud is expressly preserved by s. 5(2) of the Criminal Law Act 1977. It is defined in the leading case of *Scott* v *Metropolitan Police Commissioner* [1975] AC 819, where Viscount Dilhorne said:

> ... an agreement by two or more [persons] by dishonesty to deprive a person of something which is his or to which he is or would be or might be entitled [or] an agreement by two or more by dishonesty to injure some proprietary right of his suffices to constitute the offence ...
>
> ... it suffices if there is a dishonest agreement to expose the proposed victim to some form of economic risk or disadvantage to which he would not otherwise be exposed.

The situation in the question deprives the company of its right to sell its own product (see *R* v *Cooke* [1986] AC 909, where buffet car staff were selling their own sandwiches on British Rail trains). It is immaterial whether the company actually made a loss; because the company has been *exposed* to economic risk, therefore answer C is incorrect. Also, it is immaterial whether the customers realised that what they were drinking was not produced by the brewery, as the brewery is actually the loser in this scenario, and answer A is incorrect. Lastly, the offence is committed when the two people agree to deprive the company of profits — the fact that only one of them is employed by the brewery is not relevant, and answer B is incorrect.

Crime, para. 1.3.3.2

Answer 3.5

Answer **B** — Conspiracy to defraud involves:

> ... an agreement by two or more [persons] by dishonesty to deprive a person of something which is his or to which he is or would or might be entitled [or] an agreement by two or more by dishonesty to injure some proprietary right [of the victim] ...

There are two principal variants of this offence, although these are not mutually exclusive. The first is defined above in the leading case of *Scott* v *Metropolitan Police Commissioner* [1975] AC 819. There may or may not be an intent to deceive in such cases, and there may or may not be an intent to cause economic or financial loss to the proposed victim or victims, but it suffices if there is a dishonest agreement to expose the proposed victim to some form of economic risk or disadvantage to which he would not otherwise be exposed.

The second variant was also recognised in *Scott*, but has been more fully considered by the Privy Council in *Wai Yu-Tsang* v *The Queen* [1992] 1 AC 269. In this variant, there must be a dishonest agreement by two or more persons to 'defraud' another, by deceiving him into acting contrary to his duty.

Although the requirement for an agreement between at least two people is the same, this offence is broader than statutory conspiracy. There is no requirement to prove that the end result would amount to the commission of an offence, simply that it would result in depriving a person of something under the specified conditions or in injuring his or her proprietary right; answer C is therefore incorrect.

A good example of this offence can be found in *R* v *Hussain* [2005] EWCA Crim 1866 where the defendant pleaded guilty to conspiracy to defraud after a widespread abuse of the recently introduced postal voting system. In that case the defendant, an official Labour party candidate, collected uncompleted postal votes from households and completed them in his own favour. In that case it was shown that the end result was unlikely to have been affected by the defendant's actions, as it was likely he would have been elected in any case; however this has no effect on the commission of the offence of conspiracy to defraud. The offence is complete when an agreement is reached; answer D is therefore incorrect and is not limited to some dishonest *actus reus* like signing the forms fraudulently; answer A is therefore incorrect.

The *actus reus* of this offence is the agreement, the *mens rea* is the intent of the offender to defraud the victim (*R* v *Hollinshead* [1985] AC 975), and the dishonesty of the defendant as set out in *R* v *Ghosh* [1982] QB 1053.

Crime, para. 1.3.3.2

Answer 3.6

Answer **B** — This is a crime of specific intent, so you need to prove interference with a motor vehicle or trailer, and as such answer D is incorrect (note there is no definition of what interference is). You do, however, have to show an intention to commit theft of the vehicle/trailer, *or* theft from it *or* TADA (taking and driving away); therefore, C is incorrect. It is not necessary to show intention to commit any particular one of the further offences, and intention to commit any of them would suffice; therefore, answer A is incorrect.

Crime, para. 1.3.4.1

Answer 3.7

Answer **C** — A person cannot be guilty of conspiracy if the only other party to the supposed agreement intends to frustrate or sabotage it. As the officer clearly will frustrate the agreement, answers A and D are incorrect. This was considered by the House of Lords in *Yip Chieu-Chung* v *The Queen* [1995] 1 AC 111, where N, the appellant's only fellow conspirator in a plan to smuggle heroin out of Hong Kong, was an undercover agent working with the knowledge of the authorities. The House of Lords held that if N's purpose had been to prevent the heroin being smuggled, no indictable conspiracy would have existed. Their Lordships said:

> The crime of conspiracy requires an agreement between two or more persons to commit an unlawful act with the intention of carrying it out. It is the intention to carry out the crime that constitutes the necessary *mens rea* for the offence .... [A]n undercover agent who has no intention of committing the crime lacks the necessary *mens rea* to be a conspirator.

Conspiracy requires an agreement which will amount to or involve the commission of an offence. Where no such offence is likely, the offence is not made out. Common law conspiracy involves conspiracy to defraud only and therefore B is incorrect.

Crime, paras 1.3.3.1, 1.3.6.3

Answer 3.8

Answer **A** — A person may incite another to do an act by threatening or by pressure, as well as by persuasion, therefore answer C is incorrect. Incitement can be committed even if the incited person refuses to act, or does not commit the actual offence incited, therefore answer D is incorrect. The offence is complete when the inciter uses persuasion in an attempt to incite another to commit the offence. It is irrelevant that SCHALK took the leaflets; the offence was already committed before this action took place, and answer B is incorrect.

Crime, para. 1.3.2

Answer 3.9

Answer **A** — Section 1(1) of the Criminal Attempts Act 1981 requires the accused to have committed an act which is 'more than merely preparatory' to the offence attempted. Where trial is on indictment, it is for the judge to determine whether there is evidence on which a jury could properly find that the accused's actions did go beyond mere preparation, but it is then for the jury to decide that question as one of fact, there is no specific formula used by the courts in interpreting this requirement.

Courts have accepted an approach of questioning whether the defendant had 'embarked on the crime proper' (*R* v *Gullefer* [1990] 1 WLR 1063) but there is no requirement for him or her to have passed a point of no return leading to the commission of the substantive offence. However, to prove an 'attempt' you must show an *intention* on the part of the defendant to commit the substantive offence. So combining 'intent' with 'beyond mere preparation' takes us beyond what DUBROWSKY did. He does not commit the offence or attempted robbery; answers B, C and D are therefore incorrect.

Crime, para. 1.3.4

Answer 3.10

Answer **C** — The question of police entrapment is an emotive one. Where the line was drawn between legitimate police activity in undercover operations and the police acting as *agents provocateurs* was sometimes fuzzy. The House of Lords laid down the legal position in this issue in *R* v *Loosely*; *Attorney General's Reference (No. 3) of 2000* [2001] 1 WLR 2060, where it was held, *inter alia*:

> A useful guide is to consider whether the police did no more than present the defendant with an unexceptional opportunity to commit a crime. The yardstick for the purposes of this test is, in general, whether the police conduct preceding the commission of the offence was no more than might have been expected from others in the circumstances.

Was the officer enticing the accused to commit an offence he would not otherwise have committed? He was committing the offence of drug dealing, and was not entrapped there, but the officer goes beyond being a passive observer when he asks about the firearm. In *Loosely*, their Lordships stated:

> The police must act in good faith. Having reasonable grounds for suspicion is one way good faith may be established. It is not normally considered a legitimate use of police power to provide people not suspected of being engaged in any criminal activity with the opportunity to commit crimes. The principle is that the police should prevent and detect crime, not create it.

So the fact the operation was authorised does not negate entrapment by an individual officer (answer A is incorrect); nor does the fact that the accused seems keen to carry out the officer's request (answer B is incorrect). What is also clear is that simply going beyond what is authorised is not necessarily entrapment; it depends on the officer's action — answer D is therefore incorrect. This area of law has guidelines set down, but ultimately it is for the judge to decide if actions amount to entrapment, and whether such entrapment should lead to a stay of proceedings or not, which is why answer C states 'may be entrapment'.

Crime, para. 1.3.6.1

Answer 3.11

Answer **C** — The scenario is based on the case of *R v Bowles* [2004] EWCA Crim 1608, a case in which the defendant had been convicted of offences of dishonesty against his neighbour. The neighbour's will left her estate to charity, but following his arrest police officers found a 'new' will, fully complete except for a signature. The defendant and his wife were named as the main beneficiaries. Although the defendant's son had been overheard making reference to the fact that he was going to inherit the house, the new will had been drafted over six months earlier and there was no evidence of any steps to execute it, nor any evidence that it had ever been used. The Court of Appeal held that the making of the will was no more than merely preparatory and the defendant's conviction for attempting to make a false instrument was quashed. Answers A and D are therefore incorrect.

A defendant's intention *may* be conditional, that is, he or she may only intend to steal from a house if something worth stealing is later found inside. Answer B is therefore incorrect. The conditional nature of this intention will not generally prevent the charge of attempt being brought and the defendant's intentions will be judged *on the facts as he or she believed them to be*. However, careful drafting of the charge may be required in cases where there is doubt as to the precise extent of the

defendant's knowledge at the time he/she was caught (see *R* v *Husseyn* (1978) 67 Cr
App R 131).

Crime, para. 1.3.4

Answer 3.12

Answer **C** — Under s. 1(1) of the Criminal Law Act 1977, a person is guilty of conspiracy if he or she agrees with any other person(s) that a course of conduct will be
pursued which, if the agreement is carried out in accordance with their intentions,
either —

- (a) will necessarily amount to or involve the commission of any offence or offences by
one or more of the parties to the agreement; or
- (b) would do so but for the existence of facts which render the commission of the offence or any of the offences impossible.

Offences may sometimes be tried in our country even though they were committed
abroad. If the object of a conspiracy would amount to an offence under the jurisdiction of the relevant country *and* of England and Wales, the conspiracy may be
tried under the Criminal Law Act 1977, s. 1A. In addition, it was held in *R* v *Man-
ning* [1998] 2 Cr App R 461 that if people conspire abroad to commit offences in
England and Wales they may, under certain circumstances, be indicted under English and Welsh law even if none of the conspirators enters the jurisdiction to do so.
Answers A and D are therefore incorrect.

The 'end product' of the agreement must be the commission of an offence by
one or more of the parties to the agreement, as this isn't the case answer B is therefore incorrect. When the next meeting is held however the offence is likely to be
committed.

Crime, para. 1.3.3.1

Answer 3.13

Answer **B** — Section 1 of the Criminal Law Act 1977 states:

- (1) Subject to the following provisions of this part of this Act, if a person agrees with
any other person or persons that a course of conduct will be pursued which, if the
agreement is carried out in accordance with their intentions, either —
  - (a) will necessarily amount to or involve the commission of any offence or offences
by one or more of the parties to the agreement; or

(b) would do so but for the existence of facts which render the commission of the offence or any of the offences impossible,

he is guilty of conspiracy to commit the offence or offences in question.

For there to be a conspiracy there must be an agreement. Therefore there must be at least two people involved. Each conspirator must be aware of the overall common purpose to which they all attach themselves. If one conspirator enters into separate agreements with different people, each agreement is a separate conspiracy (*R* v *Griffiths* [1966] 1 QB 589).

A person can be convicted of conspiracy even if the other conspirators are unknown (as to the effect of the acquittal of one party to a conspiracy on the other parties, see s. 5(8) of the Criminal Law Act 1977).

However a defendant cannot be convicted of a statutory conspiracy if the only other party to the agreement is:

- his or her spouse
- a person under 10 years of age
- the intended victim

(Criminal Law Act 1977, s. 2(2)).

An indictment for conspiracy must not be misleading. An indictment alleging that the defendants conspired to supply drugs to 'another' cannot sensibly apply to a case in which the intended recipient was one of the conspirators (*R* v *Jackson* The Times, 13 May 1999; *R* v *Drew* [1999] EWCA Crim 401).

In this scenario SCIMITER has conspired to supply drugs to his co-conspirators; he therefore cannot be guilty of statutory conspiracy; answers A and C are therefore incorrect.

The other three have, however, conspired to supply controlled drugs to persons other than those who have conspired, and they are guilty; answer D is therefore incorrect.

Crime, para. 1.3.3.1

4 | General Defences

STUDY PREPARATION

There is little point in collecting evidence, arresting and charging a person only to find that they raise a specific or general defence at trial — a defence which the investigating officer could have addressed in interview or when taking witness statements. For this reason alone it is important to know what defences may exist in relation to certain offences. Similarly, as the police are under a duty to investigate fully and impartially, it is important to know what defences may be available to a defendant.

A number of offences have specific defences contained in the relevant statute, and these are (not surprisingly) called statutory defences. In addition, there are a number of 'general defences', some of which are statutory and others existing at common law. It is helpful to divide general defences into two categories:

1. Those which involve a denial of the basic requirements of *mens rea* and voluntary conduct (the defences of mistake and automatism are best regarded in this way).
2. Those which do not deny these basic requirements but which rely on other circumstances of excuse or justification, as in the defences of duress and self-defence.

The integration of the Human Rights Act 1998 and the European Convention on Human Rights into English law is also important in this area of study.

QUESTIONS

Question 4.1

SHUNZO was a small time drug dealer who believed he was some sort of underworld lord. He felt that as a major criminal there would be any number of other drug dealers after his 'turf'. This was not true at all, SHUNZO was not a threat to any of the major gang related drug dealing that took place where he lived. SHUNZO was approached by two police officers in plain clothes (suits, shirt and tie), who had a warrant for his arrest. Before they could introduce themselves SHUNZO hit out and punched one of the officers. SHUNZO believed they were two rival drug dealers out to get him.

With regards to whether SHUNZO could claim he was acting in self defence due to mistaken belief, which of the following is correct?

A SHUNZO would have to show that his belief was reasonable to claim self defence.
B SHUNZO would have to show that his belief was reasonable and that his actions were necessary to claim self defence.
C SHUNZO would be judged on whether the 'reasonable man' would believe that his actions were reasonable to claim self defence.
D SHUNZO would be judged on the circumstances as he believed them to be at the time, whether they were reasonable or not is irrelevant.

Question 4.2

AISLING and HIEN had been drinking in a nightclub all night. HIEN claimed he was an SAS soldier. They left together to go to AISLING's flat. The next morning, AISLING made an emergency call saying that he had been out all night and had returned to find an unknown man dead in his home; this male was HEIN; near the deceased's body was a sledgehammer. Under HEIN's body was found a stick, some 5 feet in length, which belonged to AISLING and which he had fashioned to resemble a samurai sword. AISLING stated that if he had killed HIEN, he might have acted in self defence in that HIEN might have attacked him with the stick, and he might have used the sledgehammer to defend himself. AISLING stated that his drunken state might have led him to believe, albeit mistakenly, that the deceased was an SAS soldier attacking him with a sword.

In relation to the claim of a mistaken belief of self defence induced by voluntary intoxication, which of the following is correct?

A This defence could only apply where the charge was murder given the specific intent required for such a charge.
B This defence could only apply where the charge was manslaughter as this is a basic intent offence.
C This defence will always be available in homicide offences, but only so far as sentencing is concerned.

D This defence will not apply as a defendant cannot rely on a mistake induced by their own voluntary intoxication.

Question 4.3

BROGAN was driving her large goods vehicle along the motorway when she collided with a car, which was stationary on the hard shoulder. The driver of the car was killed and at a subsequent trial BROGAN claimed the defence of automatism.

Which of the following best describes what 'automatism' is legally?
A Any loss of voluntary control due to some external influence.
B Total loss of voluntary control due to some external influence.
C An involuntary reflex brought about by an external influence.
D An involuntary reflex brought about by an influence, external or internal.

Question 4.4

MAPLEY has been stopped by Constable MORRIS who was driving an unmarked police vehicle. The officer, although in uniform, did not have his warrant card with him. Constable MORRIS asked MAPLEY to take a breath test as he could smell alcohol on his breath, he refused when the officer could not produce his warrant card when asked by MAPLEY. The officer tried to grab hold of MAPLEY to arrest him; MAPLEY threw him off and drove away. MAPLEY later stated he did not believe that Constable MORRIS was a real police officer.

Considering the offence of assault with intent to resist arrest only, could MAPLEY avail himself of the defence of mistake?
A Yes, provided his belief that MORRIS was not a police officer was genuinely held.
B Yes, provided his belief that MORRIS was not a police officer was genuinely held and reasonable in the circumstances.
C No, the officer was in full uniform and was not under an obligation to produce a warrant card.
D No, the officer was in uniform; MAPLEY could never have any reasonable belief that MORRIS was not a police officer.

Question 4.5

CRANSTON, aged 15, has been bullied at school by a gang of youths. The gang are well known for shoplifting in the lunch hour in the local shops. One evening, while his parents were out, CRANSTON received a phone call from one of the gang members, stating that the gang wanted him to steal a pair of trainers from a sports shop on the way into school. The caller stated that if he did not comply, he would be severely beaten the next day in school by members of the gang. CRANSTON was very scared and the next day tried to steal a pair of trainers.

In relation to any possible defence that CRANSTON might have, which of the following is correct?

A CRANSTON would not be able to rely on the defence of duress in these circumstances, as it applies to threats of death only.

B Provided CRANSTON held a genuine belief that he would be seriously injured if he did not commit the crime, he would have a defence of duress in these circumstances.

C CRANSTON would be able to rely on the defence of duress in these circumstances, as a threat was made. It is immaterial whether he believed the threat or not.

D CRANSTON would not be able to rely on the defence of duress in these circumstances, as the threat was not immediate.

Question 4.6

GLAKKEN was a drug user heavily in debt to his dealer. The dealer suggested that GLAKKEN could pay off some of his debt by collecting several bottles of 'shampoo' from a nearby town and delivering it to the dealer. GLAKKEN readily agreed, however, the dealer outlined that there was in fact no choice; he reminded GLAKKEN that he knew where he and his girlfriend lived and that he was a very violent and vengeful man. GLAKKEN collected the 'shampoo' which surprisingly turned out to be class A drugs, and GLAKKEN was arrested when found in possession of it.

Could GLAKKEN use duress as a defence?

A Yes, as his and his girlfriend's life was threatened.

B Yes, but only if he genuinely believed that the threat issued would be carried out.

C No, prior to the threat being made GLAKKEN had agreed to collect the drugs.

D No, as GLAKKKEN exposed himself to such risk with his association with drugs and the dealer.

Question 4.7

SWANSON parks his car whilst he goes into a restaurant for a meal. He meets a friend and ends up drinking more than he had intended. Believing he would be over the legal limit for driving, SWANSON returns to his car to collect his laptop computer, fully intending to get a taxi. There is now a large gang near his car. The gang are very aggressive and SWANSON fears for his personal safety. As they charge at him, he jumps into his car and drives away. He stops about half a mile further down the road, and parks the car, intending to take a taxi. However, a police officer sees SWANSON and breathalyses him, the result of which is positive. SWANSON is charged with a drink driving offence.

Will SWANSON have a defence to this offence?

A   Yes, he could claim duress.
B   Yes, he could claim duress of circumstances.
C   No, there is no defence to drink driving offences.
D   No, general defences apply to criminal offences only.

Question 4.8

Doctor HODGES keeps a quantity of cannabis at her surgery, the sole purpose of which is to dispense to sufferers of various illnesses that cause severe pain to the patient. The doctor had found that cannabis was more effective than any other proprietary medicine that was available, and that use of cannabis was the only way to reduce the severe pain that her patients were in. This was the only defence she had raised when questioned by the police about her actions.

Will the doctor have a defence of possession of controlled drugs with the intention of supplying them using a general defence?

A   Yes, provided the doctor could justify that she was conducting medical research.
B   Yes, provided the doctor reasonably believed that what she was doing was a medical necessity.
C   No, in these circumstances the doctor will have no general defence to possession with intent to supply.
D   No, because she did not raise her actions as a 'human rights' issue; in that case she may well have had a defence.

Question 4.9

Constable CROWLEY is on the tactical firearms unit, and has been called to a hostage situation. Unfortunately, the incident ends when Constable CROWLEY fatally shoots RUSSELL, who was the assailant.

In relation to the lawfulness of CROWLEY's use of lethal force, what test will be applied?

A That he had an honestly held belief that it was necessary.
B That such force was reasonable in the circumstances.
C That such force was no more than absolutely necessary.
D That such force was necessary to protect the life of another.

Question 4.10

LOXLEY is a keen archer and has permission from WARMAN to use his land for practice. WARMAN even tells him that there is a scarecrow in a field that he can fire at. LOXLEY takes his high-powered bow and fires an arrow at the scarecrow from 200 metres. Being a good shot he hits the scarecrow, but is surprised when the scarecrow falls over. He goes to investigate and is horrified to find he has just shot a rambler who had stopped to check his map.

Could LOXLEY use the defence of mistake if he was charged with murder?
A No, he was under a positive obligation to check what he was aiming at.
B No, he should have checked with the landowner if there was a public footpath.
C Yes, as he had the landowner's authority, the landowner is vicariously liable.
D Yes, as he did not have the requisite *mens rea*.

Question 4.11

The police were called to a domestic disturbance at the home of BOORMAN and his wife, DENISE. On their arrival, officers were confronted by BOORMAN, a six foot two male, of heavy build, and DENISE, who was five foot two and of slim build. DENISE had suffered a deep cut to the back of her head and claimed it was caused by BOORMAN, who had pushed her against a wall. BOORMAN claimed that he was acting in self defence, as DENISE had attacked him with a vase and that he had only pushed her away with the open palm of his hand. BOORMAN was arrested for assault by the officers.

Which of the following statements is correct in relation to what factors the court might take into consideration if BOORMAN were to claim self-defence?
A The court would not take into account the relative sizes of BOORMAN and DENISE; the issue is whether BOORMAN held a genuine belief that the force was reasonable in the circumstances.
B In the circumstances, the court would have expected BOORMAN to retreat when he perceived the threat from DENISE.
C The court would not take into account the gender of BOORMAN and DENISE; the issue is whether BOORMAN held a genuine belief that the force was reasonable in the circumstances.

D The court may take into account both the relative sizes of BOORMAN and DENISE, and the gender difference.

Question 4.12

GYSLOR was found in possession of a shotgun and on the way to commit a burglary. When he was arrested and interviewed, however, he stated that his wife was being held captive by an armed gang who threatened to kill her if he did not commit the burglary. He also stated that it was his idea and not the gang's that he should take the shotgun; his intention was to use it to resist arrest and he felt his wife's life was in danger.

Considering that GYSLOR has committed an offence contrary to s. 18 of the Firearms Act 1968 (carrying a firearm or imitation firearm with intent to resist arrest), will he be able to claim the defence of duress?

A Yes, but only if he can show that the intention to resist arrest was as a result of duress.

B Yes, in these circumstances duress is available as a defence, as this was the reason he took the shotgun.

C No, duress is not available as he was only asked to carry out a burglary, the firearms offence was his idea.

D No, the defence of duress is not available if the threat is made against a third party, unless they are present at the time of the offence.

Question 4.13

In relation to the defence of duress of circumstances, the person accused of an offence must have acted in a certain way.

In relation to what caused the person to behave as they did which of the following is correct?

A The person must be impelled to behave as they did because they themselves actually feared a criminal act being committed.

B The person must be impelled to behave as they did because a reasonable person in those circumstances would fear a criminal act being committed.

C The person must be impelled to behave as they did because a criminal act was actually being committed there and then.

D The person must be impelled to behave as they did because they perceived a threat that in itself would not amount to a criminal act.

Question 4.14

WEDDON and HOPKINS have been jointly charged with an offence of aggravated burglary. It is alleged by the prosecution that during the burglary of a dwelling house, WEDDON and HOPKINS assaulted and seriously injured the elderly occupant. WEDDON is aged 10 and HOPKINS is aged 14.

Which of the following statements is correct, in relation to criminal liability of both defendants?

A Because of their ages, the prosecution *may* be asked by the court to adduce evidence to show that both knew that what they had done was seriously wrong but only where challenged by the defence to do so.

B Both WEDDON and HOPKINS are criminally liable for the offence as charged, irrespective of their ages.

C Because of his age, HOPKINS is criminally liable; however, the prosecution *may* be asked by the court to adduce evidence that to show that WEDDON knew that what she had done was seriously wrong.

D Because of their ages, the prosecution *will always* be asked by the court to adduce evidence to show that both knew that what they had done was seriously wrong.

Question 4.15

NORSTER had driven his stepson to work although he was disqualified from driving. He claimed that he had done this because his wife had threatened to commit suicide unless he did so, as the boy was in danger of losing his job if he was late. The wife had suicidal tendencies and a doctor had told NORSTER that it was likely that she would carry out any threat to take her own life. In fact the wife had no intentions of killing herself that night; it was just her way of ensuring her son was not late for work.

In these circumstances would the defence of duress of circumstances be likely to succeed?

A Yes, as NORSTER had reasonable grounds to suppose his wife's threat was real due to the doctor's report.

B Yes, because NORSTER had an honestly held belief that his wife may carry out her threat.

C No, because there was no actual threat to NORSTER's life.

D No, because the threat made by the wife was not in fact true.

ANSWERS

Answer 4.1

Answer **D** — Section 3(1) of the Criminal Law Act 1967 provides that:

A person may use such force as is reasonable in the circumstances in the prevention of crime, or in effecting or assisting in the lawful arrest of offenders or suspected offenders or of persons unlawfully at large.

Note that it is the amount of force that has to be reasonable, not the defendant's belief. If the defendant mistakenly believes that he or she is being attacked, that belief does not have to be 'reasonable', nor do they have to show it was 'necessary'; answers A and B are therefore incorrect (*R* v *Williams* (*Gladstone*) [1987] 3 All ER 411). In such cases the defendant's actions will be judged against the circumstances as he or she believed them to be at the time, not the 'reasonable person'; answer C is therefore incorrect.

Therefore, where a defendant mistakenly believed he was being attacked by strangers and 'defended' himself against them, his actions were to be judged as though that were actually the case — even though the strangers were in fact police officers and court officials and the defendant's mistake was not an entirely reasonable one (*Blackburn* v *Bowering* [1994] 1 WLR 1324).

Crime, para. 1.4.8.2

Answer 4.2

Answer **D** — The principal restriction imposed on defences based on intoxication is that voluntary intoxication can only give rise to a defence to crimes of specific rather than basic intent as the courts have also accepted that a defendant is still capable of forming basic intent even when completely inebriated (see *DPP* v *Majewski* [1977] AC 443).

This is further complicated where the defence used relates to a mistaken belief. Although the principle that an accused who mistakenly believes he is being attacked may be able to rely on the defence of self defence this does not apply where the accused's mistake was due to voluntary intoxication (*R* v *O'Grady* [1987] QB 995). Although the actual conviction in *O'Grady* was for manslaughter (a basic intent offence), the Court of Appeal seemed clear in the view that an intoxicated mistake could not be relied upon even in relation to a crime of specific intent such as murder. This view was further endorsed by the Court of Appeal in *R* v *Hatton* (2006) 1 Cr App R 16; the court held that on the proper application of the law of precedence, the general principle that was the reason for the court's decision in *O'Grady* was not to be regarded as mere *obiter dicta* (remarks of a judge which are not necessary to reaching a decision, but are made as comments, illustrations or thoughts) so far as the law of murder was concerned. Accordingly, the court was bound by the decision, and there were no grounds to argue that the judge should have directed the jury to consider whether the defendant's drunkenness might have led him to make a mistake as to the severity of any attack to which he might have been subjected by the deceased.

The specific defence raised in this scenario cannot be raised in a case of manslaughter or murder; answers A and B are therefore incorrect. Although in manslaughter cases mitigation is allowed in sentencing, a conviction for murder leaves a judge no discretion in sentencing a defendant; answer C is therefore incorrect.

Crime, paras 1.4.3.1, 1.4.8.2

Answer 4.3

Answer **B** — Strictly speaking, automatism is not a 'defence'; it is an absence of a fundamental requirement for any criminal offence, i.e. the 'criminal conduct'. Automatism is where a defendant has total loss of control over his or her actions; in these circumstances he or she cannot be held liable for those actions. Only where this loss of control is total, are there grounds to claim a defence of automatism; answer A is therefore incorrect.

One example of this defence is the road traffic case where a swarm of bees flies into a car; other examples might include a person inadvertently dropping and damaging property when suddenly seized by cramp, or discharging a firearm as a result of an irresistible bout of sneezing. As can be seen, the influences that cause the involuntary action can be external (the bees) or internal (sneezing). However, as stated, an involuntary action alone may not suffice exclusive of total loss of control.

In *Attorney General's Reference (No. 2 of 1992)* [1993] 4 All ER 683, in circumstances mirroring this scenario, it was held that the defence of automatism requires a total destruction of voluntary control on the defendant's part. Impaired, reduced or partial control is not enough. The evidence of 'driving without awareness' (as offered by the defence) did not lay the proper evidential foundation; some control had been retained by the driver. The test is, can the defendant be said not to be driving at all? Any involuntary reflex is not a total loss of control as is required for this defence; answers C and D are therefore incorrect.

Crime, para. 1.4.2

Answer 4.4

Answer **A** — The defence of mistake will only be used to negate the *mens rea* of the offence charged. In *R* v *Lee* [2000] Crim LR 991, a case arising from an assault on two arresting police officers, the Court of Appeal reviewed the law in this area, reaffirming the following points:

- A genuine or honest mistake could provide a defence to many criminal offences requiring a particular state of mind, including assault with intent to resist arrest (*R* v *Brightling* [1991] Crim LR 364).
- A defence of mistake had to involve a mistake of fact, not a mistake of law.

Here MAPLEY is contesting a fact, not a point of law. The officer, although in uniform, did not produce a warrant card, MAPLEY would only have to show that he genuinely believed that the person who stopped him was not a police officer for the defence to succeed. The defendant need not even show that his belief was reasonable in the circumstances only that he had no 'intent'; answer B is therefore incorrect.

It is immaterial what the officer's actions were and whether they were in uniform or not, all that is required is the honest mistake, and you would have to say that not being able to produce a warrant card 'gifts' this defence to MAPLEY; answers C and D are therefore incorrect.

Crime, para. 1.4.5

Answer 4.5

Answer **D** — Generally speaking, where a person is threatened with death or serious physical injury unless he or she carries out a criminal act, he or she may use the defence of duress. Note that this includes a threat of serious injury, not just death, therefore answer A is incorrect (see *R* v *Graham* [1982] 1 WLR 294). There are, however, caveats to this general use of duress. One of these caveats is that the threatened injury must be anticipated at or near the time of the offence (i.e. not some time in the distant future). As the threat was for the following day CRANSTON could not use the defence, and answers B and C are both incorrect.

Crime, para. 1.4.6

Answer 4.6

Answer **D** — Where a person is threatened with death or serious physical injury unless they carry out a criminal act, they may have a defence of duress. However if a defendant knowingly exposes himself or herself to a risk of such a threat of death or serious physical injury, he or she cannot then claim duress as a defence. For instance, if a person joins a violent gang or an active terrorist organisation, he or she cannot then claim duress as a defence to any crimes he or she may go on to commit under threat of death or serious injury from another member or rival of that organisation (see *R v Sharp* [1987] QB 853). In *Sharp* the Lord Chief Justice held that 'where a person has voluntarily, and with the knowledge of its nature, joined a criminal organisation or gang which he knew might bring pressure on him to commit an offence, he cannot avail himself of the defence of duress'.

Although GLAKKEN was not a member of a gang as such by becoming indebted to a drug dealer he had put himself at risk and could not expect to be rescued by the courts whatever his belief; answers A and B are therefore incorrect.

Although the threat followed the agreement this would not negate the actual defence of duress, that is not what defeats the defence in this scenario, it is the association with the dealer; answer C is therefore incorrect.

Crime, para. 1.4.6

Answer 4.7

Answer **B** — Duress of circumstances is available in traffic cases, so answers C and D are incorrect. SWANSON has to show that his actions were reasonable (*R v Martin* [1989] 1 All ER 652). Here his actions could be regarded as 'reasonable', as he feared for his safety. The fact he stopped soon after supports this claim, and the defence has succeeded in similar circumstances (*DPP v Bell* [1992] RTR 335). Contrast this with *DPP v Jones* [1990] RTR 33, where a similar defence failed because the accused drove all the way home, without even checking whether he was still being chased. The facts of this question would not support a defence of 'duress' as no threat has been made, which is a necessary component of that defence, which makes answer A incorrect.

Crime, para. 1.4.7

Answer 4.8

Answer **C** — The Court of Appeal has considered this specific issue in *R v Quayle and Others* [2005] 1 WLR 3642, specifically whether a defence of medical necessity could be left to the jury in relation to offences of cultivation, production, possession,

possession with intent to supply or importation of cannabis allegedly committed for the purpose of alleviating severe pain.

In *Quayle* the Attorney General made a reference in respect of a defence of 'medical necessity', concerned as to whether or not the defence of necessity was available in respect of drugs offences such as possession of cannabis with intent to supply where the defendant intended to supply the drug for the purpose of alleviating pain from a pre-existing illness (such as multiple sclerosis).

It was also argued that the common law defence of necessity should be expanded to prevent or remove any inconsistency with statutory legislation such as the European Convention on Human Rights. Dismissing the appeals, the Court held that necessary 'medical use' claimed on an individual basis was in conflict with the purpose and effect of the legislative scheme (in particular the Misuse of Drugs Act 1971 and the relevant Regulations); answer B is therefore incorrect. No such use was permitted under the legislation, even on doctor's prescription, except in the context of ongoing trials for medical research purposes. In this scenario the doctor could not attempt to justify that her actions were for research; for this defence to work evidence of proper research and trials would have to exist; answer A is therefore incorrect.

The legislative scheme did not permit unqualified individuals to prescribe cannabis to themselves as patients or to assume the role of a doctor by obtaining, prescribing and supplying it to other 'patients'. Neither can a defendant rely on the same defence by presenting it as a 'human rights' issue (*R v Altham* [2006] EWCA Crim 7); answer D is therefore incorrect.

For the defence of necessity of circumstances to be potentially available, there has to be 'extraneous circumstances capable of objective scrutiny by judge and jury' (per *R v Hasan* [2005] UKHL 22) and the legal defences of duress by threats and 'necessity' should be confined to cases where there was an imminent danger of physical injury and pain.

Crime, paras 1.4.6, 1.4.7

Answer 4.9

Answer **C** — The test applied under s. 3(1) of the Criminal Law Act 1967 — such force as is reasonable in the circumstances — has been superseded, as far as lethal force is concerned, by Art. 2 of the European Convention on Human Rights. Under the Convention the test for such force is now no more than 'absolutely necessary';

in addition it must be strictly proportionate to the legitimate purpose being pursued. Anything other than this strict test will not be enough, making answers A, B and D incorrect.

Crime, para. 1.4.8.1

Answer 4.10

Answer **D** — The defences of mistake and inadvertence consist of a denial of the *mens rea* of the particular crime charged. The *mens rea* for murder is the intention to kill or cause grievous bodily harm. So in relation to this defence you can generalise that wherever an offence requires individual awareness of a particular element, a genuine mistake that such an element is absent will be a defence. The logic of this rule is irrefutable as applied to crimes requiring intention. If a man believes he is shooting at an inanimate object such as a scarecrow, he cannot at the same time by that very act intend to kill. Consider the offence of handling stolen goods, where particular information is required. A person who believes that the goods he buys are not stolen cannot at the same time know (or even believe) that the goods are stolen — the two states of mind are logically inconsistent with one another. However, some offences require some degree of foresight or awareness of risk, and these offences create problems for those wishing to avail themselves of this defence; they would have to show ruling out of any risk of the prohibited consequences (see *Chief Constable of Avon and Somerset Constabulary* v *Shimmen* (1986) 84 Cr App R 7). Here the accused claimed to have ruled out the risk of causing damage to a window when he aimed a martial-art-style kick in its direction, basing his view on his faith in his own prowess as an exponent of the Korean art of self defence. In other words, he claimed to believe that no damage would result from his action (the subsequent shattering of the window revealing this belief to be a sadly mistaken one). So LOXLEY, if charged with murder, would not have to show foresight of what he was aiming at, or whether there might be a person as opposed to an inanimate object in the field, where he was to use this defence; answers A and B are therefore incorrect. And even with the landowner's permission, were LOXLEY to have the requisite *mens rea* for murder, this defence would not be available; answer C is therefore incorrect.

Crime, para. 1.4.5

Answer 4.11

Answer **D** — In deciding whether or not the force used by a defendant was reasonable in the circumstances, the courts may take into account matters such as the relative height, build and strength of the defendant and the person against whom the force was used and the injuries caused. The court may also take into account the gender of the parties (see *R (on the application of Buckley)* v *DPP* [2004] EWHC 2533). In this case, the court also found that even an open-handed push could amount to unreasonable force in the circumstances. Answers A and C are therefore incorrect.

There is no requirement to let the believed attacker 'strike the first blow' (see *Beckford* v *The Queen* [1988] AC 130) *or* for the person defending themselves to retreat (see *R* v *Bird* [1985] 1 WLR 816). A 'pre-emptive' strike may be justified by the circumstances. Answer B is therefore incorrect.

Crime, para. 1.4.8.2

Answer 4.12

Answer **A** — First, let's consider the offence under s. 18 of the Firearms Act 1968 which states:

(1) It is an offence for a person to have with him a firearm or imitation firearm with intent to commit an indictable offence, or to resist arrest or prevent the arrest of another, in either case while he has a firearm or imitation firearm with him.

It is important to note that the offence asked of him is different from the offence he stands accused of; this does not mean *per se* that he cannot use the defence of duress. However, where applicable intent is a fundamental element of an offence, the accused must show that he or she had, or could only have formed that intent by reason of that duress. Without showing that the only compelling factor in the formation of the relevant intent is duress, then the defence will fail (*R* v *Fisher* [2004] EWCA Crim 1190); answer C is therefore incorrect. Note the relevant intent here is that of resisting arrest, not possession of the shotgun; therefore answer B is incorrect.

The question is whether the threat has to be directed at the accused or whether threats to third parties, especially close relatives, can suffice. There seems to be consensus amongst legal commentators on this point and certainly in principle threats to third parties should be capable of constituting duress. Even the bravest man may be prepared to risk his own neck whilst baulking at subjecting his loved ones to serious peril. Indeed there is Australian authority recognising threats to the accused's common-law wife, and in *R* v *Ortiz* (1986) 83 Cr App R 173 threats to the accused's wife or family appear to have been considered to be sufficient; answer D is therefore incorrect.

Crime, para. 1.4.6

Answer 4.13

Answer **D** — As well as cases where a person receives a direct threat in order to make them commit an offence, there may be times when circumstances leave the defendant no real alternative. In *R v Cairns* [1992] 2 Cr App R 137 the court held that the jury must ask two questions in relation to this 'necessary action':

- Was he (or might he have been) impelled to act as he did because, as a result of what he reasonably believed, he had good cause to fear he would suffer death or serious injury if he did not do so?
- If so, would a sober person of reasonable firmness and sharing the same characteristics, have responded to the situation in the way that he did?

If each question were answered with a 'yes', the defence would be made out.

In the case of *R v Jones (Margaret) & Others* [2004] EWCA 1981, the Court of Appeal considered whether a case of necessity or duress of circumstances could be made out for a person who used force in the honestly held belief that in doing so he was protecting the property of others abroad from damage that would be caused by the executive's lawful exercise of the prerogative power to wage war. The Court accepted that that the defence of necessity was available if a defendant could show that he acted to prevent an act of greater evil but there was no requirement that the act of greater evil should be unlawful. This effectively means that a person can act in duress of circumstances where the threat (or perceived threat) does not amount to a criminal act. Therefore answers A, B and C are incorrect as they relate to criminal acts or perceptions of criminal acts.

Crime, para. 1.4.7

Answer 4.14

Answer **B** — Before the Crime and Disorder Act 1998, children under 14 years of age were subject to a rebuttable presumption at common law to be 'incapable of evil' or *doli incapax*. The presumption of *doli incapax* in relation to children who were aged 10 or over but who had not yet reached 14 years of age was *rebuttable*. This meant that the prosecution could adduce evidence to show that the child defendant knew that what he or she had done was seriously wrong. If the evidence was accepted, the courts would regard that presumption as having been rebutted and the child defendant could be tried in much the same way as an adult. Some concern as to how appropriate such a presumption was in modern society led the House of Lords in *C (a Minor) v DPP* [1995] 2 WLR 383 to declare the rule to be outdated but adding that it was up to Parliament to change it. Section 34 of the Crime and Disorder Act 1998 did exactly that and abolished this second, rebuttable form of the presumption of *doli incapax*, effectively lowering the age of criminal responsibility to 10 years of age.

In relation to children under 10 years of age that presumption was, and still is irrebuttable. Consequently, no evidence to the contrary will be entertained by a court and children under 10 cannot be convicted of a criminal offence.

Since both defendants are over 10, they are both criminally liable for their actions and answers A, C and D are incorrect.

Crime, para. 1.4.10

Answer 4.15

Answer **B** — In *R* v *Martin* [1989] 1 All ER 652 Simon-Brown J stated that the principles of duress of circumstances may be summarised as:

- First, English law does in extreme circumstances recognise a defence of necessity. It can arise from objective dangers threatening the accused or others in which case it is conveniently called 'duress of circumstances'.
- Secondly, the defence is available only if, from an objective standpoint, the accused can be said to be acting reasonably and proportionately in order to avoid a threat of death or serious injury.
- Thirdly, assuming the defence to be open to the accused on his account of the facts, the issue should be left to the jury, who should be directed to determine these two questions:
  - (1) Was the accused, or may he have been, impelled to act as he did because as a result of what he reasonably believed to be the situation he had good cause to fear that otherwise death or serious injury would result?
  - (2) If so, may a sober person of reasonable firmness, sharing the characteristics of the accused, have responded to that situation by acting as the accused acted?

If the answer to both these questions was yes, then the jury would acquit: the defence of necessity would have been established. Further, the court in *Martin* was willing to contemplate the defence succeeding where an unqualified or disqualified driver took control of a car to get a person who had suffered a heart attack to hospital.

The important aspect to this defence then is that it will only avail the defendant as long as he or she is acting under compulsion of the prevailing circumstances when committing the offence. It appears that the defendant need only hold an *honest* belief that those circumstances exist without necessarily having *reasonable grounds* for that belief (see *DPP* v *Rogers* [1998] Crim LR 202) and there is no need for the threat to be 'real'. In other words there is no need for the doctor's report, provided the defendant honestly believed his wife's threat (whether it was true or not), the defence could succeed; answers A and D are therefore incorrect.

The threat does also not have to be directed against the person who commits the unlawful act; answer C is therefore incorrect.

Crime, para. 1.4.7

5 | Homicide

STUDY PREPARATION

This chapter contains the law relating to some of the most serious charges a person can face. Although these offences are still relatively rare and are usually dealt with by specialist investigators, it is important to know the constituent elements — particularly as it is often more a case of good fortune which prevents people involved in assaults and woundings from facing these more serious charges. In addition to the offences themselves, the chapter deals extensively with the special defences associated with an indictment for murder. It is worth noting that there are three different types of manslaughter offences, and it is worth learning the differences between them.

QUESTIONS

Question 5.1

QIAN has had a stormy relationship with his girlfriend, who is now 7 months' pregnant. One night, in a fit of rage, he hits her so hard she falls and bangs her head on the wall. She is taken into hospital and goes into early labour. The child is still born. When interviewed by police, QIAN admits that his intention was only to cause serious injury to the mother.

Which is the most appropriate charge relating to the death of the baby?

A Murder.
B Manslaughter.
C Grievous bodily harm owing to transferred malice of intention.
D No offence in relation to the death of the baby.

Question 5.2

KOBIS is a cruel man, and has systematically beaten his wife over many years. One night, after another battering, his wife loses any self control she had left and decides she will hurt her husband, she does not care if he lives or dies. However, afraid that he is stronger than her, she waits till he is asleep and then takes a baseball bat and strikes KOBIS on the head several times. KOBIS does not die from his injuries, but suffers irreparable brain damage. His wife is charged with attempted murder.

Which of the statements below is correct in relation to whether the wife could use any of the 'special defences'?

A His wife could be guilty of attempted murder, and could only use the defence of provocation to defend herself.

B His wife could be guilty of attempted murder, and could use either provocation or diminished responsibility to defend herself.

C His wife could be guilty of attempted murder, but could not use the special defences as her husband did not actually die.

D His wife, in these circumstances, could not be guilty of attempted murder and therefore needs no defence

Question 5.3

PIDGEON is a central heating engineer and is employed by a company. PIDGEON incorrectly fits a part when repairing a gas combi boiler and as a result it leaks carbon monoxide. Due to this leak the owner of the house dies of carbon monoxide poisoning. The company was aware that PIDGEON's work had not been up to scratch in the past, and had already issued two written warnings to him for errors in repairs he had done. Neither of the previous cases had led to any injuries though.

Considering the offence of manslaughter, which of the following is correct?

A PIDGEON could only be guilty of manslaughter by unlawful act, as due to his omission a person died unlawfully.

B PIDGEON could only be guilty of manslaughter by unlawful act, as due to his omission a person died unlawfully *or* manslaughter by gross negligence.

C PIDGEON could only be guilty of manslaughter by gross negligence due to the duty of care; the company are not culpable at all.

D PIDGEON could only be guilty of manslaughter by gross negligence due to the duty of care and the company guilty of corporate manslaughter.

Question 5.4

STEADMAN, NAYLOR and BLUNT decide they want to end their lives and form a written agreement. They intend to shoot each other in a game of Russian roulette which involves loading a gun with four bullets, one of which is a blank. They load the revolver and spin the chamber. STEADMAN fatally shoots NAYLOR in the head, and then BLUNT fatally shoots STEADMAN in the head. BLUNT then turns the gun on himself but the next bullet is blank. Thankful to be alive, BLUNT panics and runs from the scene.

In relation to suicide pacts, if BLUNT is to use this as a 'special defence' to murder, which of the following must be shown?

A Only that such a pact existed at the time BLUNT shot STEADMAN.

B That a pact existed and that BLUNT intended to shoot himself next.

C That a written agreement existed between STEADMAN and BLUNT.

D That a written agreement existed between all the parties.

Question 5.5

IVY and his common law wife had been to the local pub where they had been drinking heavily and arguing. IVY returned to their flat where he chopped wood with an axe and drank more lager. His common law wife was still in a public house drinking. When she returned to the flat she told IVY she had just had sex with another man. IVY picked up the axe, intending to leave the flat and chop some more wood, when his common law wife said, 'You haven't got the guts'. He struck her 7 or 8 times with the axe, killing her, and is charged with murder.

IVY wishes to use 'provocation' as a defence; for the purposes of the defence of provocation by what standard should he be judged?

A He will be judged on whether a 'reasonable' or ordinary person would have lost his self-control in these circumstances.

B He will be judged on whether a 'reasonable' or ordinary person, who was also drunk, would have lost his self-control in these circumstances.

C He will be judged on his own particular circumstances, particularly that he was drunk.

D He will be judged on his own particular circumstances, but not the fact that he was drunk.

Question 5.6

NEWLEY and PROTHEROE were hunting fanatics. While hunting in the local woods, NEWLEY thought he would play a joke on PROTHEROE. NEWLEY pointed his rifle at PROTHEROE, believing there were no bullets in the chamber, and pulled the trigger. However, he had not checked the gun properly and PROTHEROE was hit by a bullet in the chest. PROTHEROE was taken to the local hospital, where he subsequently died.

In relation to any homicide offences committed by NEWLEY, which of the following is correct?

A NEWLEY is guilty of murder in these circumstances, as he was reckless in his actions.

B NEWLEY is guilty of manslaughter in these circumstances, as he was reckless in his actions.

C NEWLEY is not guilty of manslaughter by an unlawful act, as he had no intention to injure PROTHEROE.

D NEWLEY is guilty of manslaughter in these circumstances, as he was negligent in relation to his gun.

Question 5.7

KACIK had been bullying his college friend CROFT for several years. CROFT was terrified of KACIK and did everything he could to stay out of his way. CROFT was standing on the platform of the railway station when he saw KACIK walking towards him in a threatening manner. In panic he ran across the railway track, but stood on the electric rail which killed him outright. In fact KACIK had not seen CROFT on the platform, his threats were directed towards another person standing near CROFT.

Is KACIK guilty of the manslaughter by unlawful act?

A Yes, as he was threatening someone, and as such committing an unlawful act; he will be guilty.

B Yes, as CROFT feared the application of immediate unlawful force, which is an unlawful act, KACIK is guilty.

C No, he did not have the relevant *mens rea* against CROFT.

D No, CROFT voluntarily stepped onto the tracks, thereby negating the unlawful intent of KACIK.

Question 5.8

SADIQUE is an ardent and devout Muslim who created audiotapes for others to listen to. These were of an inflammatory nature and urged Muslims to fight and kill, among others, Jews, Christians, Americans, Hindus and other unbelievers. He encouraged his listeners to kill. He encouraged them to wage Jihad against the enemies of Islam as he deemed them to be. When questioned by police, SADIQUE stated that when he spoke of killing, he was speaking only of killing in self defence.

Is this solicitation to murder?

A No, as he did not personally encourage killing, any solicitation to murder was done only through the tapes.

B No, as there was no specific threat against someone.

C No, as he has not coerced people to murder for him.

D Yes, as he has sought to solicit and encourage murder.

Question 5.9

MALONE owned a taxi firm which was failing financially. MALONE owned the building which contained the firm's office and decided to set fire to the building to claim from the insurance company. MALONE enlisted the help of a friend, LARIMY, who had no connection with the company, and one evening they went to the building with cans of petrol and matches. MALONE spread the petrol around the inside of the premises and lit a fire, while LARIMY stood near the door as the lookout. Unfortunately, when the petrol ignited there was an explosion which killed LARIMY and injured MALONE. MALONE was subsequently charged with manslaughter.

In relation to MALONE's liability for the offence of manslaughter, which of the following statements is correct?

A MALONE would be guilty of manslaughter by unlawful act in these circumstances.

B MALONE would not be guilty of manslaughter, as LARIMY actually assisted with the crime.

C MALONE would be guilty of manslaughter by gross negligence in these circumstances.

D MALONE would not be guilty of manslaughter; the intention was to commit arson, not to injure LARIMY.

5. Homicide

Question 5.10

SHIPLEY has been charged with an offence of murder and is due to appear in court. SHIPLEY intends pleading not guilty to murder and will ask the court to accept a plea of guilty to the offence of manslaughter on the grounds of diminished responsibility.

Which of the following is correct, in respect of the 'impairment of responsibility' that SHIPLEY must have suffered, in order to succeed with this approach?

A The impairment suffered must have been substantial and must also have been the sole cause of SHIPLEY's actions in committing the manslaughter.

B The mental impairment must have been substantial, and it must be shown that it contributed in some way to SHIPLEY's actions in committing the manslaughter.

C The mental impairment need not be substantial, provided it contributed in some way to SHIPLEY's actions in committing the manslaughter.

D The mental impairment need not be substantial, provided it can be shown that it was the sole cause of SHIPLEY's actions in committing the manslaughter.

Question 5.11

Tilly was aged 5 years and was on the at risk register for previous assaults on her by members of her family. She lived at home with her mother, and whilst her mother's boyfriend was a frequent visitor, he did not live there. Tilly's mother was aware that her boyfriend was violent particularly when drunk and had assaulted Tilly previously. One night after he returned home drunk from the pub the boyfriend was fed up with Tilly's crying and went up and shook her violently, Tilly died from injuries received from that shake.

Who could be charged with an offence contrary to the Domestic Violence, Crime and Victims Act 2004, s. 5, causing or allowing the death of a child or vulnerable adult?

A Only Tilly's mother.

B Tilly's mother provided it could be established that she foresaw the attack on Tilly.

C Only the boyfriend.

D Both Tilly's mother and her boyfriend.

Question 5.12

Constable GREAVES from the road policing unit put his vehicle into the workshops as it had defective brakes and it was returned the following day from the workshop. After a short test drive he returned the car again claiming the brakes were not right. The workshop manager, HARDEN, told the officer the brakes were fine and there would be no more repairs made to it, he told the officer he was 'getting it in the neck' from the force's fleet manager to cut costs. The officer answered a call on the motorway and whilst travelling at 150 mph the brakes fail, the resulting collision killed the officer.

Which of the following is correct in relation to the Corporate Manslaughter and Corporate Homicide Act 2007?

A Both the force and the workshop manager could be charged with causing the officer's death.

B The force, the fleet manager and the workshop manager could be charged with causing the officer's death.

C Only the force could be charged with causing the officer's death.

D No-one could be charged with causing the death as the decision was that of the workshop manager, who would not be 'senior management' as defined in the Act.

ANSWERS

Answer 5.1

Answer **D** — Murder is committed when a person unlawfully kills another human being under the Queen's Peace, with malice aforethought. 'Another human being' includes a baby who has been born alive and has an existence independent of its mother. If a person injures a baby while it is in its mother's womb and it subsequently dies from those injuries after being born, it may be appropriate to bring a charge of murder.

If the defendant intended only to cause serious injury to the mother, that intention cannot support a charge of murder in respect of the baby if it goes on to die after being born alive. It may, however, support a charge of manslaughter. This departure from the earlier law is clear from the House of Lords' ruling in *Attorney-General's Reference (No. 3 of 1994)* [1998] AC 245, a ruling that overturned the Court of Appeal's previous decision in the same case. The House of Lords ruled that the doctrine of 'transferred malice' (see chapter 1.1) does not fully apply in cases of unborn children (*in utero*). Any liability of the defendant for the subsequent death of a child that he or she injured before it was born alive will depend on the defendant's intentions at the time of causing the injury. Clearly an intention to kill the mother could be sufficient in bringing a charge of murder following the subsequent and connected death of the child.

However none of this applies where a child is still born and has never had life; answers A, B and C are therefore incorrect.

Crime, para. 1.5.2

Answer 5.2

Answer **D** — The special defences in homicide cases are just that, defences to homicide cases, where someone actually dies. Both provocation and diminished responsibility requires a fatal act, diminished responsibility is where 'a person kills or is party to the killing of another' and provocation is a defence 'on a charge of murder'; answers A and B are therefore incorrect.

This makes answer C look correct, however it should be noted that the only state of mind or *mens rea* that will support a charge of attempted murder is an *intention to kill*. Nothing less will suffice, including recklessness as to whether death would follow action, so the wife cannot be guilty of attempted murder as she was merely reckless as to an intention to kill; answer C is therefore incorrect.

Crime, paras 1.5.2, 1.5.3

Answer 5.3

Answer **C** — In order to determine whether an act constitutes the offence of gross negligence manslaughter, the prosecution must establish that:

- there was a duty of care owned by the accused to the deceased;
- there was a breach of the duty of care by the accused;
- death of the deceased was caused by breach of the duty of care by the accused;
- the breach of the duty of care by the accused was so great as to be characterised as gross negligence and therefore a crime.

In the circumstances of the question the only part that remains unanswered is the last part. The actions of PIDGEON 'could', and in a case in Cwmbran in South Wales, did lead to a conviction for gross negligence manslaughter.

So PIDGEON could be guilty of gross negligence manslaughter, but what about manslaughter by unlawful act? In order to prove manslaughter by an unlawful act (constructive manslaughter), you must prove an unlawful act by the defendant, that is, an act which is *unlawful in itself*, irrespective of the fact that it ultimately results in someone's death. The act must be inherently unlawful. An act that only becomes unlawful by virtue of the way in which it is carried out will not be enough. Clearly fitting or repairing a gas boiler is not an unlawful act; answers A and B are therefore incorrect.

It is accepted that it is possible for a company to be prosecuted for gross negligence manslaughter, so called corporate manslaughter. However there are a number of difficulties which need to be addressed if a company is to be prosecuted successfully.

For a company to be guilty of manslaughter, it is necessary to identify a 'controlling mind', who is also personally guilty of manslaughter. This person must have acted 'as the company' to the extent that his or her identification 'is the mind of the company', and will therefore hold a senior position in the company. That individual or individuals will usually be prosecuted but there may be particular circumstances whereby they are not. Even then the prosecution must still be able to demonstrate that the named individual is guilty of the offence. Therefore before the prosecution can even start to consider 'corporate manslaughter', it must first be able to identify an individual who has committed the offence.

So although in these circumstances the directors of the company may have been grossly negligent in employing someone who was clearly a danger to their customers that negligence did not extend to an act that actually led to the death of the person, so they cannot be liable for 'corporate manslaughter'; answer D is therefore incorrect.

Crime, paras 1.5.4.1, 1.5.4.2, 1.5.4.3

Answer 5.4

Answer **B** — A suicide pact is formed when a common agreement is made between two or more persons, having for its object the death of all of them. It does not have to be written, but does have to be an agreement between all involved. A suicide pact allows for a conviction of manslaughter, and not murder, where the accused was acting in pursuance of such a pact.

The defendant must show that a suicide pact had been made, *and* he or she had the intention of dying at the time the killing took place. (Therefore, answers C and D are incorrect.)

This means that the existence of the pact is not enough (answer A is therefore incorrect) — at the time of the killing there must also be an intention of dying.

Crime, para. 1.5.3.3

Answer 5.5

Answer **A** — The defence of provocation is outlined in s. 3 of the Homicide Act 1957 which states:

> Where on a charge of murder there is evidence on which a jury can find that the person charged was provoked (whether by things done or by things said or by both together) to lose his self-control, the question whether the provocation was enough to make a reasonable man do as he did shall be left to be determined by the jury; and in determining that question the jury shall take into account everything both done and said according to the effect which, in their opinion, it would have on a reasonable man.

The main questions to be considered are:

- Was the defendant actually provoked?
- Might a reasonable person have acted as the defendant did under the same circumstances?

Most problematic is what the 'reasonable person' means, and here the decisions in the courts are confusing to say the least!

The House of Lords considered this area and the competing authorities in *R v Smith (Morgan James)* [2001] 1 AC 146. That decision attempted to set out the components of the 'reasonable person' test and the factors that a jury may take into account when assessing whether or not provocation can be claimed by the defendant — factors such as those peculiar to the defendant (e.g. suffering from 'battered woman syndrome' or a personality disorder). *Morgan Smith* was a controversial decision and many legal experts disagreed with it; however even that decision, which gave some guidance, has effectively been overturned. The Privy Council (which exercised through its Judicial Committee is the provision of a final Court of Appeal for a number of Commonwealth countries who have chosen to retain it) heard an appeal from Jersey (*Attorney General for Jersey* v *Holley* [2005] UKPC 23), the House of Lords sitting as Lords of Appeal in Ordinary decided the question of the reasonable person very differently from their decision in *Morgan Smith*.

The standard that a person will be judged on for this defence now is whether having regard to the actual provocation and the jurors' view of its gravity, a person having ordinary powers of self-control would have done what the defendant did. The effect of the alcohol having no effect to this particular defence, answers B, C and D are therefore incorrect.

The only consideration is that as this is a case from Jersey how binding is it on English law; however as Professor A.J. Ashworth put it in Crim LR 2005, Dec, 966–971

> Is *Holley* binding on English courts? There may be a purist strain of argument to the effect that it is not, since it concerns another legal system (that of Jersey). However, the reality is that nine Lords of Appeal in Ordinary sat in this case, and that for practical purposes it was intended to be equivalent of a sitting of the House of Lords. It is likely that anyone attempting to argue that *Morgan Smith* is still good law in England and Wales would receive short shrift ...

Crime, para. 1.5.3.2

Answer 5.6

Answer **C** — Like most offences, homicide requires that the defendant had the required *mens rea* for the relevant 'unlawful act', which for homicide offences would lead to the death of a victim. If the defendant did not have that *mens rea*, the offence of manslaughter will not be made out and therefore answers A, B and D are incorrect. In the case of *R v Lamb* [1967] 2 QB 981, the defendant pretended to fire a revolver at his friend. Although the defendant believed that the weapon would not fire, the chamber containing a bullet moved round to the firing pin and the defendant's friend was killed. As SHIPLEY did not have the *mens rea* required for an assault his conviction for manslaughter was quashed.

Crime, para. 1.5.4.1

Answer 5.7

Answer **C** — Unlawful act manslaughter is often known as constructive manslaughter — at common law it is manslaughter to kill in the course of committing an unlawful act just as it was murder to kill in the course of committing a felony. This felony/murder rule was repealed by s.1 of the Homicide Act 1957 but the constructive malice rule is still with us.

For unlawful act manslaughter, the requirements are that:

- accused must have *caused* the death of another; *and*
- the killing must have occurred in the course of the accused's *unlawful* act; *and*
- that unlawful act must have also been *dangerous* i.e. exposing the victim to a risk of harm; *and*
- the defendant had the required *mens rea* for the relevant 'unlawful act'.

Note the '*and*': all four factors have to be present.

Did KACIK cause the death of CROFT? Arguably, yes, he did. Was it an unlawful act? If the threat amounted to a public order offence, then yes. Was the threat dangerous? It depends on the threat but again it could be. Did the defendant have the required *mens rea*? Here is where a 'weak' case dies.

Any unlawful intention of KACIK was not directed at CROFT. In *R v Arobieke* [1988] Crim LR 314 the defendant had been convicted of manslaughter on the basis that his presence at a railway station had caused the victim, whom he knew to be terrified of him, to attempt an escape by crossing the railway tracks, with the result that he was electrocuted. The Court of Appeal quashed the conviction on the ground that there had been no criminal act by the defendant, as the evidence did not show that the defendant had physically threatened or chased the deceased.

There is no *mens rea*, and therefore no offence; answers A and B are therefore incorrect.

Note if all the other factors were present, a voluntary act by the victim would not exculpate the accused. Had the accused stepped towards the victim carrying a knife, with malicious intent, and the accused had tried to escape by running over the tracks and met a similar fate to CROFT, a charge of manslaughter may well have ensued; answer D is therefore incorrect.

Crime, para. 1.5.4.1

Answer 5.8

Answer **D** — There is no requirement that the solicitation be made in person (answer A is incorrect), nor that there be a particular person under threat (answer B is incorrect). The scope of the behaviour sufficient to constitute the offence was classically identified as follows in *R v Most* (1881) 7 QBD 244 *per* Huddleston B, at p. 258:

> The largest words possible have been used — 'solicit' — that is defined to be, to importune, to entreat, to implore, to ask, to attempt to try to obtain: 'encourage', which is to intimate, to incite to anything, to give courage to, to inspirit, to embolden, to raise confidence, to make confident, 'persuade' which is to bring any particular opinion, to influence by argument or expostulation, to inculcate by argument: 'endeavour' and then, as if there might be some class of cases that would not come within those words, the remarkable words are used, 'or shall propose to', that is say, make merely a bare proposition, an offer for consideration.

This wide interpretation means that coercion is not required; therefore answer C is incorrect. The facts of this question mirror that of *R v El-Faisal* [2004] EWCA Crim 343, where the Court of Appeal upheld the conviction of El-Faisal for solicitation to murder through the production of tapes that urged Muslims to kill unbelievers.

Crime, para. 1.5.7

Answer 5.9

Answer **A** — The circumstances in the question are similar to those in *R v Willoughby* [2004] EWCA Crim 3365, where the court examined a case of arson on the defendant's own public house. In the first instance, the Court of Appeal found that provided the defendant's conduct (intentionally starting the fire) had been the cause of the death, the jury were bound to convict the defendant of manslaughter. Answer D is therefore incorrect. The defendant in *Willoughby* was found guilty, even though the victim in the case was also the accomplice in similar circumstances to this question, therefore answer B is incorrect.

The Court of Appeal examined whether or not the defendant should have been found guilty of manslaughter by gross negligence. The Court held that it was entirely unnecessary to have recourse to manslaughter by gross negligence in this case as it was a straightforward case of manslaughter by unlawful act. Answer C is therefore incorrect. However, it was also held even though the offence of manslaughter by gross negligence was unsuitable in this case, there may be occasions where the defendant could be guilty of manslaughter via either avenue.

Crime, para. 1.5.4.2

Answer 5.10

Answer **B** — Under s. 2 of the Homicide Act 1957, a defendant may be acquitted of murder, but be liable instead for manslaughter, if the person is able to show the court that he or she was suffering from such abnormality of mind (whether arising from a condition of arrested or retarded development of mind or any inherent causes or induced by disease or injury) as *substantially* impaired his/her mental responsibility for his or her acts or omissions in doing or being a party to the killing. The mental impairment suffered must be substantial and minor lapses of lucidity will not be enough. Answers C and D are therefore incorrect.

In the case of *R* v *Dietschmann* [2003] 1 AC 1209, the House of Lords accepted that a mental abnormality caused by a grief reaction to the recent death of an aunt with whom the defendant had had a physical relationship could suffice. In that case their Lordships went on to hold that there is no requirement to show that the 'abnormality of mind' was the sole cause of the defendant's acts in committing the killing. Answers A and D are therefore incorrect.

Crime, para. 1.5.3.1

Answer 5.11

Answer **D** — The Domestic Violence, Crime and Victims Act 2004, s. 5 states:

(1) A person ('D') is guilty of an offence if —
  (a) a child or vulnerable adult ('V') dies as a result of the unlawful act of a person who —
    (i) was a member of the same household as V, and
    (ii) had frequent contact with him,
  (b) D was such a person at the time of that act,
  (c) at that time there was a significant risk of serious physical harm being caused to V by the unlawful act of such a person, and
  (d) either D was the person whose act caused V's death or —
    (i) D was, or ought to have been, aware of the risk mentioned in paragraph (c),

(ii) D failed to take such steps as he could reasonably have been expected to take to protect V from the risk, and

(iii) the act occurred in circumstances of the kind that D foresaw or ought to have foreseen...

This seems very complicated at first reading, so it is important to break it down.

You will need to answer yes to all the following questions for the offence to be made out.

- Was the victim a child or vulnerable adult? Yes.
- Was the defendant a member of the same household? For these purposes a person will be a member of a particular household if they visit it so often and for such periods of time that it is reasonable to regard them as a member of it — even if they do not actually live there, so yes.
- Was there a significant risk of serious physical harm being caused to the victim by the unlawful act of such a person? Yes.
- Was the defendant the person who caused the victim's death? Yes.
- Was the defendant also — although not the person who caused the death — a member of the household? Yes.
  - If yes, were they aware of the above risk? Yes.
  - Did they fail to take steps to protect the victim from that risk? Yes.
  - Did the act occur where it was foreseen or ought to have been foreseen? Yes.

As can be seen by all the yes answers the offence is made out for both the mother and the boyfriend, the mother being culpable even in circumstances where she ought to have foreseen the attack; answers A, B and C are therefore incorrect.

Crime, para. 1.5.5

Answer 5.12

Answer C — The Corporate Manslaughter and Corporate Homicide Act 2007, s. 1 states:

(1) An organisation to which this section applies is guilty of an offence if the way in which its activities are managed or organised —
   (a) causes a person's death, and
   (b) amounts to a gross breach of a relevant duty of care owed by the organisation to the deceased.
(2) The organisations to which this section applies are —
   (a) a corporation;
   (b) a department or other body listed in Schedule 1;

(c) a police force;

(d) a partnership, or a trade union or employers' association, that is an employer.

(3) An organisation is guilty of an offence under this section only if the way in which its activities are managed or organised by its senior management is a substantial element in the breach referred to in subsection (1).

The offence is concerned with the way in which an organisation's activities were managed or organised. Under this test, the courts will examine management systems and practices across the organisation, and whether the adequate standard of care was applied to the fatal activity.

The threshold for the offence is gross negligence. The way in which the activities were managed or organised must have fallen far below what could reasonably have been expected.

The failure to manage or organise activities properly must have caused the victim's death.

A duty of care is an obligation that an organisation has to take reasonable steps to protect a person's safety. These duties exist, for example, in respect of the systems of work and equipment used by employees, the condition of worksites and other premises occupied by an organisation and in relation to products or services supplied to customers. The duty must be a relevant one. Relevant duties are set out in s. 2 of the Act and include:

• Employer and occupier duties
• Duties connected to:
  • Supplying goods and services
  • Commercial activities
  • Construction and maintenance work
  • Using or keeping plant, vehicles or other things.

• In relation to policing and law enforcement in the Act, there are some exceptions to the relevant duty of care obligation (s. 5 of the Act), these are in:

  • Operations for dealing with terrorism, civil unrest or serious disorder, that involve the carrying on of policing or law-enforcement activities where officers or employees of the public authority in question come under attack, or face the threat of attack or violent resistance, in the course of the operations.

  • Activities carried out in preparation for, or directly in support of, such operations above.

  • Training of a hazardous nature or training carried out in a hazardous way in order to improve or maintain the effectiveness of officers or employees of the public authority with respect to such operations as above.

Police services and authorities are still subject to the Act and could be prosecuted in matters where death relates to the organisation's responsibility as an employer (or to others working for the organisation) or as an occupier of premises.

The offence is concerned with the corporate liability of the organisation itself and does not apply to individual directors, senior managers or other individuals; answers A and B are therefore incorrect. It is not possible to convict an individual of assisting or encouraging this offence (s. 18).

The term 'senior management' is defined in s. 1(4) of the Act to mean those persons who play a significant role in the management of the whole or of a substantial part of the organisation's activities. This covers those individuals in the direct chain of management as well as those in, for example, strategic or regulatory compliance roles, this would include both the fleet and workshop manager; answer D is therefore incorrect.

Crime. para. 1.5.4.3

Offences relating to the misuse of drugs require a sound knowledge both of the elements of the offences and the case law that supports them. You should also understand the elements of the statutory defences that apply, and how they affect the case in question. This chapter also covers the rather complicated power to enter, search and seize granted by s. 23 of the Misuse of Drugs Act 1971, and it is well worth taking your time over this section (if you've read it you'll know what I mean!). In addition to the more usual controlled drugs, this chapter also includes the law relating to intoxicating substances.

QUESTIONS

Question 6.1

Supplying articles for administering or preparing controlled drugs is an offence contrary to the Misuse of Drugs Act 1971, s. 9A. Constable ENGLAND stops a male and finds various articles on him.

In relation to the articles which combination of articles would constitute an offence? (You should consider all the articles.)

A   A metal spoon and a hypodermic needle.

B   A tourniquet, a metal spoon and a hypodermic needle.

C   A tourniquet, a metal spoon, a lighter and a hypodermic needle.

D   A tourniquet, a metal spoon and a lighter.

Question 6.2

HINDS has a bottle of vitamin tablets in her handbag. Unknown to her, her son had put three Ecstasy tablets in the bottle that morning. Before leaving the house HINDS checks that she has the bottle in her handbag.

Which of the following is correct?

A HINDS is in possession of a controlled drug, but may not be committing an offence.

B HINDS is in possession of a controlled drug and is committing an offence.

C HINDS is not in possession of a controlled drug as she did not put them in the bottle.

D HINDS is not in possession of a controlled drug as she has no knowledge of what the tablets are.

Question 6.3

Detective Constable FISCHER is a member of the National Crime Squad. She has been involved in an undercover operation in relation to drug trafficking. STROUER is a major drug dealer and has asked FISCHER to help in the supply of cocaine. FISCHER has provisionally agreed to this to maintain her cover. In fact FISCHER has no intention of illegally supplying drugs, and the arrest of STROUER is considered as necessary.

In relation to incitement under s. 19 of the Misuse of Drugs Act 1971, which of the following is correct?

A The offence is complete when STROUER asks FISCHER to supply the drugs.

B As FISCHER has no intention of supplying the drugs, the offence is not complete.

C The offence would be complete only if FISCHER actually supplied the drugs.

D The offence is complete only if STROUER receives the drugs, and supplying is complete.

Question 6.4

MORRISON is a self-employed chemist and her partner, OLDMAN, confessed to her that he was a heroin addict, although not registered as such. MORRISON was shocked by the news, but agreed to help OLDMAN break his addiction. MORRISON took some methadone from her storeroom, and gave it to OLDMAN.

In relation to MORRISON's actions, which of the following is incorrect?

A MORRISON has committed no offence in these circumstances, as she had lawful possession of the drug.

B Even though MORRISON would normally be entitled to lawfully possess a controlled drug, she has committed an offence by supplying it to OLDMAN.

C MORRISON has committed an offence in these circumstances.

D MORRISON has committed an offence from the time she took the drug from the surgery intending to supply it to OLDMAN.

Question 6.5

CARLOS found a bag containing white powder in her son's bedroom, which she believed was cocaine. CARLOS took the powder, intending to hand it in to the police. However, as a leader of the local youth club, CARLOS decided to keep the drugs to show other youth workers, so they will be able to recognise the drug should they find any.

Would CARLOS be able to claim a statutory defence to the offence of possession of a controlled drug, under s. 5(4) of the Misuse of Drugs Act 1971?

A Yes, providing it was her intent to destroy the drugs when she took possession of them to prevent her son from committing an offence.

B No, the defence would only apply if she took possession of the drugs and subsequently destroyed them.

C No, the defence would only apply if she took possession of the drugs and subsequently delivered them to a person lawfully entitled to possess them.

D No, the defence would only apply if she took possession of the drugs and either destroyed them or delivered them to a person lawfully entitled to possess them.

Question 6.6

HILL is a customs officer working undercover. She is part of an on-going operation regarding drug supply at the 'Green Man' public house. The officer goes to the pub to make a test purchase, and is shown several wraps containing white powder by MOYLES, a suspected drug dealer. MOYLES states that the wraps contain amphetamine and will cost £30 per wrap. In fact the wraps contain baking powder, a fact of which MOYLES is unaware. The transaction takes place.

Which of the following offences, if any, does MOYLES commit?

A Possession of a controlled drug.

B Possession with intent to supply a controlled drug.

C Offering to supply a controlled drug.

D Supplying a controlled drug.

Question 6.7

MCCOURT and DAVIES are business partners. DAVIES uses her factory for the production of Ecstasy. MCCOURT ensures that the premises are not disturbed by providing 24-hour security in the factory, and also provides transportation to the factory of the raw goods required for the production of Ecstasy. MCCOURT neither visits the factory, nor has any direct contact with the security or transportation, but is aware of what happens at the factory. DAVIES never visits the factory either.

Who, if anyone, is guilty of unlawful production of a controlled drug under s. 4 of the Misuse of Drugs Act 1971?

A MCCOURT.

B DAVIES.

C Both of them.

D Neither of them.

Question 6.8

BOOYNET has long been suspected by the police of being involved in the supply of controlled drugs and a warrant has been obtained to search his premises. The police go to BOOYNET's house and, as they enter, BOOYNET takes various papers and shreds them. BOOYNET is unsure whether they are evidence or not, but is not willing to take a chance. These papers actually amounted to the only real evidence proving BOOYNET's involvement in the supply of controlled drugs.

Has BOOYNET committed an offence of obstruction under s. 23(4) of the Misuse of Drugs Act 1971?

A Yes, he was reckless as to whether the papers were evidence or not.

B Yes, he has obstructed the officers by destroying the evidence.

C No, as obstruction only applies to deliberate, physical obstruction of the officers themselves.

D No, as obstruction only applies to stop/searches in relation to drugs.

Question 6.9

Police suspect that STRONG is using her premises to allow persons to enter and smoke cannabis. Her neighbours have complained that the noise is continual, both day and night, and have asked the police if they can do something to stop the occurrence of the disorder associated with persons entering and leaving STRONG's house.

In relation to using the premises for the unlawful use, production or supply of a controlled drug which of the following is correct?

A A police officer not below the rank of superintendent may authorise the issue of a closure notice in respect of the premises in these circumstances.

B A police officer not below the rank of inspector may authorise the issue of a closure notice in respect of the premises in these circumstances.

C A closure notice can only be applied for by the local authority in these circumstances.

D No closure notice may be authorised in these circumstances.

Question 6.10

ANDERSON has a controlled drug in his pocket, which he intends to supply to someone else. Seeing a police officer in the distance, he hands the drugs to his friend, CARLOS, and says 'hold on to these for me and I will give you £20'. CARLOS agrees and takes possession of the drugs. The officer walks past them and CARLOS hands the drugs back to ANDERSON and collects his £20.

In relation to the controlled drugs, which offence(s) has CARLOS committed?

A Possession only.

B Supply only.

C Possession or supplying only.

D Possession or supplying or possession with intent to supply.

Question 6.11

MCNIFF is 16 years old and works on Saturdays in his father's shop. He sells a bottle of solvent to his school friend whom he knows is 16 years old.

Under s. 1 of the Intoxicating Substances (Supply) Act 1985 (supply of an intoxicating substance), which of the following is correct in relation to the defences available to MCNIFF?

A MCNIFF has a defence owing to his age only.

B MCNIFF has a defence as he was acting in the course of a business.

C MCNIFF has a defence owing to his age and the fact that he was acting in the course of a business.

D MCNIFF has no defence.

Question 6.12

SAUNDERS and TWEED are both drug addicts and bought a quantity of heroin together, which SAUNDERS carried back to a house. At the house, SAUNDERS divided the heroin equally and gave a share to TWEED. Unfortunately, TWEED had been drinking all day and fell asleep. SAUNDERS then injected TWEED with her own drugs while she was asleep.

At what point, if at all, does SAUNDERS commit the offence of supplying a controlled drug, under s. 4(3)(a) of the Misuse of Drugs Act 1971?

A When SAUNDERS divided the heroin and gave it to TWEED.

B Only when SAUNDERS injected TWEED with the heroin.

C On both occasions, when SAUNDERS divided the heroin and gave it to TWEED and later when TWEED was injected with the heroin.

D The offence is not committed at all, because the heroin was jointly purchased by SAUNDERS and TWEED.

Question 6.13

Travel restriction orders made under the Criminal Justice and Police Act 2001 restrict the travel of convicted drug traffickers.

For how long a period does this travel restriction order last?

A 2 years.

B 4 years.

C 10 years.

D Unlimited period; no set maximum.

Question 6.14

MAY was the sole tenant and occupier of a flat, which was raided by the police. They found MAY, along with seven others, and a number of items used for the smoking of drugs. They also found a quantity of cannabis resin. MAY admits he had given permission for drug smoking to take place. During the search of the premises the police could detect no smell of cannabis. MAY was charged with allowing the offence of permitting the smoking of cannabis, cannabis resin or prepared opium on premises under s. 8 of the Misuse of Drugs Act 1971.

Is MAY guilty of this offence?

A No, as he was not the owner of the premises.

B No, as there was no evidence actual smoking took place.

C Yes, as there was cannabis and drugs paraphernalia in the premises.

D Yes, as he admits that he gave permission for drug smoking.

Question 6.15

Police are considering a closure notice under s. 1 of the Anti-social Behaviour Act 2003, with regard to a club which has been used in connection with supplying Class A drugs.

In relation to the officer who can authorise this, and how long this individual can go back in relation to the club's activities (the officer is considering issuing the order today), which of the following is true?

A An officer of at least the rank of assistant chief constable (ACC) can authorise, and can consider the use of the club over the past month.

B An officer of at least the rank of superintendent can authorise, and can consider the use of the club over the past month.

C An officer of at least the rank of ACC can authorise, and can consider the use of the club over the past three months.

D An officer of at least the rank of superintendent can authorise, and can consider the use of the club over the past three months.

Question 6.16

Police officers are executing a warrant under s. 23 of the Misuse of Drugs Act 1971 at a house. The warrant allows for the searching of persons as well as the premises. In the house are several people, including a gas meter reader, who states he was there to read the meter. The police wish to search him, but he wants to go and read other meters.

Which of the following is true?

A They can search the meter reader, but only with his permission.

B They can search the meter reader, and can require him to remain for that purpose.

C They cannot search the meter reader, only the occupier of the premises.

D They cannot search him, only the occupier and persons present with his permission.

Question 6.17

Section 4 of the Anti-social Behaviour Act 2003 creates offences in relation to premises subject to a closure notice or order.

Which of the following would amount to one of these offences?
A Entering the premises.
B Obstructing a constable without reasonable excuse.
C Obstructing an authorised person acting within their powers.
D Remaining on the premises.

Question 6.18

RIDDICK was approached by CRAWLEY and asked to deliver a package to a nearby address. CRAWLEY gave RIDDICK £200 for taking the package. RIDDICK was very drunk at the time he was asked to take the package and did not realise that he had been given so much money. He takes the package but is stopped by police officers who have had CRAWLEY, a known drug dealer, under surveillance. The package is found to contain a very large quantity of a Class A drug and RIDDICK is charged with possession of, and possession with intent to supply, a Class A drug.

Consider RIDDICK's use of the defence under s. 28(2) of the Misuse of Drugs Act 1971 (lack of knowledge of some alleged fact) due to the fact he was drunk and he had no 'reason to suspect' what he was doing.

Which of the following is correct?
A The defence could be used for possession of the drugs, but not for the intention to supply.
B The defence could *not* be used for either charge as 'reason to suspect' is a factual test and not subject to individual peculiarities.
C The defence could be used for either charge as 'reason to suspect' is subject to individual peculiarities and is not a factual test.
D The defence could be used for intention to supply but not for mere possession of the drugs.

Question 6.19

ROONEY is a drug dealer who deals out of a public house. Police have been watching the premises and when his accomplice, STRUTHERS arrives in a van the police strike, arresting both men. In the van there is a large quantity of crack cocaine. The van belonged to ROONEY and STRUTHERS states he was just delivering the drugs to ROONEY. However ROONEY did not actually take possession of the drugs as the police raid prevented that.

For what offence(s) under the Misuse of Drugs Act 1971 will STRUTHERS be liable?

A Possession of a controlled drug, he only intended supplying ROONEY.

B Possession of a controlled drug and possession with intent to supply.

C Possession of a controlled drug and being concerned in the supply of a controlled drug.

D Possession of a controlled drug and being concerned in the supply of a controlled drug and possession with intent to supply.

ANSWERS

Answer 6.1

Answer **D** — The Misuse of Drugs Act 1971, s. 9A states:

(1) A person who supplies or offers to supply any article which may be used or adapted to be used (whether by itself or in combination with another article or other articles) in the administration by any person of a controlled drug to himself or another, believing that the article (or the article as adapted) is to be so used in circumstances where the administration is unlawful, is guilty of an offence.

(2) ...

(3) A person who supplies or offers to supply any article which may be used to prepare a controlled drug for administration by any person to himself or another believing that the article is to be so used in circumstances where the administration is unlawful is guilty of an offence.

This offence deals with the supplying of or offering to supply articles for use for preparing or administering controlled drugs. The offence is designed to address the provision of drug 'kits'. It specifically does not include hypodermic syringes, or parts of them (s. 9A(2)). So effectively it could be any article that could be used or adapted to be used in administering drugs, except as stated above hypodermic needles. As the only option that does not include a hypodermic syringe is D answers A, B and C are therefore incorrect.

Crime, para. 1.6.5.8

Answer 6.2

Answer **A** — Common law outlines possession as physical control plus knowledge of the presence of the drugs. This becomes problematical where the person in possession claims not to realise what they possessed. In these cases it needs to be shown that the person had physical control of the container together with knowledge that it contained something. HINDS knew she had a container and that it contained tablets (answers C and D are therefore incorrect). This simply means that HINDS was in possession of controlled drugs, not that she was committing an offence under the 1971 Act, therefore answer B is incorrect. It is clear from various case authorities that the basic elements are that a person 'knows' that they are in possession of something which is in fact a controlled substance. As answer C states that she is committing an offence for simply possessing the drugs, it is incorrect. She may commit an offence, as outlined in answer A; however, she could avail herself of the statutory defences available.

Crime, paras 1.6.3.1, 1.6.3.2, 1.6.3.3

Answer 6.3

Answer **A** — The definition of this offence under s. 19 of the Misuse of Drugs Act 1971 is 'for a person to incite . . . another to commit [an offence under this Act]'. This clearly covers all sections, not just supplying.

Although the offence of incitement exists for most other offences generally, the 1971 Act makes a specific offence of inciting another to commit an offence under its provisions.

On the arguments in *DPP* v *Armstrong* [2000] Crim LR 379, it would seem that a person inciting an undercover police officer may commit an offence under this section even though there was no possibility of the officer actually being induced to commit the offence, and therefore answer B is incorrect. As the offence is committed at the time the incitement is made and is not conditional on either the supply or receipt of the controlled drugs, answers C and D are incorrect.

Crime, para. 1.6.5.17

Answer 6.4

Answer **A** — Section 5 of the Misuse of Drugs Act 1971 states:

(3) Subject to section 28 of this Act, it is an offence for a person to have a controlled drug in his possession, whether lawfully or not, with intent to supply it to another in contravention of section 4(1) of this Act.

It is important to note that the lawfulness or otherwise of the possession is irrelevant; what matters here is the lawfulness of the intended supply. If a vet, or a police officer or some other person is in lawful possession of a controlled drug but they intend to supply it unlawfully to another, this offence will be made out.

This is a crime of specific intent and the intention to supply would have to be proven, as it is in the question. Consequently, MORRISON commits an offence, making answers B, C and D actually correct in law. The question, though, asks you what is incorrect, and therefore answer A is actually the correct answer.

Crime, para. 1.6.5.6

Answer 6.5

Answer **D** — Defences are provided by s. 5(4) of the Misuse of Drugs Act 1971, which states:

> In any proceedings for an offence under subsection (2) above in which it is proved that the accused had a controlled drug in his possession, it shall be a defence for him to prove —
>
> (a) that, knowing or suspecting it to be a controlled drug he took possession of it for the purpose of preventing another from committing or continuing to commit an offence in connection with that drug and that as soon as possible after taking possession of it he took all such steps as were reasonably open to him to destroy the drug or to deliver it into the custody of a person lawfully entitled to take custody of it;
>
> (b) that, knowing or suspecting it to be a controlled drug he took possession of it for the purpose of delivering it into the custody of a person lawfully entitled to take custody of it and that as soon as possible after taking possession of it he took all such steps as were reasonably open to him to deliver it into the custody of such a person.

It can be seen from the above that once CARLOS had taken possession of the drugs, she would then be expected *either* to destroy them *or* deliver them to a person lawfully entitled to possess them — answers B and C are incorrect, because the defence is available to a person who does either of these things.

The issue of intent under s. 5(4)(b) above was examined in the case of *R v Dempsey and Dempsey* [1986] 82 Cr App R 291. In this case it was held that the defendant must prove that it was his or her *sole* intention at the time of taking possession of the drug to deliver it to a person lawfully entitled to possess it. However, even though it was CARLOS's intent to hand the drugs in to the police when she actually took possession of the drugs, she later changed her mind and did not do so. From the point that she changed her mind, she was in unlawful possession of the drugs and would not be able to rely on the defence provided by s. 5(4) above. Answer A is therefore incorrect.

Crime, para. 1.6.4.1

Answer 6.6

Answer **C** — For the offences of possession, possession with intent to supply and supply, the prosecution would need to prove that the substance in question is in fact a controlled drug. Answers A, B and D are therefore incorrect. For the offence of offering to supply under s. 4(3)(c) of the 1971 Act, it does not matter whether the accused had a controlled drug in his or her possession or had easy access to a controlled drug.

Crime, para. 1.6.5.2

Answer 6.7

Answer **C** — The meaning of 'produce' and 'concerned in production' is defined by s. 37 of the Misuse of Drugs Act 1971, which states:

(1) ... 'produce', where the reference is to producing a controlled drug, means producing it by manufacture, cultivation or any other method, and 'production' has a corresponding meaning; ...

Being concerned in production requires the accused to take an identifiable role in the production. Both MCCOURT and DAVIES take an identifiable role in the production in that, although they never visit the premises, they have guilty knowledge of its function and, but for their actions, the production may not take place. This makes option C the only possible correct answer.

Crime, para. 1.6.5.1

Answer 6.8

Answer **B** — This offence is complete where the person obstructs someone carrying out stop/search procedures and also executing a warrant, and therefore answer D is incorrect. In *R v Forde* (1985) 81 Cr App R 19, it was held that a person only committed this offence if the obstruction was intentional, that is to say the act viewed objectively, through the eyes of a bystander, did obstruct the constable's search, and viewed subjectively, that is to say through the eyes of the accused himself, was intended so to obstruct. BOOYNET knew he was intentionally obstructing the officers and, even though he was unsure of the outcome, recklessness does not apply (answer A is incorrect). Section 23(4)(b) of the Misuse of Drugs Act 1971 states that the offence includes a person who 'conceals from a person acting in the exercise of his powers under subsection (1) above any such books, documents ...'. So, as books and documents are included, answer C is incorrect.

Crime, para. 1.6.6.2

Answer 6.9

Answer **D** — Section 1 of the Anti-social Behaviour Act 2003 states:

> This section applies to premises if a police officer not below the rank of superintendent (the authorising officer) has reasonable grounds for believing —
>
> (a) that at any time during the relevant period the premises have been used in connection with the unlawful use, production or supply of a Class A controlled drug, and
>
> (b) that the use of the premises is associated with the occurrence of disorder or serious nuisance to members of the public.

As can be seen closure notices only apply to circumstances surrounding the unlawful use, production or supply of a Class A controlled drug, and as cannabis is not Class A in these circumstances a closure notice cannot be authorised; answers A, B and C are therefore incorrect.

Although in relation to the drug usage it is the police who authorise closure notices this must be done in consultation with the local authority (s. 1(2)(a)); there is also a general power for local authorities to make a closure order in relation to noise and nuisance being caused in connection with the use of premises under s. 40 of the 2003 Act.

Crime, para. 1.6.5.10

Answer 6.10

Answer **D** — In its simplest form, where one person hands over a controlled drug to another, there can be said to be a supply. Where a person leaves a controlled drug with another for safekeeping, the situation is trickier. Fortunately, the House of Lords have given direction in this area in two cases: *R v Maginnis* [1987] AC 303 and *R v Dempsey and Dempsey* (1986) 82 Cr App R 291. The outcome of these cases is that if the person looking after the drugs for another is in some way benefiting from that activity, then the return of those drugs to the depositor will amount to 'supplying' and the offences of supplying or possession with intent to supply will be applicable as well as simple possession. None of these offences need stand alone in the circumstances outlined in the question, and therefore answers A, B and C are incorrect.

Crime, para. 1.6.5.3

Answer 6.11

Answer **D** — Section 1 of the Intoxicating Substances (Supply) Act 1985 defines the defence in subs. (2) as:

> in proceedings against any person for an offence under subsection (1) above it is a defence for him to show that at the time he made the supply or offer he was under the age of 18 and was acting otherwise than in the course or furtherance of a business.

So on the one hand MCNIFF does have a defence in that he is 16; but this does not stand alone as the statute says 'under the age of 18 *and*' — that 'and' makes answer A incorrect. The second part of the subsection concerns 'acting otherwise than in the course or furtherance of a business' and as MCNIFF was acting in the course of or in furtherance of a business, he is not afforded this defence and answers B and C are incorrect.

Crime, para. 1.6.7

Answer 6.12

Answer **A** — It is an offence under s. 4(3)(a) of the Misuse of Drugs Act 1971 to supply a controlled drug to another. It has been held that dividing up controlled drugs which have been jointly purchased *will* amount to 'supplying' (*R v Buckley* (1979) 69 Cr App R 371).

Further, injecting another with his or her own controlled drug has been held *not* to amount to 'supplying' in a case where the defendant assisted pushing down the plunger of a syringe that the other person was already using. Parker CJ's comments in that case suggest that simply injecting another person with their own drug would not amount to 'supplying' (*R v Harris* [1968] 1 WLR 769). It may, however, amount to an offence of 'poisoning' under s. 23 of the Offences Against the Person Act 1861.

Answers B, C and D are therefore incorrect.

Crime, paras 1.6.5.2, 1.6.5.3

Answer 6.13

Answer **D** — The introduction of the Criminal Justice and Police Act 2001, ss. 33–37, allows any criminal court (but effectively, given the sentencing restriction, this means the Crown Court) to impose a travel restriction order on an offender who is convicted of a drug trafficking offence. The offender has to have been sentenced by that court to a term of imprisonment for four years or more

(s. 33(1)). The effect of the order is to restrict the offender's freedom to leave the United Kingdom for a period specified by the court, and it may require delivery up of his passport. The minimum duration of a travel restriction order is two years, starting from the date of the offender's release from custody. There is no maximum period prescribed in the legislation, therefore answers A, B and C are incorrect. The court must always consider whether such an order should be made and must give reasons where it does not consider such an order to be appropriate (s. 33(2)).

Crime, para. 1.6.6.3

Answer 6.14

Answer **B** — Section 8 of the Misuse of Drugs Act 1971 states:

A person commits an offence if, being the occupier or concerned in the management of any premises, he knowingly permits or suffers any of the following activities to take place on those premises, that is to say:
(a) producing or attempting to produce a controlled drug in contravention of section 4(1) of this Act;
(b) supplying or attempting to supply a controlled drug to another in contravention of section 4(1) of this Act, or offering to supply a controlled drug to another in contravention of section 4(1);
(c) preparing opium for smoking;
(d) smoking cannabis, cannabis resin or prepared opium.

As can be seen, it applies to occupiers and not just owners; answer A is therefore incorrect. It does, however, require that it was necessary to establish that the activity of smoking had taken place and not merely that the permission had been given (*R v August*, *The Times*, 15 December 2003); answer D is therefore incorrect. It is also not sufficient that the drugs and paraphernalia were present — it seems the police may have timed their raid a bit too soon as no smoking had taken place — answer C is therefore incorrect.

Crime, para. 1.6.5.9

Answer 6.15

Answer **D** — Section 1 of the Anti-social Behaviour Act 2003 deals with premises where drugs are used unlawfully:

(1) This section applies to premises if a police officer not below the rank of superintendent (the authorising officer) has reasonable grounds for believing —

(a) that at any time during the relevant period the premises have been used in connection with the unlawful use, production or supply of a Class A controlled drug, and
(b) that the use of the premises is associated with the occurrence of disorder or serious nuisance to members of the public.

So it is a superintendent who authorises, not an assistant chief constable (ACC); answers A and C are incorrect. The relevant period over which the officer can consider the use of the club is also defined in the Act by s. 1(10): 'The relevant period is the period of three months ending with the day on which the authorising officer considers whether to authorise the issue of a closure notice in respect of the premises'. So three months, and not one month, is the appropriate period; answer B is therefore incorrect.

Crime, para. 1.6.5.10

Answer 6.16

Answer **B** — The secret is in the wording of the warrant: if the warrant only allows for searching of premises, that in itself will not give authority to search people on the premises unless the officer can point to some other authority allowing that search (see *Chief Constable of Thames Valley Police* v *Hepburn*, The Times, 19 December 2002). However, does that searching extend to everybody on the premises, even those there for an ancillary purpose? The Divisional Court has held that it is reasonable to restrict the movement of people within the premises to allow the search to be conducted properly (see *DPP* v *Meaden*, The Times, 2 January 2004). So the police can search the meter reader without his permission and can restrict his movements; answers A, C and D are therefore incorrect. After all, the officers only have his word that he is there to read meters!

Crime, para. 1.6.6.1

Answer 6.17

Answer **C** — Section 1 of the Anti-social Behaviour Act 2003 relates to closure notices. The police have power to close down premises being used for the supply, use or production of Class A drugs where there is associated serious nuisance or disorder. Section 4 of the Anti-social Behaviour Act 2003, which deals with offences relating to those closure notices, states:

(1) A person commits an offence if he remains on or enters premises in contravention of a closure notice.

(2) A person commits an offence if —
    (a) he obstructs a constable or an authorised person acting under section 1(6) or 3(2),
    (b) he remains on premises in respect of which a closure order has been made, or
    (c) he enters the premises.

There is a statutory defence courtesy of s. 4(4):

(4) But a person does not commit an offence under subsection (1) or subsection (2)(b) or (c) if he has a reasonable excuse for entering or being on the premises (as the case may be).

Therefore the offence is only complete where the person enters or remains on the premises with no reasonable excuse; answers A and D are therefore incorrect. This reasonable excuse defence does not exist where a constable or authorised person is obstructed; answer B is therefore incorrect as the offence is made out irrespective of any reasonable excuse proffered by the accused.

Crime, para. 1.6.5.14

Answer 6.18

Answer **B** — Section 28(2) allows a defence where the defendant did not know, suspect or have reason to suspect the existence of some fact which is essential to proving the case. In relation to this defence RIDDICK could discharge the evidential burden by showing that he neither knew, nor suspected that the package contained a controlled drug, and that he neither knew nor suspected that he was supplying it to another. Both of these elements would be facts, which the prosecution would have to allege in order to prove the offence.

However external factors can impact on this defence. For example if RIDDICK knew the person to be a local drug dealer, or the reward for his errand was suspiciously big (say £200!), then he may not be able to discharge this, albeit evidential, burden.

However it has been held that the test for 'reason to suspect' is an objective (factual) one (*R v Young* [1984] 1 WLR 654). Consequently, where a 'reason to suspect' was not apparent to a defendant because he or she was too intoxicated to see it, the defence will not apply. So if you're offered a package to deliver whilst drunk. . .

Consequently answers A, C and D are incorrect.

Crime, para. 1.6.4.3

Answer 6.19

Answer **A** — Obviously STRUTHERS will be liable for possession, he is in possession of what in fact is a controlled drug and offers no defence to that possession.

The concept of supplying another with a drug generally conjures up something along the lines of a straightforward sale or exchange. It has been held that, where a person holds on to a controlled drug belonging to another for a short while and then hands it back, there is no 'supply' (although there may be unlawful possession) (*R v Dempsey and Dempsey* (1986) 82 Cr App R 291). If the person looking after the drugs for another is in some way benefiting from that activity, then the return of those drugs to the depositor *will* amount to 'supplying', and the offences of supplying or possession with intent to supply will be applicable (*R v Maginnis* [1987] AC 303). In the question there is no indication of benefit to STRUTHERS, therefore there can be no supply.

Being concerned in the supply of a controlled drug involves an actual 'supply', in this case the police prevented that by arresting the person prior to the supply.

So STRUTHERS is only liable for possession of the controlled drug; answers B, C and D are therefore incorrect.

Crime, para. 1.6.5.3

7 | Offences Against the Person

STUDY PREPARATION

This chapter deals with non-fatal offences against the person. This chapter examines the definition of assault and battery; it also addresses the offences of common assault, actual and grievous bodily harm, and the differences between them. Of particular importance in this area is the required element of state of mind (*mens rea*) and how that differs between offences.

Specific confrontation in relation to police officers, designated and accredited persons is considered.

This chapter should be read in conjunction with CPS Charging Standards.

QUESTIONS

Question 7.1

HAWKINS is angry when the police attend at her house to arrest her son, and she follows the police out to their police car as they escort her son. Before they can stop her HAWKINS jumps into the back seat of the police car next to her son and locks the door, refusing to leave; she is also very abusive to the officers verbally. Eventually she gets out of the police car and starts to walk off, still shouting obscenities at the officers. One of the officers approaches her and takes hold of her arm; she bites the officer and runs into her house, shutting the door behind her. The officers enter the premises by force and arrest HAWKINS for an offence of assaulting a police officer contrary to s. 89 of the Police Act 1996.

In relation to this which of the following is correct?

A The officers had lawful power to take hold of HAWKINS' arm as she was committing a breach of the peace.

B The officers had lawful grounds to arrest HAWKINS for assaulting a police officer, but had no power of entry to her house to effect it.

C The officers had lawful grounds to arrest HAWKINS for assaulting a police officer, and there is a lawful power of entry to her house to effect it.

D The officers had no lawful grounds to arrest HAWKINS and no power to enter even if the arrest had been lawful.

Question 7.2

DENNY is fed up with her neighbour lighting fires that make her house smell. To stop it happening again DENNY places a used hair spray aerosol can in the drum her neighbour uses to burn rubbish. The can states that it should not be disposed of in a fire, or left near a naked flame. Her neighbour lights a fire and the can explodes in her face causing minor burns.

Has DENNY assaulted her neighbour?

A Yes, provided it can be shown that she had read the warning on the can, or was aware of a risk.

B Yes, provided it can be shown that a 'reasonable man' would have accepted it was reckless putting the aerosol can in the drum.

C No, there was no direct application of force applied by DENNY.

D No, as her neighbour did not apprehend the immediate infliction of unlawful force, he did not know the can was there.

Question 7.3

YOUNG takes her children to their dentist, WALKER. She consents to the children receiving fillings. During the procedure YOUNG becomes concerned that WALKER is either drunk or drugged and reports the matter to the police. During the investigation it transpires that WALKER is taking drugs prescribed for a psychiatric illness, and for that reason he was suspended by the General Dental Council 2 months ago. The police are considering charging WALKER with assault.

Has WALKER unlawfully assaulted the children?

A No, YOUNG has given true consent.

B No, any formal medical practice is not an assault.

C Yes, YOUNG has given consent obtained by fraud.

D Yes, WALKER is suspended and no longer covered by law as it relates to consent.

Question 7.4

GREENING is a store detective employed by a major retail chain. He witnesses a theft of a £200 cashmere sweater and follows the suspect, STEWART, outside the shop. GREENING holds STEWART and asks him to return to the shop as he has items for which he has not paid. STEWART pulls a knife and threatens GREENING with it. GREENING backs off and STEWART makes good his escape.

Has STEWART committed an offence of assault with intent to resist arrest under s. 38 of the Offences Against the Person Act 1861?

A No, as it applies to police officers making arrests only.

B No, as it applies to assaults involving actual injury only.

C Yes, as it applies to lawful arrests made by a person other than a constable.

D Yes, but only because s. 38 is triable only at Crown Court.

Question 7.5

Constable WILCE wishes to question BOON about an alleged assault. The officer attends at BOON's home address and tells him the nature of the incident. Believing that he is about to be arrested, BOON grabs hold of Constable WILCE's arm and pulls him into the doorway; he then slams the door on the officer's arm and makes good his escape. As a result of this attack, Constable WILCE's arm is broken in two places. When interviewed, BOON states that he did not intend to cause the injury, but accepts that his conduct presented a risk of some harm to the officer.

Which of the following statements is correct?

A This would not amount to a s. 18 assault, as there was no malice, i.e. premeditation.

B This would not amount to a s. 18 assault, as there was no intention to cause serious harm.

C This would amount to a s. 18 assault, as BOON intended to prevent his lawful arrest.

D This would not amount to a s. 18 assault, as BOON had not actually been arrested.

Question 7.6

BACHMAN has fallen out with his girlfriend following a heated argument. He sees her in town one afternoon with another man. BACHMAN's girlfriend is walking next to her 10-year-old child. BACHMAN punches his girlfriend on the nose, break-ing it and making it bleed. The child burst into tears fearful that he will be punched next, fearing for his life the other man runs off.

In relation to this action, which of the following is correct?

A BACHMAN has committed battery on his girlfriend and assaulted the child and the other male.

B BACHMAN has committed battery on his girlfriend and assaulted the child only.

C BACHMAN has committed battery on his girlfriend only.

D BACHMAN has committed battery on all 3 of them.

Question 7.7

KNOWLES is having an argument with TYNE in the street, opposite the police sta-tion. TYNE picks up a large piece of wood and raises it above his head. He says to KNOWLES, 'How dare you swear at me? If we weren't opposite the nick I'd let you have this.'

Which of the following statements is correct?

A TYNE has committed an assault as he threatened to use immediate force.

B TYNE has committed an assault as he picked up a weapon.

C TYNE has not committed an assault as force was not actually used.

D TYNE has not committed an assault as his threat was negated by his words.

Question 7.8

EUSTACE is a Police Community Support Officer (PCSO), employed by her local Police Authority. Whilst on patrol she meets KACZYNSKI, who takes exception to her presence and wrestles her to the ground. BROWN, a member of the public and very community-minded, tries to pull KACZYNSKI off EUSTACE and KACZYNSKI re-sponds by pushing BROWN over.

Which of the following is true in relation to the Police Reform Act 2002?

A KACZYNSKI has committed an offence of assaulting a designated or accredited person in relation to both EUSTACE and BROWN and can be arrested where that is deemed necessary by a police officer.

B KACZYNSKI has committed an offence of assaulting a designated or accredited person in relation to EUSTACE only and can be arrested where that is deemed necessary by a police officer.

C KACZYNSKI has committed an offence of assaulting a designated or accredited person in relation to both EUSTACE and BROWN, and there is no power of arrest as it is not an indictable offence.

D KACZYNSKI has committed an offence of assaulting a designated or accredited person in relation to EUSTACE only, and there is no power of arrest as it is not an indictable offence.

Question 7.9

Constable MURPHY is a black officer. She is making an arrest for a public order offence when the suspect pushes her to the ground, saying 'fuck you black bitch, get back to the jungle where you belong'. Constable MURPHY is hurt but her injuries do not amount to a s. 47 assault.

The behaviour demonstrated by the offender amounts to racial or religious hatred. In relation to that, which of the following is true?

A In these circumstances the offender can *only* be charged with assault on police or assault with intent to resist arrest.

B The offender cannot be charged with a racially aggravated assault as this only applies to at least a s. 47 offence.

C The offender can be charged with racially aggravated common assault as the offence is made out.

D The offender can be charged with racially aggravated assault on police as the offence is made out.

Question 7.10

KADAR is infected with the HIV virus, and has unprotected sex with a woman he met in a nightclub. The woman consents fully to have sex with KADAR, and it was her idea not to use a condom. She contracts HIV as a direct result of this sexual encounter with KADAR.

Has KADAR committed an offence under s. 20 of the Offences Against the Person Act 1861?

A Yes, in these circumstances the offence is made out.

B Yes, provided the prosecution can show that KADAR had the relevant intent.

C No, as the woman should have been aware of the risk of having unprotected sex.

D No, as the woman consented to have sex and to have it unprotected.

Question 7.11

BRIDEWELL is facing a criminal prosecution for assault at the Crown Court. The incident occurred while BRIDEWELL was playing a football game, during which he tackled another player late, after the ball had been kicked out of play. The other player sustained a broken leg as a result of the tackle. BRIDEWELL has pleaded not guilty to the offence; his defence being that, by playing football, the injured person had 'consented' to harm being done to him.

In deciding whether BRIDEWELL's actions were criminal or not which of the following is correct?

A The level at which the game was being played is not relevant as to whether it was an assault or not.

B The state of mind of BRIDEWELL at the time of the incident is not relevant as it was a sporting event.

C Any previous incidents between BRIDEWELL and the injured person during the game are irrelevant to whether it is a criminal assault.

D The type of sport being played and the extent of risk of injury to the participants are irrelevant as to whether it is a criminal matter or not.

Question 7.12

The Children Act 2004 sets out to protect children from 'unreasonable punishment' by parents and carers.

Which of the following statements is correct, in relation to chastisement that *cannot* be justified as reasonable punishment under the above Act?

A The battery of a child under 17 cannot be justified if the injuries amount to an offence under ss. 18 or 20 of the Offences Against the Person Act 1861.

B The battery of a child under 18 cannot be justified if the injuries amount to an offence under ss. 18 or 20, or under s. 47 of the Offences Against the Person Act 1861.

C The battery of a child under 18 cannot be justified if the injuries amount to an offence under ss. 18 or 20 of the Offences Against the Person Act 1861.

D The battery of a child under 17 cannot be justified if the injuries amount to an offence under ss. 18 or 20, or under s. 47 of the Offences Against the Person Act 1861.

Question 7.13

PLANTZ has been knocked over by a car and has sustained injuries as a result of this deliberate act.

In relation to a possible 'assault' charge contrary to Offences Against the Person Act 1861 which of the following is correct?

A Although there are injuries, only relevant driving offences can be considered.

B An assault charge could be preferred as long as the injuries amounted to actual bodily harm (s. 47).

C An assault charge could be preferred as long as the injuries amounted to grievous bodily harm (s. 20).

D An assault charge could be preferred as long as the injuries amounted to grievous bodily harm with intent to do him grievous bodily harm (s. 18).

Question 7.14

PLEGGE and his girlfriend were having a stormy time in their relationship. PLEGGE was very upset when he discovered that she had been having an affair with her beauty therapist, who had helped manicure and keep her very long and polished nails. It had taken over two years to get her nails to the point where she thought they were perfect. Whilst she slept PLEGGE took some nail clippers and cut off one nail from each of his girlfriend's hands; needless to say she was less than happy and complained to the police that she had been assaulted.

In the circumstances as outlined above, would the actions of PLEGGE amount to an assault?

A This could only ever amount to a common assault, as she was asleep when the nails were cut.

B This could have amounted to assault occasioning actual bodily harm, but only if the girl had been awake and resisted the cutting.

C This could amount to assault occasioning actual bodily harm in these circumstances.

D This is not an assault at all; the nail beyond the cuticle is dead tissue, and in any event can be grown again.

Question 7.15

Constable CALDICOT was called to a road traffic collision, where a vehicle had driven into a wall and two men were seen running away from the scene. Constable CALDICOT made a search and saw PAINTER nearby. The officer questioned

PAINTER about his movements, but he refused to answer any questions at all; however the officer could smell intoxicants. The officer discovered that PAINTER was the registered owner of the vehicle from documents in his wallet and, under s. 172 of the Road Traffic Act 1988, the officer asked for the name and address of the driver at the time of the collision, again with no verbal response from PAINTER. He was eventually arrested for providing a positive sample of breath. Prior to being charged the police obtained irrefutable evidence that it was the other man who was driving, and not PAINTER. In actual fact PAINTER had sold the vehicle to the man who had been driving but he omitted to tell the police that.

Consider the offence of obstructing a police officer contrary to s. 89 of the Police Act 1996; in these circumstances has PAINTER committed this offence?

A Yes, for refusing to answer the direct questions asked only, but not for omitting to volunteer information.

B Yes, for refusing to answer the direct questions asked only, and also for omitting to volunteer information.

C No, the offence of obstruction cannot be committed by simply failing to answer questions or by omitting to volunteer information.

D No, as there must be at least some form of physical resistance, even where refusing to answer questions or by omitting to volunteer information.

Question 7.16

SELF separated from his wife when she became pregnant by another man 3 months ago. He has instructed a solicitor, TERRIGHTY, to represent him at divorce proceedings and has written a letter to TERRIGHTY. Part of the letter stated, 'I do not wish to take the child's life after it is born but ... the Law will take its course after I get rid of it, and I hope prison won't be too bad'.

Which of the following statements is correct?

A This would be a threat to kill provided the solicitor feared it would be carried out.

B This would be a threat to kill provided SELF intended that it would be believed.

C This would not amount to a threat to kill, as the threat is not immediate or in the immediate future.

D This would not amount to a threat to kill, as the threat is merely implied and not direct.

Question 7.17

KNIGHT is a member of the crew of a lifeboat and is a member of the Royal National Lifeboat Institute. One night his pager goes off and he starts to make his way to the harbour. On the way his path is blocked by his neighbour with whom he is in dispute over a hedge boundary. The neighbour hinders KNIGHT in attending the lifeboat call out.

Has the neighbour committed an offence contrary to s. 2 of the Emergency Workers (Obstruction) Act 2006?

A Yes, provided KNIGHT was on way to an actual emergency, and life was endangered due to the neighbour's actions.

B Yes, even if the call out was a false call and no actual life was endangered.

C No, as KNIGHT was no actually assaulted the offence is not made out.

D No, lifeboat personnel are not covered by this particular piece of legislation.

ANSWERS

Answer 7.1

Answer **D** — It is critical to the offence of assaulting a police officer contrary to s. 89 of the Police Act 1996 that the officer was acting in the execution of his or her duty when assaulted. Given the almost infinite variety of situations that police officers may find themselves in, it is difficult to define the precise boundaries of the execution of their duty; however through decided cases the courts have assisted to define what is, and more importantly, what is not lawful execution.

In *R (on the Application of Hawkes)* v *DPP* [2005] EWHC 3046, the defendant was convicted of assaulting a police officer in the execution of his duty after the police had gone to her home address to arrest her son. After the arrest, the defendant followed her son into a police car and refused to get out. She was given a warning and was verbally abusive, and only got out of the car when a second police car arrived. The defendant then started to walk towards her house but a police officer took hold of her arms. She bit the police officer on the arm. The prosecution case was that the police officer had arrested her for a breach of the peace and that the assault had occurred in the execution of that duty. The defendant argued that the prosecution case had been that she had actually committed a breach of the peace whilst she had been sitting in the police car. It was not a case of a threatened breach; accordingly, there was a requirement to establish some sort of violent conduct. Allowing her appeal, the Divisional Court held that the defendant had exhibited nothing more than an aggressive manner and that, while her conduct may have given rise to an imminent threat of violence, there was no evidence to suggest that it involved any violence justifying the conclusion that she had actually committed a breach of the peace in the presence of the police officer. In the circumstances, her arrest had been unlawful and the conviction for assaulting a police officer in the execution of his duty could not stand.

This question of the lawfulness of any arrest will become even more important to this offence (s. 89) in light of the re-wording of s. 24 of the Police and Criminal Evidence Act 1984, following the Serious Organised Crime and Police Act 2005. An offence contrary to s. 89 is a summary only offence, therefore the general power of entry under s. 17(1) of the Police and Criminal Evidence Act 1984 will not apply.

There is no power of arrest as no offence has been committed, and in any case there is no power of entry to effect the arrest (even had it been lawful); answers A, B and C are therefore incorrect.

Crime, para. 1.7.3.3

Answer 7.2

Answer **A** — Assault and battery are, strictly speaking, two separate things. What people generally think of as being an 'assault' (e.g. a punch on the nose) is a 'battery', that is, the infliction of unlawful force on someone else. While it would cover a punch on the nose, an 'assault' in its proper legal sense has a much wider meaning and includes any act whereby the defendant 'intentionally — or possibly recklessly — causes another person to apprehend immediate and unlawful personal violence' (*Fagan* v *Metropolitan Police Commissioner* [1969] 1 QB 439). Although the terms have distinct legal meanings they are often referred to as simply 'assaults' or 'common assault'.

In this case a battery has taken place, and therefore there is no need to show any fear in the victim, the *actus reas* and *mens rea* of a 'battery' is what is required to prove the offence; answer D is therefore incorrect.

The term battery, or the application of 'force', creates a misleading impression as a very small degree of physical contact will be enough. That force can be applied directly or indirectly and placing the can in the drum is enough; answer C is therefore incorrect.

The *mens rea* needed to prove a 'basic' assault is either:

- an intention to cause apprehension of immediate unlawful violence, or
- subjective recklessness (i.e. foresight) as to that consequence.

In this case to prove the offence it would have to be shown that the accused recognised there was risk that injury could be caused by her actions, yet still went ahead and took that risk. The 'reasonable man' test does not apply to an assault; answer B is therefore incorrect.

Crime, paras 1.7.2.2, 1.7.2.5

Answer 7.3

Answer **A** — This question deals with consent and broadly follows the outline of the circumstances in the case of *R* v *Richardson* [1999] QB 444. In that case it was held that a dentist's failure to inform patients that the General Dental Council had suspended him did not affect the true 'consent' given for medical treatment (answer D is incorrect). In *Richardson*, Otton LJ held that there had been no deception as to the identity of the dentist, or the nature of the act carried out, and this therefore could not vitiate consent and there could be no assault. Consent obtained by fraud would relate to the identity of the dentist as a trained dentist, which is not the case here, and answer C is therefore incorrect. Consent to medical treatment is true consent, but going beyond agreed treatment could be an assault, e.g. the indecent touching of the patient, and thus answer B is incorrect.

Crime, para. 1.7.2.6

Answer 7.4

Answer **C** — On a literal reading of s. 38 of the Offences Against the Person Act 1861, the only *actus reus* required is that of common assault, making answer B incorrect, whereas the *mens rea* is that of common assault, coupled with an intent to resist or prevent one's own, or another person's, lawful arrest or detention. Nevertheless, it is firmly established that the arrest or detention in question must in fact be lawful (*R* v *Self* [1992] 3 All ER 476; *R* v *Lee* [2000] Crim LR 991) and this is an essential element. The person making the arrest (or trying to) need not be a police officer as s. 110 of the Serious Organised Crime and Police Act 2005 gives a power of arrest to a person other than a constable where an indictable offence has been committed. As s. 38 is an either way offence it fits within the Serious Organised Crime and Police Act 2005 definition of 'indictable offence', which makes answers A and D incorrect.

Crime, para. 1.7.3.2

Answer 7.5

Answer **C** — 'Maliciously' does not need premeditation but rather amounts to subjective recklessness, and the suspect admits this. He accepts that there was a risk of harm. He does not have to foresee the degree of harm and therefore answer A is incorrect. This offence has two strands:

- An intention to cause serious harm; *or*
- An intention to resist or prevent lawful apprehension.

Where, in contrast, it is alleged that the defendant merely intended to resist arrest, etc., malice becomes an important further element to be proved, and therefore answer B is incorrect. It applies to intention to prevent as well as resist arrest, and not just when someone has actually been arrested, and therefore D is incorrect.

Crime, para. 1.7.6.3

Answer 7.6

Answer **A** — A battery requires the unlawful application of force upon the victim, an assault requires an act which caused the victim to apprehend the immediate infliction of unlawful force. So the girlfriend has been 'battered' and the other two assaulted; answers B, C and D are therefore incorrect.

Crime, para. 1.7.2.2

Answer 7.7

Answer **D** — Words used by the accused may indicate that no real attack is imminent, even where the circumstances might suggest otherwise. This principle has been clearly established since the very ancient case of *Tuberville* v *Savage* (1669) 1 Mod 3, where, in the course of a quarrel with S, T placed his hand on the hilt of his sword (an act which might ordinarily have been construed as an assault) and exclaimed, 'If it were not assize time, I would not take such language from you'. 'Assize time' meant that the judges were in town, and no doubt T feared being arrested and tried. The same principle applies on the facts of this question where TYNE makes a 'qualified' threat to KNOWLES (answers A and B are therefore incorrect). As a point of interest the older the case law the better law it is, as it has stood the test of time, over 330 years in this case! There can be assault where no force is used, i.e. threats making the other person fear immediate attack, and therefore answer C is incorrect.

Crime, para. 1.7.2.3

Answer 7.8

Answer **A** — Section 46(1) of the Police Reform Act 2002 states:

(1) Any person who assaults —
    (a) a designated person in the execution of his duty,
    (b) an accredited person in the execution of his duty, or
    (ba) an accredited inspector in the execution of his duty, or
    (c) a person assisting a designated or accredited person or an accredited inspector in the execution of his duty,
    is guilty of an offence.

Provided the designated or accredited person was acting in the execution of his or her duty, it is an offence to assault either that person or anyone assisting him or her, therefore answers B and D are incorrect as they state that only the PCSO is assaulted.

By virtue of the Serious Organised Crime and Police Act 2005 all offences are arrestable where deemed necessary by a police officer because certain criteria are met. However powers of arrest are also extended to 'any person' but only where an indictable offence is involved, s. 46(1) of the Police Reform Act is summary only; answer C is therefore incorrect.

Crime, para. 1.7.3.5

Answer 7.9

Answer **C** — Although the offences of assault on police (s. 89 of the Police Act 1996) and assault with intent to resist arrest (s. 38 of the Offences Against the Person Act 1861) are perfectly valid for this instance, given the racially aggravated factors a more serious charge is appropriate. Also answer A says can *only* be charged, pre-cluding any other offence such as common assault, which is not true, and for that reason answer A is incorrect. In *R v Jacobs* [2001] 2 Cr App R (S) 174, a female police officer was subjected to repeated verbal racial abuse by a female suspect who had been arrested and taken to the police station. Bennett J commented that 'police of-ficers are entitled to be protected, just as any other members of the public, from racial abuse'. And the Crime and Disorder Act 1998 extends this racially aggravat-ing factor to various levels of assault, common assault being one of them (s. 29(1)(c) of the 1998 Act), therefore answer B is incorrect. It does not extend such offences to the Police Act, however, and there is no such offence of racially aggravated assault on police; answer D is therefore incorrect.

Crime, para. 1.7.3.1

Answer 7.10

Answer **A** — Section 20 of the Offences Against the Person Act 1861 does not re-quire intent to commit grievous bodily harm (GBH), that is a s. 18 offence, and the prosecution only have to show that the accused unlawfully and maliciously inflic-ted GBH, therefore answer B is incorrect. Certainly contracting HIV could be said to be an 'injury resulting in some permanent disability' and as such amounts to GBH; the issue here is consent. In *R v Dica* [2004] EWCA Crim 1103, it was held that recklessness to consent, as such, was not in issue. In *Dica* the defendant had unpro-tected sex with two women, knowing he was HIV positive. Although both women were willing to have sexual intercourse with the defendant, the prosecution's case was that their agreement would never have been given if they had known of the defendant's condition. The defendant stated that he told both women of his condition, and that they were nonetheless willing to have sexual intercourse with him. However, the judge ruled that whether or not the complainants knew of the defendant's condition, their consent, if any, was irrelevant and provided no defence, since *R v Brown* [1994] 1 AC 212 deprived the complainants of the legal capacity to consent to such serious harm. In *Brown* it was held that sado-masochistic acts which occurred in private and which were consented to could found charges under the 1861 Act, ss. 20 and 47, if the injuries, though not permanent, were neither transient nor trifling. So, irrespective of the victim's willingness to place herself at risk, or to consent to sexual activity, KADAR has committed the offence; answers C and D are therefore incorrect.

Crime, paras 1.7.6.2, 1.7.4.2

Answer 7.11

Answer **C** — The Court of Appeal examined the issue of 'consent to injury' in the case of *R v Barnes* [2004] EWCA Crim 3246. The case was similar to the circumstances in this question and, while accepting that the tackle was hard, the defendant claimed that it had been a fair challenge and that the injury was caused accidentally. The Court held that, if the actions of the defendant had been within the rules of the game being played, it would be a firm indication that what had occurred was not criminal.

However, in relation to the *Barnes* case, the Court held that the threshold level was an objective one to be determined by:

- the type of sport being played;
- the level at which it was being played;
- the nature of the 'act';
- the degree of force used;
- the extent of risk of injury to the participants; and
- the state of mind of the defendant.

The issue of whether there had been any previous incidents between the accused and the injured person during the game was not considered during this ruling; therefore since all the other issues listed are matters that the Court *did* consider, answers A, B and D are incorrect.

Crime, para. 1.7.2.6

Answer 7.12

Answer **B** — Section 58 of the Children Act 2004 provides that the battery of a person under 18 years of age (not 17, therefore answers A and D are incorrect) cannot be justified on the ground that it constituted reasonable punishment in relation to an offence under ss. 47, 18 or 20 of the Offences Against the Person Act 1861. Since all three of the above offences are covered, answers A and C are incorrect.

Crime, para. 1.7.2.7

Answer 7.13

Answer **B** — The Court of Appeal has held, in the case of *R v Bain* [2005] EWCA Crim 07, that there is nothing wrong on principle in charging a driver with causing grievous bodily harm as well as dangerous driving in appropriate circumstances; answer A is therefore incorrect. It follows that bringing about other forms of lasting or significant injury with a motor vehicle could also be so charged, leaving the starting point at actual bodily harm (s. 47); consequently answers C and D are incorrect.

Crime, para. 1.7.6

Answer 7.14

Answer **C** — It must be shown that 'actual bodily harm' was a consequence, directly or indirectly, of the defendant's actions. Such harm can include shock (*R v Miller* [1954] 2 QB 282) and mental 'injury' (*R v Chan-Fook* [1994] 1 WLR 689).

So what is 'actual bodily harm'? In *DPP v Smith* [1961] AC 290, it was noted that the expression needed 'no explanation' and, in *Chan-Fook*, the court advised that the phrase consisted of 'three words of the English language which require no elaboration and in the ordinary course should not receive any'. So actual bodily harm appears to mean what it says. But that is not necessarily as clear as it sounds.

In *DPP v Smith (Ross Michael)* [2006] EWHC 94 the Divisional Court took the view that in light of there being no prior decisions directly in point, cutting off a person's hair can amount to actual bodily harm; answer D is therefore incorrect.

The Court was of the view that:

> It is necessary to look at definitions because there is nothing to assist us in the decided cases. In ordinary language, 'harm' is not limited to 'injury', and according to the Concise Oxford Dictionary extends to 'hurt' or 'damage'. According to the same dictionary, 'bodily', whether used as an adjective or an adverb, is 'concerned with the body'. 'Actual', as defined in the authorities, means that the bodily harm should not be so trivial or trifling as to be effectively without significance.

Sir Igor Judge (President of the Queen's Bench Division) stated in *Smith (Ross Michael)*:

> In my judgment, whether it is alive beneath the surface of the skin or dead tissue above the surface of the skin, the hair is an attribute and part of the human body. It is intrinsic to each individual and to the identity of each individual. Although it is not essential to my decision, I note that an individual's hair is relevant to his or her autonomy. Some regard it as their crowning glory. Admirers may so regard it in the object of their affections. Even if, medically and scientifically speaking, the hair above the surface of the scalp is no more than dead tissue, it remains part of the body and is attached to it. While it is so attached, in my judgment it falls within the meaning of 'bodily' in the phrase 'actual bodily harm'. It is concerned with the body of the individual victim.

This case is identical to this scenario as nails and hair would be said to be synonymous. So although also being a common assault, there would be a case to answer for a s. 47 assault, and this is the case whether the person was asleep or awake; answers A and B are therefore incorrect.

Crime, para. 1.7.6.1

Answer 7.15

Answer **B** — Under s. 89(2) of the Police Act 1996, any person who resists or wilfully obstructs a constable in the execution of his or her duty, or a person assisting a constable in the execution of his or her duty, shall be guilty of an offence.

Resistance suggests some form of physical opposition; obstruction does not and may take many forms; answer D is therefore incorrect. Obstruction has been interpreted as making it more difficult for a constable to carry out his or her duty (*Hinchcliffe* v *Sheldon* [1955] 1 WLR 1207) and refusing to answer an officer's questions is not obstruction (*Rice* v *Connolly* [1966] 2 QB 414) — *unless the defendant was under some duty to provide information*. In this scenario the defendant was under not only a duty, but a legal requirement, to provide information; answer C is therefore incorrect.

Similarly, obstruction can be caused by omission but only where the defendant was already under some duty towards the police or the officer, and by omitting to provide information that he had that he was under a duty to disclose would be evidence of 'obstruction' by omission; answer A is therefore incorrect.

Crime, para. 1.7.3.4

Answer 7.16

Answer **B** — There are two factors to be proved in the offence of threats to kill contrary to s. 16 of the Offences Against the Person Act 1861: that the threat was made and that it was made with the intention that the person receiving it would fear that it would be carried out. It does not matter whether the person whose life is threatened so fears, or whether the person receiving the threat has such a fear; therefore answer A is incorrect. An implied threat will suffice (see the facts of *R v Solanke* [1969] 3 All ER 1383) and therefore answer D is incorrect. The threat may be to kill another person at some time in the future and therefore answer C is incorrect. A threat to a pregnant woman in respect of her unborn child is not sufficient if the threat is to kill it before its birth. But if it is a threat to kill the child after its birth, then that would appear to be within the section (*R v Tait* [1990] 1 QB 290).

Crime, para. 1.7.5

Answer 7.17

Answer **B** — Section 1 of the Emergency Workers (Obstruction) Act 2006 states:

(1) person who without reasonable excuse obstructs or hinders another while that other person is, in a capacity mentioned in subsection (2) below, responding to emergency circumstances, commits an offence.

There are a number of persons named in subs. (2) and in s. 1(2)(f) we have:

(f) that of a member of the crew of a vessel operated by —
  (i) the Royal National Lifeboat Institution, or
  (ii) any other person or organization operating a vessel for the purpose of providing a rescue service,
  or a person who musters the crew of such a vessel or attends to its launch or recovery.

Emergency circumstances are defined by the 2006 Act, but of course, like most of us, members of the emergency services do not have the gift of foresight so it is hard to tell if any call out is an actual emergency, or that life is actually endangered. The point of the Act is to protect those members of the emergency services going about their business; answer A is therefore incorrect.

RNLI staff are included and the legislation goes beyond assaults to include obstruction and hindrance; answers C and D are therefore incorrect.

Crime, para. 1.7.4.1

8 | Miscellaneous Offences Against the Person

STUDY PREPARATION

This chapter goes on to look at less frequently occurring, yet very serious offences. These are offences such as torture, kidnapping, poisoning and hostage taking.

You are tested on what the constituent parts of these offences are, together with what 'intent' is required to prove the offence has been committed.

You may only ever come across one of these offences on the pages of an examination booklet, but your understanding of them is nevertheless vital, if only for that one time you do come across them!

QUESTIONS

Question 8.1

MOORE stopped his car at a bus stop and told a lone woman waiting for the bus that the bus had broken down about half a mile down the road (this was not in fact true). He offered the woman a lift. She accepted, but then asked to be let out of the car after a short distance. MOORE refused and kept the woman in his car. He reached his house and forced her down into the basement.

At what point, if any, does MOORE 'kidnap' the woman?

A   He does not kidnap her, she consents to get in the car.
B   He kidnaps her when she first gets into the car.
C   He kidnaps her when he refuses to let her out.
D   He kidnaps her when he takes her into his house.

Question 8.2

WILSON sees a young couple out walking on the common. He approaches the girl and tells her that he is a police officer and is taking her to be searched for drugs, he tells the boyfriend to go home. He then walks her to his car about 25 metres away. Her boyfriend, suspecting something is not right, returns with two other friends and rescues the girl prior to WILSON putting her in his car. WILSON is not a police officer and had an unlawful purpose in mind.

Has WILSON committed the offence of kidnapping?

A Yes, as he has taken the girl away without her consent.

B Yes, as he has taken the girl away without her consent and had an unlawful purpose.

C No, as the girl went willingly with him.

D No, as he never really took her anywhere as they were still on the common.

Question 8.3

NEWING has had enough of her neighbour DUKE playing loud music at all hours of the day and night. One morning she took DUKE's milk from his doorstep. NEWING crushed 8 sleeping tablets prescribed for her own use and put them in the milk, returning the bottle to DUKE's doorstep. NEWING knew exactly what she was doing and intended to make DUKE ill. The effects of the tablets were reduced by the milk, however, and they simply made DUKE fall asleep.

Has NEWING committed the offence of poisoning with intent under s. 24 of the Offences Against the Person Act 1861?

A Yes, as NEWING intended to injure, aggrieve or annoy DUKE.

B No, as the drugs are not 'noxious things'.

C Yes, provided that NEWING was at least reckless to any injury caused.

D No, as DUKE's life was never in danger.

Question 8.4

MAILLING is the mayor of a small town and a strong advocate of European monetary union. Whilst leaving the town hall he sees KUILOUS writing graffiti all over the town hall, in more than 20 places prior to being seen by MAILLING. It stated, 'you can stick your Euros up your arse MAILLING'. Incensed at this criminal damage (which would be more than £5,000), MAILLING makes an arrest and takes his prisoner back up into his office. In there he makes KUILOUS squat in the corner of his office and leaves him there for an hour. MAILLING then asks all 15 members of staff to come into the room at look at KUILOUS. They all laugh at him causing him extreme humiliation. MAILLING calls the police and KUILOUS is arrested by the police for criminal damage.

Which of the following statements is true?

A MAILLING has not committed torture, as there was no real physical suffering by KUILOUS.

B MAILLING has not committed torture, as he is not acting in the performance of his public duties.

C MAILLING has committed torture, as he is a public official and has subjected KUILOUS to degrading treatment.

D MAILLING and his staff members have all committed torture.

Question 8.5

FRAMPTON is not a very popular boss amongst his colleagues. At the office party he is drinking lager, and leaves his half drunk glass on the side whilst he goes to the toilet. His colleagues drink a little of his drink and one then urinates in it at the enticing of the rest. The intention is only to annoy FRAMPTON not to injure him. Suspecting something is amiss on his return FRAMPTON leaves prior to drinking the lager.

Considering the offence of poisoning with intent (contrary to s. 24 of the Offences Against the Person Act 1861), which of the following is correct?

A The offence is not made out as there was no intent to injure or harm FRAMPTON.

B The offence is not made out as urine is not a noxious substance as defined in this Act.

C The offence is made out, but only by the person who urinated in the drink.

D The offence is made out and by all the colleagues involved in the incident.

Question 8.6

BRAWTY is a member of an animal rights group. To further their cause he waits outside the home address of someone who works in an animal testing laboratory and forcibly takes her to a warehouse. BRAWTY then telephones the head of the laboratory and states he will continue to confine BRAWTY till all the animals in the laboratory are released. BRAWTY also states that no harm will come to the worker, she will just not be released till his demand is met.

Considering s. 1 of the Taking of Hostages Act 1982, has this offence been committed?

A Yes, from the moment the worker was taken with the necessary intent.

B Yes, as soon as a threat not to release the worker was issued.

C No, the threat was not made to a State or international governmental organisation.

D No, as there was no threat to kill or injure the worker.

ANSWERS

Answer 8.1

Answer **B** — Kidnapping is defined at common law as 'the taking or carrying away of one person by another without the consent of the person so taken or carried away, and without lawful excuse'.

The issue here is consent, and certainly the woman consents to get into the car. However, the Court of Appeal held in *R v Cort* [2003] 3 WLR 1300, that if the consent is obtained by fraud, as it was here through the lies told, then this would not be true consent. Without such consent, the offence is made out when the woman gets in the car and, as MOORE has kidnapped her, answer A is incorrect. Although he further detains her, this is more the offence of false imprisonment, and happens after she is kidnapped; answers C and D are therefore incorrect.

Crime, para. 1.8.5

Answer 8.2

Answer **A** — Kidnapping is defined at common law as follows:

> It is an offence at common law to take or carry away another person without the consent of that person and without lawful excuse.

The required elements of this offence are the unlawful taking or carrying away of one person by another by force or fraud (*R v D* [1984] AC 778). These requirements go beyond those of mere restraint needed for false imprisonment. Parents may be acting without lawful excuse, for instance, if they are acting in breach of a court order in respect of their children.

The taking or carrying away of the victim must be without the consent of the victim. If the victim consents to an initial taking but later withdraws that consent, the offence would be complete. If the consent is obtained by fraud, the defendant cannot rely on that consent and the offence — or attempted offence — will be made out (see *R v Cort* [2003] 3 WLR 1300); answer C is therefore incorrect. There is no limit as to how far the taking should be; answer D is therefore incorrect.

There need only be a 'taking'; the purpose is irrelevant which makes answer B incorrect.

Crime, para. 1.8.5

Answer 8.3

Answer **A** — The offence is one of specific intent, and recklessness is not sufficient, so answer C is incorrect. In *R v Marcus* [1981] 2 All ER 833, the Court of Appeal held that a substance which might be harmless in small quantities could be 'noxious' if the quantity administered was sufficient to injure, aggrieve or annoy (answer B is incorrect). Section 24 is distinguished from s. 23 of the 1861 Act, in that the latter requires proof of a consequence — namely, the endangering of a person's life or the infliction of grievous bodily harm — and therefore answer D is incorrect.

Crime, paras 1.8.3, 1.8.3.1

Answer 8.4

Answer **B** — MAILLING does not appear to be acting in the performance or purported performance of his duties, and therefore cannot be guilty of torture (answer C is incorrect). It might be argued that he saw his actions as being part of his civic managerial duties, but this is unlikely to succeed. The meaning of 'severe pain or suffering' does not have to amount to grievous bodily harm, actual bodily harm or any standard measured by degree of injury. Indeed, the wording of s. 134(3) of the Criminal Justice Act 1988 provides that the pain or suffering may be purely mental. It is the severity of the pain rather than whether or not identifiable injury results that should be considered, though evidence of injury would be admissible evidence of the severity of the pain. Answer A is therefore incorrect. The arguments against the actions of MAILLING falling within the scope of his public duties apply even more clearly to the actions of his staff, and therefore answer D is also incorrect.

Crime, para. 1.8.2

Answer 8.5

Answer **D** — The Offences Against the Person Act 1861, s. 24 states:

> Whosoever shall unlawfully and maliciously administer to or cause to be administered to or taken by any other person any poison or other destructive or noxious thing, with intent to injure, aggrieve, or annoy any such person, shall be guilty of a misdemeanour...

As can be seen intention to annoy is enough, it need not extend as far as intent to injure; answer A is therefore incorrect. Whether a substance is noxious will depend on both its quality and quantity and is not specifically defined (I suppose a test would be if someone urinated in your drink would you find it noxious?); answer B is therefore incorrect.

The offence is committed by the 'poisoner' as well as those who cause it to be administered; answer C is therefore incorrect.

Crime, para. 1.8.3.1

Answer 8.6

Answer **B** — Section 1 of the Taking of Hostages Act 1982 states:

(1) A person, whatever his nationality, who, in the United Kingdom or elsewhere —
    (a) ...
    (b) in order to compel a State, international governmental organisation, or person to do or abstain from doing any act, threatens to kill, injure or continue to detain the hostage,
commits an offence.

So the threat can be made to a single person, as well as a State or international governmental organisation; answer C is therefore incorrect. It is also sufficient to merely threaten further detention, although threats to kill and injure are also there, they are not exclusive; answer D is therefore incorrect.

The offence is complete *after* the taking, when the further threat is issued; answer A is therefore incorrect. This makes the title of the Act a little misleading, as the mere taking of a hostage would be a kidnap and the point of 'taking' in this offence is to compel another to do or abstain from an act.

Crime, para. 1.8.6

9 | Sexual Offences

STUDY PREPARATION

Sexual offences cover a wide range of activities. In answering these questions there is a real need first of all to identify who is doing what to whom. Usually the key to the offences that arise from such activities is to be found in:

- the ages of the parties;
- the intent of the offender;
- the consent of the victim;
- the accompanying circumstances.

Until fairly recently sexual offences were subject to an Act almost half a century old — ask yourself, have sexual activity and attitudes changed since then? The existing framework was described as 'archaic, incoherent and discriminatory'. The resulting Sexual Offences Act 2003 is a landmark statute that repealed almost all of the Sexual Offences Act 1956 and many other statutory provisions enacted since, delivering, in effect, a new criminal code of sexual offences. The Sexual Offences Act 2003 not only introduces a considerable number of new offences and criminalises certain types of conduct not previously subjected to the written law, it also substantially redefines many sex crimes, incorporating new terms and language deemed more appropriate to contemporary society.

QUESTIONS

Question 9.1

HILL goes on a blind date and as they get on so well he invites her back to his house. At the house the girl initially agrees to have sexual intercourse with him, and they then both consume a lot of alcohol; the girl is very drunk. HILL goes to the bathroom to get a condom, and prior to his return the girl falls asleep on the bed. HILL has sex with her while she sleeps.

Has HILL committed rape?
A No, as she agreed to sex prior to falling asleep and never negated that consent.
B No, as her drunkenness was self-induced and she never negated consent to sex.
C Yes, even though she agreed when she was awake she may not agree at the time HILL had sex with her.
D Yes, but the onus is on the prosecution to prove beyond doubt that there was no consent.

Question 9.2

JHEETA meets a woman and begins to have a full sexual relationship with her, but she calls off the relationship. JHEETA starts sending texts to her threatening harm to her if she doesn't have sex with him again; she reports the matter to Constable THOMAS. The officer begins to investigate the matter; however JHEETA sends the girl a text purporting to be from Constable THOMAS stating that she should continue to have sex with JHEETA until she has concluded her investigation. The girl believes the text and has sex several more times with JHEETA.

In these circumstances has JHEETA committed rape?
A Yes, as the girl is deceived as to the nature of the act.
B Yes, as the girl is deceived as to the identity of the text sender.
C No, as the girl was not deceived by the nature of the intercourse.
D No, as the girl was not deceived by the identity of JHEETA.

Question 9.3

TANNOCK is driving his children to a local theme park and is driving on the motorway. His car is passed by a bus on a 'hen party' one of the females exposes her breast and another 'moons' her buttocks at the car. TANNOCK laughs and is very happy this happened, however his 10-year-old daughter is distressed by the incident.

In relation to exposure contrary to s. 66 of the Sexual Offences Act 2003, which of the following is correct?
A Both females are guilty of exposure as they have offended a girl, who is covered by the legislation.

B Only the female exposing her buttocks is guilty as exposing breast is not covered by the legislation.

C Neither female is guilty of the offence as it is only exposing genitals that is covered by the Act.

D Neither female is guilty as they were on the bus and not in a public place.

Question 9.4

TIMOTHY is 15 years of age, but is a mature boy who looks older than he is. He has been infatuated with his neighbour's 25-year-old daughter for some time, and wishes to have sex with her. One night they are alone in TIMOTHY's house and he starts to seduce her; she freely consents. They do not have sexual intercourse, but she masturbates TIMOTHY.

Which of the following is correct?

A The woman has committed a sexual assault.

B The woman has committed an offence of sexual activity with a child.

C The woman has committed no offence, as the boy consented to the act.

D The woman has committed no offence, as no intercourse took place.

Question 9.5

MCNALLY and his girlfriend, who are both 17 years of age, are in their bedroom and are joined by MCNALLY's younger brother, who is 13 years of age. Whilst the brother watches, MCNALLY and his girlfriend participate in mutual masturbation and oral sex. They both know the child is present, and both are getting sexual gratification from the fact they are being watched by the brother. The brother is not offended and enjoys watching.

Is this engaging in sexual activity in the presence of a child contrary to s. 11 of the Sexual Offences Act 2003?

A Yes, as they are over 17 years of age.

B Yes, because the brother is under 14 years of age.

C No, because they are not 18 years of age or over.

D No, because the child is not offended, nor forced to watch.

Question 9.6

TRITON invites GRAHAM, who is 19 and suffering from a severe mental disorder, back to his house. TRITON then asks GRAHAM to take all his clothes off, which he willingly does. Because of his mental disorder GRAHAM is unable to refuse involvement in sexual activity. TRITON then tries to penetrate GRAHAM anally, which GRAHAM has freely agreed to. TRITON only just manages to penetrate GRAHAM, then gives up and sends GRAHAM home.

In order to prove the offence of sexual activity with a person with a mental disorder (s. 30), what does the prosecution have to show?

A That TRITON knew GRAHAM suffered from a mental disorder.

B That TRITON knew GRAHAM suffered from a mental disorder and knew he was unlikely to refuse his advances.

C That TRITON used inducements to get GRAHAM to agree to the touching.

D That TRITON coerced GRAHAM into agreeing to the touching.

Question 9.7

MCMANUS' computer was found to contain thousands of indecent images of children. Most had been downloaded via an Internet file-sharing system whereby members installed software allowing files, held in their shared folder, to be accessed and downloaded directly into shared folders of other members whilst connected to the Internet. Only 6 of all the files downloaded were found in the defendant's shared folder, in respect of which he was charged with 6 counts of possessing indecent photographs or pseudo-photographs of a child with a view to their being distributed or shown by himself or others, contrary to s. 1(1)(c) of the Protection of Children Act 1978.

The defendant contended that he did not intend to distribute or show the photographs to others and, once downloaded, he usually moved the files into folders not accessible to other members. The 6 files in the shared folder had not yet been moved due to the process he used to download and move images in bulk.

Considering the offence contrary to s. 1(1)(c) of the Protection of Children Act 1978, has MCMANUS committed this offence?

A The images in the shared folder were possessed with a view to their being distributed, and he is guilty.

B The images are being held in a file that could be accessed by other members and MCMANUS is aware of this, and therefore he is guilty.

C The images are stored with a view to moving them to a private folder and as such he is not guilty of this offence.

D The images are not stored with an intention of allowing the distribution of them and as such he is not guilty of the offence.

Question 9.8

MORTLEY, 22 years old, is a convicted child sex offender currently on parole. He is seen by concerned parents every day of the week standing outside a local primary school. He says or does nothing, but is always outside the school when the children are released.

What is the fullest extent to which a risk of sexual harm order (RSHO) may be made to protect children?

A To protect all the children at the school who are at risk from MORTLEY.
B To protect a particular child at the school who is at risk from MORTLEY.
C To protect any child in the locality who is at risk from MORTLEY.
D To protect any child anywhere who is at risk from MORTLEY.

Question 9.9

CORNELIUS lives with his prostitute girlfriend and has recently encouraged her to go to work as a prostitute for DIBLEY, a local drug dealer. CORNELIUS hopes that in providing his girlfriend, DIBLEY will supply him with cheap drugs in the future, which is likely. CORNELIUS receives no money from DIBLEY for the deal. His girlfriend is happy with this arrangement, as she will make more money working for DIBLEY.

Has CORNELIUS committed an offence of controlling prostitution for gain under s. 53 of the Sexual Offences Act 2003?

A No, there has been no gain as yet, only future hopes of gain.
B No, as CORNELIUS's girlfriend is not forced into prostitution.
C Yes, as there will be future financial advantage.
D Yes, as the prostitute will make money and she lives with CORNELIUS.

Question 9.10

MOOLES and his female secretary, MAKINS, attended a conference in Blackpool. While they were in the bar, MOOLES asked his secretary if she wanted to try some new sex drug to aid her enjoyment, as she enjoyed being overpowered. She agreed and MOOLES put it in her drink. They went upstairs to MOOLES' bedroom and started to have consensual sex. However the drug she took stupefied MAKINS and she passed out. MOOLES continued until he ejaculated.

Has MOOLES committed rape if MAKINS were to make such a complaint?

A Yes, as MOOLES administered a substance which was capable of causing the complainant to be stupefied.

B Yes, as MAKINS was unconscious MOOLES should have stopped.

C No, as MAKINS agreed to take the drug that ultimately stupefied her.

D No, as clearly MAKINS had consented to sex prior to passing out.

Question 9.11

BENTHURST and his girlfriend DYER are having anal sex in a toilet cubicle in a men's toilet. Another man enters the toilet and hears what he clearly believes to be a couple having sex; he laughs and leaves the toilet.

Regarding sexual activity in a public lavatory, which of the following is true?

A This offence is not made out because no one was offended or disgusted.

B This offence is not made out as they are not engaged in homosexual sex.

C This offence is made out only because it involves anal sex.

D This offence is made out and both are guilty of it.

Question 9.12

LANE was given a caution for being a common prostitute, and asks you if she can dispute the interpretation of her actions as being 'soliciting'.

Which of the following is correct?

A No, she cannot dispute the caution, as it is not an official caution for an offence.

B No, she cannot dispute the caution, as it is only recorded in a police held register.

C Yes, she can apply to a court within 7 days of the caution.

D Yes, she can apply to a court within 14 days of the caution.

Question 9.13

FOWLER is a convicted paedophile, and notified police of his home address. He has stayed with a friend some 300 miles from his home address; he stayed with this friend for 3 days, 2 months ago, and now intends spending another 3 days with him. He has not notified police of the address of his friend.

Should he now notify police that he is staying with his friend?

A No, as he is not staying there for 7 days.

B No, as he has not stayed there for 7 days in the last year.

C Yes, he must notify police of any place he is staying, for any period.

D Yes, he is away from his notified address for more than 2 days.

Question 9.14

BUTCHER is a man who wishes to pay a prostitute for sexual intercourse. He has never done this before and is a bit unsure of what to do. He gets into his car and drives to a residential area he believes, mistakenly, to be a well-known red light area. He notices a lone woman standing near the bus stop; he stops beside her and says, 'Are you doing business?' Not knowing what he means she says, 'No I'm waiting for a bus, what sort of business are you looking for?' Confused, BUTCHER drives straight home.

Which of the following is correct?

A He has committed an offence of kerb-crawling as his behaviour is likely to cause annoyance to the woman.

B He has committed an offence of kerb-crawling as he has solicited the woman from his car.

C He has not committed an offence of kerb-crawling as the woman was not offended.

D He has not committed an offence of kerb-crawling as he did not intend to cause annoyance to the woman.

Question 9.15

LINTERN has a 15-year-old daughter, FAY, who looks older than her age. LINTERN introduced FAY to his friend, GREGORIOUN, who is a pimp. Between them, LINTERN and GREGORIOUN persuaded FAY to become a prostitute. She agreed and went out with GREGORIOUN on weekends only, and solicited in the street for prostitution. FAY's mother was aware of what was happening to her daughter and encouraged her, but refused to accept any money from what the child earned.

In relation to offences under s. 48 of the Sexual Offences Act 2003 of causing or inciting child prostitution, which of the following is true?

A GREGORIOUN has committed the offence, but LINTERN has not.

B LINTERN has committed the offence, but GREGORIOUN has not.

C LINTERN and GREGORIOUN have committed the offence in these circumstances.

D LINTERN, GREGORIOUN and the child's mother have committed the offence.

Question 9.16

POTTER downloaded some pornographic pictures of children under the age of 16 from the Internet. He took them to work and lent them to his friend, BOYD, who returned them the next day.

Who has committed an offence in relation to the photographs?

A Both: POTTER for possessing and distributing photographs; BOYD for being in possession of them.

B Only POTTER, for possessing and distributing the photographs to another person.

C Both POTTER and BOYD for possession, as photographs cannot be distributed to just one person in this way.

D Both POTTER and BOYD for possession, as the offence of distributing does not include lending.

Question 9.17

PAVETT is a woman employed as a cleaner at an NHS hospital specialising in mental health. She is sexually very active and is caught one morning having sexual intercourse with a male patient, who was receiving treatment for a mental disorder at the hospital as an outpatient. The man is a regular outpatient, and PAVETT frequently sees him on a daily basis. Consider s. 39 of the Sexual Offences Act 2003, on care workers causing or inciting sexual activity.

In relation to PAVETT's actions, which of the following is correct?

A She has committed this offence as she is a care worker.

B She has committed the offence; even though she is not a care worker, the man is an outpatient.

C She has not committed the offence as she is not a care worker.

D She has not committed the offence because the man is an outpatient.

Question 9.18

STREETER is very keen to have sexual intercourse with BETTY. She tells him she is only interested in his friendship and wants nothing more than that. One night STREETER decides that she will have sex with him if he forces the issue, so he hides outside her bedroom window on the ledge, intent on entering and having sex with BETTY. He intends to force her to have sex, although he honestly believes she wants to. He breaks the window and enters the house. However, she is not in the house.

Which of the following is true in relation to the Sexual Offences Act 2003, regarding STREETER's intent?

A STREETER commits an offence when he breaks the bedroom window.

B STREETER commits an offence when he hides outside the bedroom window.

C STREETER does not commit an offence, as he has an honest belief and no sex took place.

D STREETER does not commit an offence, as Betty was not in the house.

Question 9.19

REYNOLDS, aged 48 years, owns a sweet shop, which he uses to further his paedophilic desires. He sees BEN, who is 12 years old, in the shop and has desires to touch him sexually. He arranges to meet BEN later in the local park. He has never met BEN before. He walks to the park at about 7 pm, and meets BEN by the swings. BEN realises something is wrong and runs off before REYNOLDS can touch him.

At what point, if any, does REYNOLDS commit an offence under s. 15 of the Sexual Offences Act 2003, on child grooming?

A When he arranges to meet the child.

B When he starts walking to meet the child.

C When he first meets the child in the park.

D He does not commit the offence as he has not previously communicated with the child.

Question 9.20

RICH is a biology teacher at the local high school, and ELAINE is a 16-year-old pupil in his class. They are very friendly and ELAINE adores RICH, and they converse frequently in an Internet chatroom. RICH sends indecent still photographs in an e-mail to ELAINE's school computer terminal from his; they are very explicit pictures. ELAINE loves the pictures and is not in the least concerned by them. RICH receives sexual gratification from knowing that ELAINE looks at the pictures, and if questioned by the school he will say it is part of a sex education programme.

Has RICH committed an offence under s. 19 of the Sexual Offences Act 2003 on abuse of position of trust causing a child to watch a sexual act?

A Yes, but only because ELAINE is a pupil in his class.

B Yes, but only because of the sexual gratification he gets.

C No, this offence only applies to a child under 16 years of age.

D No, because they are still pictures and not a 'moving image'.

Question 9.21

FOWLER is the manager of a gym, and has recently been subject to a number of thefts of personal property from clients using the sun beds. To combat this he gets permission from all the clientele to install a hidden camera in this area. The clients agree to the camera recording the activities in this area of the gym, and for it to be viewed by the police should a further theft occur. No permission was obtained for FOWLER to view the recording 'live'. All the clientele also agree to wear underwear during the time the camera is installed. A camera is installed and begins to record; unknown to the clientele FOWLER has a fetish about women walking round in their underwear and although his original intention was to try to catch the thief he now starts to watch the recording 'live' expressly for his own sexual gratification.

In these circumstances had FOWLER committed an offence of voyeurism contrary to s. 67 of the Sexual Offences Act 2003?

A No, as he has permission from the clients to film them and as such cannot commit this offence.

B No, as the persons using the sun beds are wearing underwear and not exposing any part of their 'private' areas.

C Yes, although he had permission to film he did not have permission to view the video 'live'.

D Yes, as the clientele were unaware of the purpose formed after the camera was installed he commits this offence.

Question 9.22

GREENLEES has been convicted of possessing indecent photographs of a child, and has changed his home address since being released from prison, having served his sentence.

How should this notification of change of address be made?

A It must be personally at the police station.

B It can be by sending written notification.

C It can be by sending written notification or by telephoning the station.

D It must be by written notification.

Question 9.23

A Sexual Offences Prevention Order is made with a view to prohibiting a defendant from doing 'anything' described in that order.

To what sort of activity does this 'anything' apply?

A Any criminal activity relating to his previous convictions.

B Any criminal activity; the person does not have to have previous convictions.

C Any criminal activity or civil wrong; the person does not have to have previous convictions.

D Any criminal activity or civil wrong.

Question 9.24

A 17-year-old male has been made subject to a Notification Order by virtue of the Sexual Offences Act 2003 and the court has further ordered a parental direction. The young male has failed to comply with the order by not attending at the police station to report a change of address. His parents tried many times to get him to attend at the police station, even trying to physically take him there.

Has an offence been committed by the parent made subject of the parental direction in relation to an offence of failure to notify contrary to s. 91 of the Sexual Offences Act 2003?

A Yes, as they failed to comply with the parental direction irrespective of their actions.

B Yes, as they failed to comply with the parental direction as they should have attended at the police station themselves with the change of address.

C No, only the male subject to the order commits an offence of failure to notify; a parental order does not apply to this notification.

D No, as the offence is only committed by a person with no reasonable excuse and the parents are likely to have such excuse.

Question 9.25

WILIAMS is a 32-year-old female. She was walking down the street when a male, JONES approached her and said 'any chance of a blow job darling?'. WILIAMS walked away, but was approached again by JONES who asked if she was shy or a lesbian. JONES then tried to pull WILIAMS towards him by grabbing at a pocket that was located at the side seam of WILIAMS's trousers. WILIAMS is greatly offended by this and she believes it to be sexual.

Is this an offence of sexual touching contrary to s. 3 of the Sexual Offences Act 2003?

A No, because JONES did not touch a part of the body itself as is required by the legislation.

B No, because JONES did not touch a sexual organ as is required by the legislation.

C Yes, because of the purpose of JONES' actions and 'touching' includes clothing.

D Yes, because WILIAMS thought that it was sexual and 'touching' includes clothing.

Question 9.26

STRACHAN receives an email from a friend that includes an attachment he knows contains pornographic images. He downloads and then opens the attachment, which is several pages long. He views adult females engaged in various sexual activities and then leaves the room where the computer is. On the page after the one he was looking at are several images of children that are indecent in content. STRACHAN is unaware that there are sexually explicit pictures of children in the attachment, and has not seen them himself.

Has STRACHAN committed an offence contrary to s. 160 of the Criminal Justice Act 1988?

A Yes, because he downloaded images he knew would contain pornographic material, irrespective of his knowledge of its contents.

B Yes, because he has opened the attachment containing the pornographic images, irrespective of his knowledge of its contents.

C No, but only because he had not seen the images of the children.

D No, provided he had no cause to suspect it to be an indecent photograph of a child and he had not seen the images.

Question 9.27

GREENHAUGH was convicted of a sex offence in Northern Ireland and given a caution. The offence he committed would be subject to notification requirements as set out in sch. 3 of the Sexual Offences Act 2003. GREENHAUGH has moved into your local area.

In relation to notification requirements which of the following is correct?

A GREENHAUGH must fulfill the requirements as he was cautioned for a relevant offence; this applies to offence committed in England, Wales and Northern Ireland.

B GREENHAUGH must fulfill the requirements as he was cautioned for a relevant offence; this applies to offence committed anywhere in the United Kingdom.

C GREENHAUGH need not fulfill the requirements as this relates to offences committed in England and Wales only and subject to a caution therein.

D GREENHAUGH need not fulfill the requirements as this relates to convictions only and not cautions or conditional discharges.

Question 9.28

PUDDY meets a woman in a bar and asks her back to his house. He intends to have sexual intercourse with her, but believes she might resist so he puts sleeping tablets in her drink. The woman becomes drowsy and lies down on the sofa.

PUDDY goes over to her and takes hold of the belt on her jeans and moves her hips up and down in simulated sexual intercourse. At that moment his flatmate arrives home, PUDDY calls a taxi and puts the woman in it.

Which, if any, of the following offences, is PUDDY mostly likely to be charged with?

A An offence of attempted rape as he has administered drugs for that purpose.
B An offence of sexual assault by touching.
C An offence of causing a person to engage in sexual activity.
D No offence under the Sexual Offences Act, although possibly a common assault.

Question 9.29

LLOYD is a GP in a health clinic and has been arrested and charged with several offences of sexual touching, contrary to s. 3 of the Sexual Offences Act 2003. Complaints have been made by several women that during examinations LLOYD inserted a finger into their vaginas unnecessarily and that this was done to obtain sexual gratification. In interview, LLOYD claimed that the touching was not at all sexual, and that it formed part of the examinations.

What would need to be shown by the prosecution, for LLOYD's actions to fall within the definition of 'sexual', under s. 78 of the Sexual Offences Act 2003?

A That whatever LLOYD's purpose, the actions were sexual, by their very nature.
B That LLOYD received sexual gratification from the touching.
C That because of their nature the actions may be sexual and because of the circumstances or the purpose of any person in relation to them, they are sexual.
D That LLOYD received sexual gratification from the touching and a reasonable person would consider the actions to be sexual.

Question 9.30

PARISH has recently had gender reassignment surgery where the penis was removed and replaced with a surgically constructed vagina. Whilst out in a pub PARISH meets a man she finds very attractive, and she invites him back to her flat.

They begin kissing and PARISH allows the male to digitally penetrate her vagina, the male then removes a small dildo from his back pocket and starts to use it to penetrate PARISH's vagina, she asks him to stop as she does not want to risk damaging her reconstructive surgery. She firmly tells him 'no', but he does so anyway, laughing.

Which of the statements below is correct in relation to a sexual assault contrary to s. 2 of the Sexual Offences Act 2003?

A   A surgically constructed vagina is not included in this offence.

B   This offence is only committed by using a body part for penetration, not an inanimate object.

C   The offence here is not committed as PARISH agreed to digital penetration.

D   The offence is committed as PARISH did not consent to penetration by the dildo.

Question 9.31

GREENING is a registered sex offender and the police are carrying out a risk assessment in relation to his re-offending. They have visited his address in order to carry out this risk assessment; however he has never been in. Apart from this it seems that GREENING has been acting in compliance with his notification requirements. The police are considering whether they have a power of entry into the address to carry out a risk assessment.

In relation to this which of the following is correct?

A   They can apply for a search warrant provided there have been at least 2 failed attempts to enter a specified premise.

B   They can apply for a search warrant provided there have been at least 3 failed attempts to enter a specified premise.

C   They cannot apply for a search warrant as the person seems to be in compliance with his notification requirements.

D   They cannot apply for a search warrant as there is no power to search the address to carry out a risk assessment.

Question 9.32

Constable MCHENRY is on patrol when he comes across an elderly lady who has fallen and possibly broken her ankle, she is being cared for by a paramedic. She seems confused and doesn't know where she is. The paramedic wants to take her to hospital but she is refusing stating she wants to go home.

Considering the Mental Capacity Act 2005, which of the following is correct?

A Provided the paramedic believes the person does not have the capacity to make a decision about hospital treatment only he can forcibly take her to hospital.

B Provided the police officer believes the person does not have the capacity to make a decision about hospital treatment only he can forcibly take her to hospital.

C Provided either the paramedic or the police officer believes the person does not have the capacity to make a decision about hospital treatment either can forcibly take her to hospital.

D There is no power forcibly to take the person to hospital as the person is lucid enough to make the decision that they want to go home.

ANSWERS

Answer 9.1

Answer **C** — The Sexual Offences Act 2003 still has consent as a key issue in rape. 'Consent' is defined by s. 74 as follows: 'For the purposes of this Part, a person consents if he agrees by choice, and has the freedom and capacity to make that choice.'

Sections 75 and 76 of the 2003 Act apply to rape, and s. 75 provides for presumptions that the person did not, in certain circumstances, consent *per se*:

(1) The circumstances are that —
   (a) any person was, at the time of the relevant act or immediately before it began, using violence against the complainant or causing the complainant to fear that immediate violence would be used against him;
   (b) any person was, at the time of the relevant act or immediately before it began, causing the complainant to fear that violence was being used, or that immediate violence would be used, against another person;
   (c) the complainant was, and the defendant was not, unlawfully detained at the time of the relevant act;
   (d) the complainant was asleep or otherwise unconscious at the time of the relevant act. . .

This means that as the girl was asleep when intercourse took place, and HILL knew she was asleep, the complainant will be presumed *not* to have consented to the act and the defendant will be presumed *not* to have reasonably believed that the complainant consented.

Answer A is incorrect because, even though earlier consent was given, at the time of the act consent was presumed absent, even though the girl's condition was due to self-intoxication (which also makes answer B incorrect). This places an evidential burden upon the defendant, and not the prosecution, which makes answer D incorrect. The judge must be satisfied that the defendant can produce 'sufficient evidence' to justify putting the issue of consent before a jury; lack of such evidence will result in a direction to the jury to find the defendant guilty.

Crime, paras 1.9.3, 1.9.3.3

Answer 9.2

Answer **C** — Rape requires the absence of consent and as such both ss. 75 and 76 of the Sexual Offences Act 2003 (evidential presumptions of consent) must apply. The scenario of this question relates to s. 76. It is important to emphasise the fact that s. 76 deals with situations where the defendant either:

(i) deceives the victim regarding the nature and purpose of the act or
(ii) deceives the victim regarding the identity of the person who is carrying out the act.

If the deception does not relate to either of these aims then s. 76 has no application. For example, in *R v Harvinder Jheeta* [2007] EWCA Crim 1699, the defendant deceived the complainant into having sex more frequently than she would have done otherwise. In these circumstances the conclusive presumptions under the Sexual Offences Act 2003 had no relevance as the complainant had not been deceived as to the nature or purpose of the sexual intercourse. She knew what the nature of the sexual act was and she knew who JHEETA was, the deception as to the sender of the text is of no relevance. As she knew the nature of the act and the identity of the person carrying out the act this cannot be rape; answers A and B are therefore incorrect.

Even if the girl had known JHEETA personally had he stated that sex would improve her complexion then s. 76 would apply and it could be rape; answer D is therefore incorrect.

Crime, paras 1.9.3, 1.9.3.3

Answer 9.3

Answer **C** — The Sexual Offences Act 2003, s. 66 states:

(1) A person commits an offence if —
(a) he intentionally exposes his genitals, and
(b) he intends that someone will see them and be caused alarm or distress.

This offence requires only the intentional exposure of the genitals with the dual intention of their being seen by someone else and that this other person will be caused alarm or distress.

There is no need to show that the defendant acted for sexual gratification and simply exposing the genitals out of loutish behaviour will suffice if the other ingredients are present.

The offence is not restricted to public places and there is no need to show that anyone saw the genitals or was alarmed or distressed; answer D is therefore incorrect.

This offence is gender-neutral, which means that women can be guilty of exposure. It also means that a man or boy can be a victim as well as a woman or a girl. The offence only applies to the genitals, not the buttocks, so the act of 'mooning' will not be covered. A woman who exposes her breasts will not be guilty of an offence under s. 66; answers A and B are therefore incorrect.

Crime, para. 1.9.7.1

Answer 9.4

Answer **B** — Section 9 of the Sexual Offences Act 2003 makes it an offence for a person aged 18 or over intentionally to engage in sexual touching of a child under 16. Whether or not the child consented to the sexual activity is irrelevant, so answer C is therefore incorrect; but this is not the case in sexual assaults where lack of consent must be established, so answer A is therefore incorrect. 'Touching' is defined by s. 79(8) of the 2003 Act and basically covers all forms of physical contact, including penetration. You must also understand what is meant by 'sexual', and s. 78 defines it. Subsection (a) covers activity that the reasonable person would always consider to be sexual because of its nature; this may be sexual intercourse, but it may also be masturbation. Subsection (b) covers activity that the reasonable person would consider, because of its nature, may or may not be sexual, depending on the circumstances, or the intentions of the person carrying it out or both: for example, digital penetration of the vagina may be sexual, or it may be carried out for a medical reason. Provided the reasonable person views the activity as sexual then full intercourse does not have to be shown, so answer D is therefore incorrect.

Crime, para. 1.9.5.1

Answer 9.5

Answer **C** — Section 11 makes it an offence for a person aged 18 or over intentionally to engage in sexual activity when a child under 16 is present, or in a place from which he can be observed by the child, the purpose of which is for obtaining sexual gratification from the presence of the child. 'Sexual' is defined by s. 78. The offence is met where the child is under 16 years of age, therefore answer B is incorrect; and is committed by those who are aged 18 or over, therefore answer A is incorrect. The offence is committed even where the child apparently consents to watching the sexual act, and does not need to cause offence; answer D is therefore incorrect.

This offence is intended to cover the situation where someone seeks sexual gratification not from the sexual act itself, but rather from the fact that he is performing that act in the presence or intended presence of a child. The motive of sexual gratification is a necessary safeguard intended to avoid capturing those who engage in sexual activity in front of a child for a legitimate reason. For example, a teacher who sexually kisses his partner just outside the school gates could be deemed to be engaging in sexual activity intentionally in front of a child, and might otherwise be caught by the offence. Note that in the circumstances of the question an offence contrary to s. 13 of the 2003 Act would have been committed as the assailant was under 18, but you were asked specifically about s. 11.

Crime, para. 1.9.5.2

Answer 9.6

Answer **B** — Sections 30 to 33 of the Act deal with offences where the victim is unable to refuse to engage in or to watch a sexual activity because of, or for a reason related to, a mental disorder. It is a requirement of these offences that the offender knew, or could reasonably have been expected to know, that the victim had a mental disorder *and* that because of it he was likely to be unable to refuse. Note the *and*, which means that both elements of the offender's guilty knowledge have to be shown, therefore answer A is incorrect. Section 30 makes it an offence intentionally to touch someone sexually when that person, because of, or for a reason related to, a mental disorder is unable to refuse. The s. 78 definition of 'sexual' applies, and touching means all physical contact, including touching with any part of the body, with anything else and through anything, for example, through clothing. It includes penetration (s. 78(9)). Using inducements and/or threats and deceptions are separate offences in themselves (ss. 34 to 37) and are not requirements for this offence; answers C and D are therefore incorrect.

Crime, para. 1.9.6.2

Answer 9.7

Answer **C** — Section 1(1)(c) of the Protection of Children Act 1978 states:

(1) Subject to sections 1A and 1B, it is an offence for a person —
  (c) to have in his possession such indecent photographs or pseudo-photographs, with a view to their being distributed or shown by himself or others
    . . .

In these days of computer integration the storing and sharing of indecent images has attracted the attention of the courts as the law attempts to decipher the purpose that offenders have such images electronically stored. Note however that no specific intention to distribute is required, the requisite *mens rea* being 'a view to'; answer D is therefore incorrect.

Such IT issues were considered in *R v Dooley* [2005] EWCA Crim 3093 which mirrors the scenario of this question. The defendant maintained that he had intended to remove the pictures from the shared folder. The appeal turned on the judge's preliminary ruling on the meaning of 'with a view to' under s. 1(1)(c). The Court of Appeal agreed with the judge's ruling that there was a distinction between 'with the intention of' and 'with a view to' — where a defendant had knowledge that images were likely to be accessed by other people, any images would be downloaded 'with a view to distribute'. If one of the reasons the defendant left the pictures in the shared folder was so others could have access to them, he would be in possession of the images 'with a view to their being distributed'. However, as the court accepted that the defendant did not leave the pictures in the shared folder for that reason his conviction could not stand; answers A and B are therefore incorrect.

The court believed that 'with a view to' required more than the knowledge that the files could be accessed; as an analogy (although not a great one!) the court considered that 'a general may foresee the likelihood of his soldiers being killed in battle, but he surely does not send his troops into battle with a view to their being killed'.

Crime, para. 1.9.5.8

Answer 9.8

Answer **D** — The legislation states that a risk of sexual harm order (RSHO) may prohibit the defendant from doing anything which is necessary to protect a particular child, a group of children or children in general from sexual harm. It goes beyond a risk to any child or all of the children that go to the school, so answers A and B are therefore incorrect. Indeed, such an order can extend beyond the locality where the person is, so answer C is therefore incorrect. Although a RSHO can be made to protect a particular child or a group of children, it extends to children in general (provided they are under 16 years of age) who may be at risk of sexual harm from MORTLEY.

Crime, para. 1.9.9.24

Answer 9.9

Answer **C** — Section 53 makes it an offence for a person intentionally to control another person's activities relating to prostitution, in any part of the world, where it is done for, or in the expectation of, gain for himself or a third party. Clearly CORNELIUS is controlling his girlfriend's activity, even although she is happy to go along with it, and it was done with a view to gain, therefore answer B is incorrect. 'Gain' is defined by s. 54 of the Act as any financial advantage, including the discharge of a debt or obligation to pay, or the provision of goods or services (including sexual services) for free, or at a discount. It also covers the goodwill of any person likely to bring such a financial advantage. So this would cover CORNELIUS inciting his girlfriend to work as a prostitute for DIBLEY, where CORNELIUS expects this will lead to DIBLEY providing him with cheap drugs at a later date. This future gain therefore makes answer A incorrect. It is immaterial that CORNELIUS will be in a household with extra income due to his girlfriend's 'activities'; the offence is complete with the goodwill, and answer D is therefore incorrect.

Crime, para. 1.9.10.2

Answer 9.10

Answer **B** — The Sexual Offences Act 2003, s. 1 states:

(1) A person (A) commits an offence if —
    (a) he intentionally penetrates the vagina, anus or mouth of another person (B) with his penis,
    (b) B does not consent to the penetration, and
    (c) A does not reasonably believe that B consents.

However this has to be seen to be a continuing consent. The Sexual Offences Act 2003, s. 75 states:

(1) If in proceedings for an offence to which this section applies it is proved —
    (a) that the defendant did the relevant act,
    (b) that any of the circumstances specified in subsection (2) existed, and
    (c) that the defendant knew that those circumstances existed,
    the complainant is to be taken not to have consented to the relevant act unless sufficient evidence is adduced to raise an issue as to whether he consented, and the defendant is to be taken not to have reasonably believed that the complainant consented unless sufficient evidence is adduced to raise an issue as to whether he reasonably believed it.

Clearly initially the female consented to sex whilst conscious, however when she became unconscious the parameters change and s. 75 kicks in again, in particular s. 75(2). These conditions relate to:

(d) the complainant was asleep or otherwise unconscious at the time of the relevant act;

(e) ...

(f) any person had administered to or caused to be taken by the complainant, without the complainant's consent, a substance which, having regard to when it was administered or taken, was capable of causing or enabling the complainant to be stupefied or overpowered at the time of the relevant act.

In relation to (f) this is not an issue as the complainant consented to taking the drug, however when it affected her as it did (d) becomes effective. This is where the continuing consent applies, could MOOLES really state that MAKINS had consented to have sex whilst unconscious, and as such she could not make decisions about MOOLES ejaculating inside her. Without this evidence, continuing to have sex with a person who is asleep or unconscious may well be rape; answers A, C and D are therefore incorrect.

Crime, paras 1.9.3.3

Answer 9.11

Answer **D** — Section 71 of the 2003 Act makes it an offence for a person to engage in sexual activity in a public lavatory. It is not necessary for anyone to have been alarmed or distressed by this activity, therefore answer A is incorrect. This offence can be committed by a male or female against a male or female, which is a change from the old offence of gross indecency, therefore answer B is incorrect. The definition of 'sexual' in s. 71 is idiosyncratic, as s. 71(2) states that 'for the purposes of this section, an activity is sexual if a reasonable person would, in all the circumstances but regardless of any person's purpose, consider it to be sexual'. The difference is that it is unlikely that the third party who witnesses the activity will have information about the purpose of the defendant. For this reason, the sexual activity is limited to that which a reasonable observer would see as unambiguously sexual. This is a wide definition, and includes more than just anal sex; answer C is therefore incorrect.

Crime, para. 1.9.7.3

Answer 9.12

Answer **D** — A person *can* dispute the caution, therefore answers A and B are incorrect. He or she must apply to the court within 14 days of the caution, therefore answer C is incorrect.

Crime, para. 1.9.10.4

Answer 9.13

Answer **B** — Sections 80 to 92 of the Sexual Offences Act 2003 re-enact, with amendments, Part 1 of the Sex Offenders Act 1997, which established a requirement on sex offenders to notify certain personal details to the police. This process is commonly known as 'registration', often referred to loosely as creating a 'sex offenders register'.

Section 84 sets out the requirements on a relevant offender to notify the police of changes to notified details. Under s. 84(1)(c), an offender must notify the police within 3 days, of the address of any premises he has stayed at within the UK, besides his home address, for a 'qualifying period'. This place might be a friend's or relative's house, or a hotel where he has stayed. A qualifying period is defined by s. 84(6) as a period of 7 days, or 2 or more periods, in any 12 months, which taken together amount to 7 days. It is an accumulative period of 7 days, not 7 days straight, therefore answer A is incorrect; and for the same reason answer D is incorrect. It is not so exacting as to expect any change of address to be notified, therefore answer C is incorrect.

Crime, para. 1.9.9.5

Answer 9.14

Answer **A** — To prove the offence of kerb-crawling you have to show that the person solicited a woman either persistently, or in circumstances likely to cause annoyance. Although it can be committed from a motor vehicle, it must meet either of the two tests mentioned, so answer B is incorrect. On the subject of persistent soliciting, the prosecution must prove more than one act, i.e. separate approaches to more than one person, or two invitations to the same person. In essence, there must be a degree of repetition.

We now need to examine annoyance; it is sufficient if there was a likelihood of nuisance to other persons in the neighbourhood. BUTCHER's intention is of no consequence; answer D is therefore incorrect. In determining that likelihood, the character of the area is taken into account, e.g. how common is its use by prostitutes and its residential nature (*Paul* v *DPP* (1989) 90 Cr App R 173). Answer C is incorrect in that, even though the woman propositioned was not insulted, other people might have been; given that it is a residential area, this is more than likely. Ask yourself this: would the woman, or any other person in the area, have been annoyed had they known BUTCHER'S motives?

Crime, para. 1.9.10.4

Answer 9.15

Answer **D** — Section 48 makes it an offence for a person intentionally to cause or incite a child under 18 into prostitution or involvement in pornography in any part of the world. The prostitution or pornography itself does not need to take place for the offence to be committed. This offence is targeted at the recruitment into prostitution or pornography of a child who is not engaged in that activity at the time. The offence would be committed where a 'pimp' makes a living from the prostitution of others and encourages new recruits to work for him. It could also cover the situation where the defendant forces the victim to take part in child pornography for any reason.

Unlike the equivalent adult offence at s. 52, there is no requirement that the prostitution or pornography must be done for the gain of any of the persons involved, therefore FAY'S mother is as culpable as the others. All three persons have incited the child, therefore answers A and B and C are incorrect.

Crime, para. 1.9.5.11

Answer 9.16

Answer **A** — There are two offences here. The first offence is under the Protection of Children Act 1978, of taking, making, distributing, showing, publishing, advertising and possessing with intent to distribute indecent photographs.

The second offence is committed under the Criminal Justice Act 1988, which added the offence of mere possession of such photography.

Therefore, offences would be committed in this scenario by the person distributing, POTTER, and the people possessing, both POTTER and BOYD (answer B is incorrect).

The offence of distribution is to 'another person'; there is no requirement to distribute to more than one person (answer C is incorrect).

Distributing *will* include lending, which is why answer D is incorrect.

Crime, para. 1.9.5.8

Answer 9.17

Answer **A** — Section 39 makes it an offence for a care worker intentionally to cause or incite another person to engage in sexual activity when that person has a mental disorder and he is involved in his care. It will cover a range of behaviour, including the care worker causing or inciting the victim to have sexual intercourse with him, or causing or inciting the victim to masturbate a third person. The offence is committed if incitement takes place, even if sexual activity does not actually happen because, for example, a relative of the victim intervenes to prevent it. The Act goes on to define what is meant by 'care worker'; it is defined broadly to cover circumstances where a relationship exists because one person has a mental disorder and another person is regularly involved (or likely to be involved) face-to-face in their care, and that care arises from the mental disorder, whether on a primary or ancillary level, and whether on a paid or voluntary basis. It can include, for example, not only doctors, nurses and social workers, but also receptionists, cleaning staff, advocates or voluntary helpers. PAVETT *is* a care worker, therefore answers B and C are incorrect. Section 42(3) states *inter alia* that if the man is a patient for whom services are provided by a National Health Service body then he is included in this offence. The fact he is an outpatient is irrelevant; therefore answer D is incorrect.

Crime, para. 1.9.6.5

Answer 9.18

Answer **A** — There are two relevant offences where a person is premeditating a sexual offence. So what offence is intended? STREETER clearly intends (although he may not realise it) to commit rape. Under the 2003 Act, rape differs from the offence in the Sexual Offences Act 1956, in that it requires that the defendant does not have a 'reasonable belief' in consent, rather than that he does not have an 'honest belief' in consent. STREETER's belief is not reasonable, so he will commit rape; answer C is therefore incorrect.

There are two preparatory offences to consider: trespass with intent to commit a sexual offence (s. 63); and committing an offence with intent to commit a sexual offence (s. 62). For an offence under s. 63, the person must be 'on any premises where he is a trespasser'. Whilst STREETER is outside the bedroom window he is not a trespasser; answer B is therefore incorrect. When he breaks the window he has committed a criminal offence, and with the required intent an offence (s. 62) is committed regardless of whether or not the substantive sexual offence is committed; answer D is therefore incorrect.

Crime, paras 1.9.8.1, 1.9.8.2

Answer 9.19

Answer **D** — Section 15 makes it an offence for a person aged 18 or over to meet intentionally, or to travel with the intention of meeting, a child aged under 16 in any part of the world, if he has met or communicated with that child on at least two earlier occasions, and intends to commit a 'relevant offence' against that child either at the time of the meeting, or on a subsequent occasion. An offence is not committed if he reasonably believes the child to be 16 or over. The stumbling block to the offence in this question is the lack of a previous meeting. Had there been such previous meeting or communication then the offence would be complete as soon as REYNOLDS started travelling towards the meeting, and again when he actually does meet BEN. Note that simply arranging a meeting would not be captured by this offence; answer A is therefore incorrect. Because of the lack of two earlier communications, answers B and C are incorrect. The section is intended to cover situations where an adult establishes contact with a child through, for example, meetings, telephone conversations or communications on the Internet, and gains the child's trust and confidence so that he can arrange to meet the child for the purpose of committing a 'relevant offence' against the child ('relevant offences' are offences under Part 1 of this Act). The course of conduct prior to the meeting that triggers the offence may have an explicitly sexual content, such as entering into conversations with the child about the sexual acts he wants to engage in when they meet, or sending images of adult pornography. However, the prior meetings or communication need not have an explicitly sexual content and could, for example, simply involve giving the child swimming lessons or selling him sweets.

Crime, para. 1.9.5.4

Answer 9.20

Answer **B** — This offence mirrors that under s. 12 of causing a child to watch a sexual act, with the addition of the perpetrator being in a position of trust. There is a significant difference, however, in that for the abuse of position of trust offences, the child may be 16 or 17 (under 16 for the s. 12 offence); therefore answer C is incorrect. A position of trust is defined by s. 21 of the Act, and in relation to someone in education subs. (5) states:

> This subsection applies if A looks after persons under 18 who are receiving education at an educational institution and B is receiving, and A is not receiving, education at that institution.

'Receiving education at an educational institution' is defined by s. 22(4)(a) as:

...he is registered or otherwise enrolled as a pupil or student at the institution.

'Looks after persons under 18' is a wide caveat, which extends this section beyond the actual teacher/pupil relationship within a specific lesson; therefore answer A is incorrect.

Lastly, s. 12 outlines that it is an offence for a person aged 18 or over intentionally to cause a child, for the purposes of his own sexual gratification, to watch a third person engaging in sexual activity, or to look at an image of a person engaging in a sexual act. The act can be live or recorded, and there is no need for the child to be in close physical proximity to the sexual act. An example would be where he sends a child indecent images over the Internet. In order for an offence to be committed, the adult must act for his own sexual gratification. This ensures that adults showing children sex education material, either in a school or in another setting, will not be liable for this offence. However, this will not be an excuse if the act was done purely for sexual gratification. The term 'image' means a moving or still image, and includes an image produced by any means and, where the context permits, a three-dimensional image; therefore answer D is incorrect.

Crime, para. 1.9.5.5

Answer 9.21

Answer **D** — The offence of voyeurism is divided into three parts:

- The first offence involves a defendant observing another doing a private act with the relevant motive of gaining sexual gratification.
- The second offence deals with people operating equipment such as hoteliers or landlords using webcams to enable others to view live footage of their residents or tenants, in each case for the sexual gratification of those others.
- The third offence deals with the recording of the private act with the intention that the person doing the recording or another will look at the image and thereby obtain sexual gratification.

The three offences described above require proof that the victim does not consent to the observing, recording or operating of the relevant equipment for the purpose of the defendant or another's sexual gratification. The accused must know that the victim does not consent to his recording the act with that intention. It follows that consent to recording given by the victims for another purpose will not avail the accused; answers A and C are therefore incorrect.

A 'private act' is defined as where they are in a place which, in the circumstances, would reasonably be expected to provide privacy, and:

- their genitals, buttocks or breasts are exposed or covered only with underwear;
- they are using a lavatory; or
- they are doing a sexual act that is not of a kind ordinarily done in public.

So the fact that the persons could be seen in underwear makes this a 'private act' and within the scope of s. 67; answer B is therefore incorrect.

Crime, para. 1.9.7.2

Answer 9.22

Answer **A** — Section 87 of the Sexual Offences Act 2003 deals with the method of notification and related matters. It states:

(1) A person gives a notification under section 83(1), 84(1) or 85(1) by —
  (a) attending at such police station in his local police area as the Secretary of State may by regulations prescribe or, if there is more than one, at any of them, and
  (b) giving an oral notification to any police officer, or to any person authorised for the purpose by the officer in charge of the station.

The person must attend within the period of 3 days beginning with any change of his home address. The only option is personal attendance; answers B, C and D are therefore incorrect.

Crime, para. 1.9.9.8

Answer 9.23

Answer **D** — A Sexual Offences Prevention Order:

(a) prohibits the defendant from doing anything described in the order, and
(b) has effect for a fixed period (not less than 5 years) specified in the order or until further order (Sexual Offences Act 2003, s. 107(1)).

Such an order can cover any activity by the offender at all, whether that activity amounts to a criminal offence or a civil wrong, provided it is shown necessary for the purpose of protecting the public, or any particular members of the public, from serious sexual harm from the defendant. As it includes civil wrongs, answer A is incorrect.

A chief officer of police may by complaint to a magistrates' court apply for an order under this section in respect of a person who resides in his police area, or who the chief officer believes is in, or is intending to come to, his police area, if it appears to the chief officer that the person is a qualifying offender. A 'qualifying offender' is defined in s. 106(6) as a person who:

(a) has been convicted of an offence listed in Schedule 3 (other than at paragraph 60) or in Schedule 5,
(b) has been found not guilty of such an offence by reason of insanity,
(c) has been found to be under a disability and to have done the act charged against him in respect of such an offence, or
(d) in England and Wales or Northern Ireland, has been cautioned in respect of such an offence.

So the person does have to have previous convictions; therefore answers B and C are incorrect.

Crime, para. 1.9.9.16

Answer 9.24

Answer **D** — An offence is committed under s. 91 where the relevant person fails, without reasonable excuse, to comply with the notification requirements under the 2003 Act, the relevant person being the offender, and also the person who is subject to a parental direction; answer C is therefore incorrect. Under this direction the parent must ensure that the young offender attends at the police station with them when notification is being given. This does not mean that they can attend and give notification themselves, the person subject to the order must personally attend; answer B is therefore incorrect.

Reasonable excuse will be a question of fact for the court, but it is more than likely that given the circumstances of this case the parents will have such excuse, having done all they can to ensure attendance of their son, and will therefore not have committed the offence; answer A is therefore incorrect.

Crime, para. 1.9.9.12

Answer 9.25

Answer **C** — New legislation usually takes time to find precedents; given the number in its predecessor it is not surprising that the Sexual Offences Act 2003 has already started!

The Court of Appeal in *R* v *H*, *The Times*, 8 February 2005 has held that the touching of an individual's clothing was sufficient to amount to 'touching' under s. 3; answers A and B are therefore incorrect.

It also confirmed that where touching was not by its nature 'sexual' it was appropriate to ask the jury to consider two questions:

- Would the jury, as twelve reasonable people, consider that the touching could be sexual?
- Would the jury, as twelve reasonable people and in all the circumstances of the case, consider that the purpose of the touching had in fact been sexual?

An affirmative answer to both questions led to a finding that the touching, in similar circumstances to this scenario, was sexual and the accused properly convicted. It is the circumstances of this scenario, or JONES' purpose in relation to it, that is important in what is 'sexual', not the victim's belief (which would be important, of course, but not definitive). A conviction could arise where the victim felt that the act was not sexual applying the test in *H*; therefore answer D is incorrect.

Crime, para. 1.9.4.2

Answer 9.26

Answer **D** — Possession of indecent photographs of children is an offence contrary to the Criminal Justice Act 1988, s. 160.

Section 160 of the 1988 Act penalises possession, even though the possessor does not intend that the photograph or pseudo-photograph be distributed. Clearly STRACHAN has the images in his possession.

However, a defendant has a defence to a charge under s. 160 if they can prove that they had a legitimate reason for having the photograph in their possession, or that they had not themselves seen the photograph, *and* neither knew nor had any reason to suspect that it was indecent, or that the photograph was sent to them without any prior request by them, and that they did not keep it for an unreasonable time.

A person who suspects that images in his possession are indecent but shows that he had no reason to suspect that they were images of children may rely on this statutory defence. So held the Court of Appeal in *R* v *Collier* [2004] EWCA Crim 1411.

Hooper LJ, in the reserved judgment of the court, said that the defence in s. 160(2)(b) would be made out if a defendant proved that he had not seen the indecent photograph of a child alleged in the charge against him *nor* had he had any cause to suspect it to be an indecent photograph of a child. Answer C is therefore incorrect. So, although knowing the general content of the attachment when downloading and opening it, not knowing its specific content permits the defence. Answers A and B are therefore incorrect.

Crime, para. 1.9.5.8

Answer 9.27

Answer **A** — The notification applies where:

- they are convicted of an offence listed in Schedule 3 — this covers most of the commonly occurring sex offences;
- they are found not guilty of such an offence by reason of insanity;
- they are found to be under a disability and to have done the act charged against them in respect of such an offence; or
- they are cautioned in respect of such an offence, not only in England and Wales but for an offence in Northern Ireland as well.

Note that Scotland is not included in this legislation and as it is part of the United Kingdom answer B is therefore incorrect. As can be seen it applies to cautions as well as convictions and does include Northern Ireland; answers C and D are therefore incorrect.

In a decision relating to the former legislation, the Court of Appeal has confirmed that conditional discharges count as 'convictions' and therefore a person receiving such a punishment was subject to the notification requirements (*R* v *Longworth* [2004] EWCA Crim 2145). The reasoning behind this decision is likely to be applied to the notification requirements under the Sexual Offences Act 2003 set out below (although the Court of Appeal expressly declined to speculate on this point). The reasoning behind the finding that conditional discharges were 'convictions' in *Longworth* was because s. 14(1) of the Powers of Criminal Courts (Sentencing) Act 2000 provides that a discharge is to be regarded as a conviction 'for the purposes of the proceedings in which the order was made' and the Court of Appeal held that the notification requirements (under the old legislation) fell within the scope of those purposes; answer D is therefore again incorrect.

Crime, para. 1.9.9.2

Answer 9.28

Answer **B** — The mental element in attempted rape is the same as that required for the full offence, namely intent to have sexual intercourse and the absence of reasonable belief in consent. It is not necessary to prove that the accused had gone so far as to attempt physical penetration of the vagina, anus or mouth. It suffices if acts be proved which the jury could regard as more than merely preparatory (*Attorney General's Reference (No. 1 of 1992)* [1993] 1 WLR 274). Clearly administering drugs in the circumstances outlined is preparatory, and indeed following the guidance of the case cited above, PUDDY would not have to go too much further to be guilty of attempted rape, as in *R v Gullefer* [1990] 1 WLR 1063, in which Lord Lane CJ stated that the crucial question was whether the accused had 'embarked upon the crime proper', but that it was not necessary that the accused should have reached a 'point of no return' in respect of the full offence. PUDDY has not and answer A is therefore incorrect.

An offence of causing a person to engage in sexual activity is committed where a person intentionally *causes* another person to engage in a sexual activity, i.e. a man forcing someone else to masturbate him. This is not the case here and answer C is therefore incorrect.

It is in fact sexual touching; in that PUDDY has intentionally 'touched' the woman, and by any reasonable person's view that touching is sexual. Although it is only her clothing he touched the Court of Appeal in *R v H, The Times*, 8 February 2005 has held that the touching of an individual's clothing was sufficient to amount to 'touching'; answer D is therefore incorrect.

Crime, para. 1.9.4.3

Answer 9.29

Answer **C** — Section 78 of the Sexual Offences Act 2003 provides that penetration, touching or any other activity will be sexual if a reasonable person would consider that:

(a) whatever its circumstances or any person's purpose in relation to it, it is sexual by its very nature; or
(b) because of its nature it *may* be sexual and because of its circumstances or the purpose of any person in relation to it, it is sexual.

Therefore, activity under (a) covers things that a reasonable person would always consider to be sexual (e.g. masturbation). The activity under (b) above covers things that may or may not be considered sexual by a reasonable person depending on the circumstances or the intentions of the person carrying it out (or both). The example of a doctor inserting a finger into a vagina might be sexual under certain circumstances, but if done for a purely medical purpose in a hospital, it would not be. Since LLOYD's actions would not always be considered sexual by their nature, answer A is incorrect.

If the activity would not appear to a reasonable person to be sexual, then it will not meet either criteria and, irrespective of any sexual gratification the person might derive from it, the activity will not be 'sexual'. Answers B and D are therefore incorrect.

Crime, paras 1.9.2.1, 1.9.4.2

Answer 9.30

Answer **D** — As with rape, s. 79(3) of the Sexual Offences Act references to a vagina include a surgically constructed vagina; answer A is therefore incorrect. The penetration may be penetration with a part of the offender's body, for example, a finger or a fist, or with anything else, for example, a dildo or a sharp object, the term 'anything else' will include an animal or other living organism; answer B is therefore incorrect.

Consent is an on-going criterion, whilst she may have freely consented to one activity, on-going consent to that activity, or any other activity can be withdrawn at any time. Failure to conform to withdrawal of consent would be an assault; answer C is therefore incorrect.

Crime, para. 1.9.4.1

Answer 9.31

Answer **A** — Section 96B of the Sexual Offences Act 2003 (inserted by s. 58 of the Violent Crime Reduction Act 2006) provides a power of entry and search to risk assess sex offenders subject to the notification requirements; answer D is therefore incorrect.

The power enables the police to gather all the information they need about a relevant offender for the purposes of assessing the risks he poses, even if he is in apparent compliance with the notification requirements (answer C is therefore incorrect) and there are insufficient grounds to believe he has committed a new substantive offence.

Under the section, the police are allowed to seek a warrant from a magistrate's court to enter and search, by force if necessary, the last notified address of a registered sex offender (or a place where there are grounds to believe the offender resides or can be regularly found) where there have been 2 failed attempts to enter a specified premises, for the purposes of assessing the risks he poses, note two and not three; answer B is therefore incorrect. The application must be made by a senior police officer, not below the rank of superintendent. The senior police officer should attend court in person to apply for the warrant.

A warrant will only be issued by a magistrate if they are satisfied that the following conditions have been met:

- that the offender is a relevant offender (i.e. an offender subject to the notification requirements);
- that the offender is not: remanded or committed to custody by order of a court; serving a sentence of imprisonment or a term of service detention; detained in hospital; or outside the UK;
- that the address of each set of premises to which the warrant relates is either the home address which was last notified in accordance with Part 2 of the Sexual Offences Act 2003, or there are reasonable grounds to believe that the registered sex offender resides there or may regularly be found there;
- that it is necessary for the constable to enter and search the premises for the purpose of assessing the risk posed by the offender;
- that on at least two occasions, a constable has sought entry to the premises in order to search them for that purpose and has been unable to obtain entry for that purpose.

The warrant may also authorise entry to and search of premises on more than one occasion if, on the application, the magistrate is satisfied that it is necessary to authorise multiple entries for the purpose of risk assessment. When a warrant authorises multiple entries, the number of entries authorised may be unlimited or limited to a maximum.

If more than one address is to be searched, then the constable will need to attempt (and fail) to enter each address for which the warrant is sought.

In circumstances where a constable has been allowed into the premises to search for the purposes of risk assessment, but not allowed into parts of the premises (e.g. a particular room), this will count as being 'unable to obtain entry' for the purposes of risk assessment.

As a warrant does not grant a power of seizure, where evidence of a crime is found during the course of a search under such a warrant, constables can use their general power of seizure under s. 19 of PACE.

Crime, para. 1.9.9.14

Answer 9.32

Answer **C** — The Mental Capacity Act 2005 was brought into force to provide a statutory framework to empower and protect vulnerable people who are not able to make their own decisions. It covers a wide range of decisions in all areas of life and provides protection from legal liability for acts done in connection with care and treatment if done in a person's best interests and in keeping with the Act. Importantly, it can provide police officers with a power to act in a person's best interests, effectively as if they had the person's consent, although the power is not just given to police officers, but anyone acting in the person's best interest; answers A and B are therefore incorrect.

The Mental Capacity Act 2005, s. 5 states:

(1) If a person (D) does an act in connection with the care or treatment of another person (P), the act is one to which this section applies if —
    (a) before doing the act, D takes reasonable steps to establish whether P lacks capacity in relation to the matter in question, and
    (b) when doing the act, D reasonably believes —
        (i) that P lacks clarity in relation to the matter and
        (ii) that it will be in P's best interests for the act to be done.
(2) D does not incur any liability in relation to the act that he would not have incurred if P —
    (a) had had capacity to consent in relation to the matter, and
    (b) had consented to D's doing the act.
(3) ...
(4) ...

The Mental Capacity Act 2005, s. 6 states:

(1) If D does an act that is intended to restrain P, it is not an act to which section 5 applies unless two further conditions are satisfied.
(2) The first condition is that D reasonably believes that it is necessary to do the act in order to prevent harm to P.
(3) The second is that the act is a proportionate response to —
    (a) the likelihood of P's suffering harm, and
    (b) the seriousness of that harm.

(4) For the purposes of this section D restrains P if he —
   (a) uses, or threatens to use, force to secure the doing of an act which P resists, or
   (b) restricts P's liberty of movement, whether or not P resists.

(5) ...

(6) ...

(7) ...

This legislation provides a statutory footing for the actions of police officers when they are called to deal with an individual who lacks capacity. If no offence has been committed by the individual then the officer can act in that person's best interests in connection with care and treatment. Where the officer has used the capacity test (set out in s. 5) force can be used to move that person from one place to another. Simply put, the 'capacity test' is the question, 'Does this person have the capacity to make this decision at this time?' If the decision is that the person lacks capacity then the officer can act in the individual's best interests, and this would include forcibly removing them to hospital if that was in their best interest; answer D is therefore incorrect.

Crime, para. 1.9.6.11

10 | Child Protection

STUDY PREPARATION

It is important that officers recognise the significance of some victims particularly children and their vulnerabilities. Operational officers deal with situations involving these persons on a daily basis; it is important to recognise your powers. Make sure you know the differences between the two offences under the Child Abduction Act 1984 (person connected and not connected to a child). The emotive issue of child cruelty is also covered here as well as legistation aimed directly at child protection, e.g. The Children Act 2004.

QUESTIONS

Question 10.1

TORRES was born in Spain but lives in the UK. He is separated from his wife, KATE, and their 4-year-old son, ANDREW. KATE has custody of ANDREW and has refused to let TORRES take ANDREW to see his grandparents in Spain. TORRES arranged for his brother to pick up ANDREW from school one Friday and take him to Spain. He intended meeting them there, when he finished work later that evening. He knew KATE would not consent, but intended to return ANDREW at the end of the weekend.

In relation to offences that might have been committed under the Child Abduction Act 1984, which of the following is correct?

A   Only TORRES is guilty of an offence; his brother is not 'connected with the child'.

B   Only TORRES' brother is guilty of an offence; he physically took ANDREW out of the UK.

C   Both TORRES and his brother are guilty of offences in these circumstances.

D   Neither person is guilty, as they intended to return ANDREW to the UK.

Question 10.2

MURTY, aged 18, was a single parent, who had a baby aged 16 months. One winter, the baby developed a severe case of influenza, which resulted in hypothermia. Eventually the baby died. The baby had been ill for some time, and MURTY had not taken her to the doctor. MURTY was lawfully arrested for the offence of child cruelty, when she reported the death to the police.

What would the prosecution have to prove in order to convict MURTY of this offence?

A That her actions in denying medical care were wilful.
B That she was reckless in denying medical care to the child.
C That she intended to deny medical care to the child.
D That her denying medical care for the child included a positive act.

Question 10.3

JUDAVICH invited a 15-year-old girl, whom he reasonably believed to have attained the age of 16, back to his house. He had consensual sex with her that night. The following morning he was telephoned by the police who were looking for the girl, who had been reported missing by her foster parents. At this time JUDAVICH was made aware that the girl was in fact 15, however he made no effort to return her, and indeed hid her when the police arrived at his house to look for her. He was later arrested.

Considering only s. 2 of the Child Abduction Act 1984, which of the following charges, if any, would be most appropriate in these circumstances?

A An offence contrary to s. 2(1)(a) is the most appropriate charge in these circumstances.
B An offence contrary to s. 2(1)(b) is the most appropriate charge in these circumstances.
C An offence contrary to either s. 2(1)(a) or s. 2(1)(b) is the most appropriate charge in these circumstances.
D No charge should be preferred as the defendant reasonably believed the girl to be over 16 at the time of the taking.

Question 10.4

STUART is 2 years old and is in bed with his elder brother who is 16 years of age. The elder brother had drank half a bottle of vodka and is very drunk. Unfortunately in the morning the child has suffocated and died. At the post mortem it is discovered that the child choked on a peanut that the brother had dropped in the bed when he went in there.

Considering only s. 1(2)(b) of the Children and Young Persons Act 1933, has the elder brother committed the offence of child cruelty?

A   Yes, as he is 16 years of age and was under the influence of drink when he went to bed and the child is under 5 years of age.

B   Yes, as he is 16 years of age and was under the influence of drink when he went to bed and the child is under 3 years of age.

C   No, as he has not reached 17 years of age and is not responsible for the child.

D   No, as the suffocation was caused by a blockage of the airways by an object.

Question 10.5

ANITA, aged 15, agreed to babysit her neighbours' 2-year-old child, while her neighbours went out for the evening. During the evening, ANITA's boyfriend rang her and asked if he could see her. ANITA checked that the child was asleep, then slipped out of the house to meet her boyfriend. She had been gone from the house for about half an hour, when neighbours found the child wandering down the street in his pyjamas. The child was not injured during the incident.

In relation to the Children and Young Persons Act 1933, which of the following is correct?

A   ANITA has committed an offence of child cruelty through her neglect.

B   ANITA has committed an offence of child cruelty as her actions are wilful.

C   ANITA does not commit an offence of child cruelty in these circumstances.

D   ANITA does not commit an offence of child cruelty as the child was not injured.

Question 10.6

STERN had committed an offence against a child, and had a disqualification order imposed on him under the Criminal Justice and Court Services Act 2000, which prevents unsuitable people from working with children. He is aware he is so disqualified. STERN was asked by a neighbour, O'BRIEN, who runs an under-11 football team, if he was willing to be the kit manager. The only involvement STERN would have would be collecting the kit and washing it ready for the next game. STERN agrees to take on the post. O'BRIEN is aware that STERN is so disqualified, but does not realise what this means.

In relation to applying for a position while disqualified contrary to s. 35 of the Criminal Justice and Court Services Act 2000 which of the following is correct?

A STERN does not commit the offence, as he did not *apply* for the position; he was *offered* it and he *accepted* it.

B STERN does not commit the offence as 'position' only relates to regulated positions not voluntary ones.

C STERN does commit the offence as he has accepted a voluntary position working with children. O'BRIEN commits no offence.

D STERN does commit the offence as he has accepted a voluntary position, as does O'BRIEN when she offered it.

Question 10.7

Child cruelty is covered by s. 1 of the Children and Young Persons Act 1933 which outlines what would amount to the criminal offence of child cruelty.

Which of the following is correct?

A The offence can only be committed by a positive act and not by omission.

B The acts must have occurred in a manner that caused unnecessary suffering or injury to health.

C The acts must have occurred in a manner that caused unnecessary suffering or injury to health with intention to do so.

D The acts must have occurred in a manner likely to cause unnecessary suffering or injury to health, there is no need to show that any such suffering or injury actually came about.

Question 10.8

LILLEY has 3 children who are profoundly deaf; he himself suffers from Usher's Syndrome, which means that he has tunnel vision and night blindness. He is registered blind, and has been without a valid driving licence since it was withdrawn on medical grounds by the DVLA. Despite this, LILLEY regularly drove his children to school, but has been warned by social services that this must stop, and he had agreed it would. Two days later social services had information that LILLEY had driven the children several hundred miles to be assessed by another school for deaf children. On learning what had happened, the family's social worker instructed the council's legal department to apply for an emergency protection order (EPO) pursuant to s. 44 of the Children Act 1989, which was granted. The police were informed and they intercepted the vehicle on the motorway being driven home with the children as passengers. The officers invoked their powers under s. 46 of the Children Act 1989 and took the children into police protection.

In relation to police action, which of the following is correct?

A The officers should not have invoked police protection whilst an EPO was in place.

B The police should only have invoked police protection whilst an EPO was in place where there are compelling reasons to do so.

C The police are entitled to invoke a police protection whilst an EPO was in place and this could never be unlawful.

D The police are entitled to invoke a police protection whilst an EPO was in place as the statutory scheme accords primacy to the EPO procedure.

Question 10.9

Section 46 of the Children Act 1989 deals with the protection of children in certain situations.

In relation to the section, which of the following statements is correct?

A A constable or social worker may remove a child to suitable accommodation.

B A constable in uniform may remove a child to suitable accommodation.

C A constable may only remove a child to a police station or hospital.

D A constable may remove a child to suitable accommodation.

Question 10.10

JUSTIN is 11 years old and is living with his 20-year-old sister, although she has no parental responsibility for him. JUSTIN becomes subject to police protection in line with s. 46 the Children Act 1989.

Which of the following is correct in relation to whether the designated officer can allow the sister to have contact with JUSTIN whilst in police protection?

A No one from the family is allowed to have contact with JUSTIN whilst in police protection.

B Only a parent or someone with parental responsibility is allowed to have contact with James whilst in police protection.

C The sister could be allowed contact provided the designated officer believes it to be reasonable and in the child's best interest.

D The sister must be allowed contact provided the designated officer believes it to be reasonable and in the child's best interest.

Question 10.11

An 11-year-old child has been made subject of an emergency protection order under s. 44 of the Children Act 1989 taken out by social services and has been placed into temporary foster care. The child's father contacts her on her mobile phone and tells her that if she comes back to the family home she will be safe and taken away on a special holiday to see her grandmother who lives in France.

Has the father committed an offence of acting in contravention of a protection order?

A Yes, as the father has induced, assisted or incited the child to run away from foster care.

B Yes, as the father has induced, assisted or incited the child to run away from foster care and intends taking the child abroad.

C No, as the child wasn't directly in 'care' within the local authority area as foster care is not 'care' for the purposes of the legislation.

D No, as the offence would only be complete if the child actually leaves, or is taken away from the foster care by the father.

Question 10.12

PRINCE is the divorced father of 3 children aged 16, 14 and 12. He takes them on a skiing holiday to France for a week with the consent of his wife, and at the end of that time he calls her to say he will not be returning the children to her, he is going to settle in France with them.

Considering the offence under s. 1 of the Child Abduction Act 1984 (abduction by person connected with a child) only, which of the statements below is correct?

A PRINCE commits the offence in relation to all 3 children and has no defence.

B PRINCE commits the offence in relation to the 2 younger children and has no defence.

C PRINCE commits the offence, but would have a defence as he is out of the United Kingdom for a period of less than one month.

D PRINCE does not commit this offence at all in these circumstances.

Question 10.13

MAYNARD has applied to be a school governor; the head teacher has some concerns over his suitability and is considering referring the case to the Independent Barring Board. The actual job would entail working approximately 3 days in a 30-day period.

In relation to the Safeguarding Vulnerable Groups Act 2006 which of the following is correct?

A The case should not be referred as being a school governor is not a regulated activity under the Act.

B The case should not be referred as regulated activity under the Act is for more than 3 days in a 30-day period.

C The case should be referred as this would fit the criteria for referral as laid down in the Act.

D The case should be referred provided the head teacher has factual information to support her concerns.

ANSWERS

Answer 10.1

Answer **C** — There are two offences under the Child Abduction Act 1984 that deal with taking a child under the age of 16.

Under s. 1 of the Act, an offence takes place where a person connected with a child under the age of 16 takes or sends the child out of the UK without the appropriate consent. This offence *may only be committed by a 'connected person'*; who will include the child's parent, father even if the parents are not married, the legal guardian, or a person with a residence order or lawful custody order.

As TORRES' brother does not fall within this group, he cannot commit this offence. However, to take ANDREW lawfully out of the UK, TORRES would require the consent of the mother/guardian/person with a residence order or person with custody.

Obviously TORRES did not have consent to take ANDREW out of the UK, and even though he did not actually take him, he committed the offence by sending him. Sending can include 'causing', or 'inducing', a child to go with another, which is why answer B is incorrect.

Under s. 2 of the Act, a person commits an offence if, without lawful authority or reasonable excuse, he takes or detains a child under the age of 16 so as to remove him from the lawful control of any person having lawful control of the child; or so as to keep him out of the lawful control of any person entitled to lawful control of the child (which would include KATE). This offence may be committed by a person *who is not a 'connected person'*, and would be committed by the brother (which is why answer A is incorrect).

There is no requirement for the abduction to be permanent (making answer D incorrect).

Crime, paras 1.10.4.1, 1.10.4.2

Answer 10.2

Answer **A** — The circumstances in the question may amount to neglect, but the prosecution must prove that this was *wilful* (not reckless or intentional, which is why answers B and C are incorrect). The issue of *mens rea* was addressed in the case of *R v Sheppard* [1981] AC 394. Lord Diplock explained that:

...the jury must be satisfied (1) that the child did in fact need medical aid at the time at which the parent is charged with failing to provide it (the *actus reus*) and (2) either that the parent was aware at the time that the child's health might be at risk if it were not provided with medical aid, or that the parent's unawareness of this fact was due to his not caring whether the child's health was at risk or not (the *mens rea*).

There may be an element of 'objective recklessness' in the defendant's behaviour. However, the definition requires proof that a person was wilful in his or her actions.

Answer D is incorrect, as the offence can be committed either by a positive act, *or* by an omission.

Crime, para. 1.10.5

Answer 10.3

Answer **B** — This offence (s. 2 of the Child Abduction Act 1984) requires the taking or detaining of a child under 16 years. This will include keeping a child in the place where he/she is found and inducing the child to remain with the defendant or another person. The distinction between subss. (a) and (b) is important.

In *Foster* v *DPP* [2004] EWHC 2955 the victim was a 15-year-old girl who at the time of the offence was living with foster parents who had lawful control of her for the purposes of the Act. On 1 March the defendant had consensual sexual intercourse with her and the circumstances of that case mirror this scenario.

In *Foster* a charge contrary to s. 2(1)(a) was laid. The trial judge had held that the operative act of removal took place the following morning when the defendant learned that she was under 16 and thereafter took no steps to return her and the defendant was convicted and appealed by way of case stated.

The defendant, on appeal, submitted that the offence under s. 2(1)(a) could not have been committed the day he invited the girl to his house on the ground that for the *actus reus* of the offence, not knowing the girl was underage, he had a statutory defence and in the morning the girl was no longer in the lawful control of the foster parents.

The Queen's Bench Division allowed the appeal, on the grounds that the removal from lawful control contrary to s. 2(1)(a) was completed on the day the girl went to the defendant's house, at which time he had a defence, as he believed the girl had attained the age of 16.

The *mens rea* for an offence contrary to s. 2 was an intentional or reckless taking or detention of a child under the age of 16, the effect or objective result of which was to remove or keep that child within the meaning of s. 2(1)(a) or s. 2(1)(b) respectively. The word 'remove' for the purpose of s. 2(1)(a) was intended to convey a substitution of the authority by an accused for that of the person lawfully having it. Physical removal from a particular place was not required. Section 2(1)(a) required the child there and then to be in the lawful control of someone entitled to it when taken or detained, whereas s. 2(1)(b) required only that the child be kept out of the lawful control of someone entitled to it when taken or detained. There was a distinction between removal from a person having control contrary to s. 2(1)(a) and keeping from a person entitled to control contrary to s. 2(1)(b).

The court also held that the failure to return the girl after discovering her true age did not constitute an offence under s. 2(1)(a) as she was at that time no longer in the foster parents' lawful control.

The circumstances of the scenario of the question could only lead to a charge under s. 2(1)(b); answers A and C are therefore incorrect.

At trial the prosecution had conceded that the defendant's lack of knowledge of the girl's age provided a defence up to the point of that knowledge, however a charge of s. 2(1)(b) could not be answered using the statutory defence if it was committed when the defendant became aware of the girl's correct age; answer D is therefore incorrect.

Crime, paras 1.10.4.3, 1.10.4.4

Answer 10.4

Answer **D** — Section 1(2) of the Children and Young Persons Act 1933 states:

(b) where it is proved that the death of an infant under three years of age was caused by suffocation (not being suffocation caused by disease or the presence of any foreign body in the throat or air passages of the infant) while the infant was in bed with some other person who has attained the age of sixteen years, that other person shall, if he was, when he went to bed, under the influence of drink, be deemed to have neglected the infant in a manner likely to cause injury to its health.

As the suffocation was caused by a blockage of the airways by an object the offence is not made out.

The ages of the child and the brother are therefore irrelevant; answers A, B and C are incorrect.

Crime, para. 1.10.5

Answer 10.5

Answer **C** — To be guilty of an offence under s. 1 of the Children and Young Persons Act 1933, an accused must have been over the age of 16 at the time of the offence, and must have 'had responsibility' for the child or young person in question. Although s. 1 creates just one offence, it may take a number of different forms. It may take the form of positive abuse (assault, ill-treatment, abandonment or exposure) or of mere neglect, or it may take the form of causing or procuring abuse or neglect. The abuse or neglect in question must be committed 'in a manner likely to cause unnecessary suffering or injury to health', but the offence is essentially a conduct crime rather than a result crime. It need not therefore be shown that any such injury was caused (answer D is therefore incorrect). ANITA's actions may well have amounted to an offence under the Act, but she is outside the scope of the legislation by virtue of her age; answers A and B are therefore incorrect.

Crime, para. 1.10.5

Answer 10.6

Answer **D** — Section 35 states:

(1) An individual who is disqualified from working with children is guilty of an offence if he knowingly applies for, offers to do, accepts or does any work in a regulated position.

(2) An individual is guilty of an offence if he knowingly —
   (a) offers work in a regulated position to, or procures work in a regulated position for, an individual who is disqualified from working with children, or
   (b) fails to remove such an individual from such work.

(3) It is a defence for an individual charged with an offence under subsection (1) to prove that he did not know, and could not reasonably be expected to know, that he was disqualified from working with children.

There are two offences associated with being a disqualified person. The first offence arises where a disqualified person knowingly applies for, offers to do, accepts or does any work in a regulated position. Given the specific defence available (s. 35(2)), it would seem that the requirement of 'knowingly' here relates to the act of applying, offering or accepting work in a regulated position. Answer A is therefore incorrect. Regulated positions are generally those where the person's normal duties include working with children, whether in the public, private or voluntary sectors, and also in certain senior management roles such as social services and children's charities. Amongst the examples given by the Home Office is voluntary work at a children's football club. Answer B is therefore incorrect.

The second offence arises where a person offers or procures work in a regulated position for a person who is disqualified from working with children or fails to remove such an individual from that work. This offence is clearly aimed at employers, though it would clearly extend beyond those circumstances and it does not have the statutory defence available. This seems slightly odd given that, of the two, a prospective employer is far less likely to know of the implications of a person's disqualification than the person disqualified. Therefore answer C is incorrect.

Crime, para. 1.10.2.1

Answer 10.7

Answer **D** — It is an offence of child cruelty when a person, in relation to a child:

wilfully assaults, ill-treats, neglects, abandons, or exposes him, or causes or procures him to be assaulted, ill-treated, neglected, abandoned, or exposed, in a manner likely to cause him unnecessary suffering or injury to health...

(Children and Young Persons Act 1933, s. 1)

The above section creates only one single offence, albeit one that can be committed in many different ways, by both positive acts and omission (see *R* v *Hayles* [1969] 1 QB 364); answer A is therefore incorrect. Although any aspect of neglect must be shown to have occurred in a manner likely to cause unnecessary suffering or injury to health, there is no need to show that any such suffering or injury actually came about; answers B and C are therefore incorrect.

Crime, para. 1.10.5

Answer 10.8

Answer **B** — This scenario mirrors the case of *Langley* v *Liverpool City Council and Chief Constable of Merseyside* [2006] 1 WLR 375. In that case the police invoked their powers under s. 46 of the Children Act 1989 despite an EPO being in existence that the social services were going to raise when the children returned home.

The Court of Appeal considered the proper approach in these circumstances to be as follows:

• There is no express provision in the Act prohibiting the police from invoking s. 46 where an EPO is in place and it is not desirable to imply a restriction which prohibits a constable from removing a child under s. 46 where he or she has reasonable cause to believe that the child would otherwise be likely to suffer significant harm; answer A is therefore incorrect.
• The s. 46 power to remove a child can therefore be exercised even where an EPO is in force in respect of the child.

- Where a police officer knows that an EPO is in force, he or she should not exercise the power of removing a child under s. 46, unless there are compelling reasons to do so.
- The statutory scheme accords primacy to the EPO procedure under s. 44 because removal under that section is sanctioned by the court and involves a more elaborate, sophistic-ated and complete process of removal than under s. 46; answer D is therefore incorrect.
- Consequently, the removal of children should usually be effected pursuant to an EPO, and s. 46 should only be invoked where it is not reasonably practicable to execute an EPO.
- In deciding whether it is practicable to execute an EPO, the police should always have regard to the paramount need to protect children from significant harm.
- Failure to follow the statutory procedure may amount to the police officer's removal of the child under s. 46 being declared unlawful; answer C is therefore incorrect.

Crime, para. 1.10.6

Answer 10.9

Answer **D** — Section 46 states that where a constable has reasonable cause to be-lieve that a child would otherwise be likely to suffer significant harm, he or she may remove that child to suitable accommodation and keep him or her there. Answer A is incorrect, as the section allows only a constable to remove the child (known as police protection). There is no requirement for the officer to be in uniform (an-swer B is therefore incorrect). The section does not specify that the child should only be taken to a police station or hospital (although these may be suitable places); the child may be taken to any suitable accommodation (which is why answer C is incorrect).

Crime, para. 1.10.6

Answer 10.10

Answer **C** — The Children Act s. 46(10) states:

Where a child has been taken into police protection, the designated officer shall allow —
(a) the child's parents;
(b) any person who is not a parent of the child but who has parental responsibility for him;
(c) any person with whom the child was living immediately before he was taken into police protection;
(d) any person in whose favour a contact order is in force with respect to the child;

(e) any person who is allowed to have contact with the child by virtue of an order under section 34; and

(f) any person acting on behalf of any of those persons,

to have such contact (if any) with the child as, in the opinion of the designated officer, is both reasonable and in the child's best interests.

So clearly it is the decision of the designated officer what, if any, contact should be had with the child whilst in police protection considering:

- what is reasonable.
- what is in the child's best interest.

So there is no 'must' about the sister's contact and therefore answer D is incorrect.

Contact would be allowed to those persons fitting the criteria of s. 10 and extends beyond parents or those with parental responsibility; answer B is therefore incorrect. However contact can, and should be allowed; answer A is therefore incorrect.

JUSTIN's sister would fit the criteria laid out in s. 46(10)(c).

Crime, para. 1.10.6.1

Answer 10.11

Answer **A** — Acting in contravention of a protection order or power exercised under s. 46 of the Children Act 1989 (police protection power) is an offence contrary to s. 49 of the 1989 Act

Section 49 of the Children Act 1989 states:

(1) A person shall be guilty of an offence if, knowingly and without lawful authority or reasonable excuse, he —

(a) takes a child to whom this section applies away from the responsible person;

(b) keeps such a child away from the responsible person; or

(c) induces, assists or incites such a child to run away or stay away from the responsible person.

So the offence is complete when a person induces, assists or incites a child to run away, and does not necessarily involve actually taking the child away, although that action is also an offence under this section; answer D is therefore incorrect. In this section 'the responsible person' means any person who for the time being has care of him by virtue of the care order, the emergency protection order, or s. 46, as the case may be, this would include the foster carer; answer C is therefore incorrect.

The legislation does not mention an intention to take the child abroad, referring only to taking the child, or inducing the child to leave the place they were put if they were in care, subject to an EPO or police protection powers (s. 49(2)); answer B is therefore incorrect.

Crime, para. 1.10.6.2

Answer 10.12

Answer **D** — Section 1 of the Child Abduction Act 1984 states:

(1) Subject to subsections (5) and (8) below, a person connected with a child under the age of 16 commits an offence if he takes or sends the child out of the United Kingdom without the appropriate consent.

So the offence itself only relates to children under 16; for that reason alone answer A is incorrect.

The offence can only be committed by a person 'connected with' the child, and this is defined in s. 1(2) of the Child Abduction Act 1984, which would include the children's father.

Such a person must either take, or be responsible for sending, the child out of the United Kingdom himself. This offence is not committed by holding the child within the jurisdiction, nor where the child is lawfully taken out the country and return is then refused; answers A, B and C are therefore incorrect.

Had the father taken the children to France without the consent of the mother then the offence may have been committed. This would have led to the various defences kicking in, one of which is that he is out of the United Kingdom for a period of less than one month. However as the offence was not committed no defence is necessary.

Crime, para. 1.10.4.1

Answer 10.13

Answer **C** — The Safeguarding Vulnerable Groups Act 2006 was passed as a result of the Bichard Inquiry arising from the Soham murders in 2002, when schoolgirls Jessica Chapman and Holly Wells were murdered by Ian Huntley (their school caretaker). The Inquiry questioned the way which employers recruit people to work with vulnerable groups and particularly the way background checks are carried out. The purpose of the scheme is to minimise the risk of harm posed to children and vulnerable adults by those that might seek to harm them through their work (paid or unpaid). It seeks to do this by barring unsuitable individuals not just on the basis of referrals but also at the earliest opportunity as part of a centralised vetting process that all those working closely with children and/or vulnerable adults will need to go through, the referral is not limited by actual information known; answer D is therefore incorrect. The whole tenet of the Act is that it will be preventative rather than reactive and rather than just providing a snapshot of an individual on the day the check is made, it will be able to react to new information about a person. This will allow an individual to be barred as soon as information justifying this is at hand.

Regulated activities will apply to most individuals working with children. It is broadly defined and covers what might be called 'frontline' activity where individuals have direct contact with children and vulnerable adults. Regulated activities will include:

- Any activity which involves contact with children or vulnerable adults and is of a specified nature on an intensive, frequent or overnight basis e.g teaching, training, care, supervision, advice, treatment or transport.
- Any activity allowing contact with children or vulnerable adults and is in a specified place on an intensive or frequent basis e.g. schools or care homes.
- Fostering (public or private) and childcare.
- Certain defined positions of responsibility e.g. school governor, director of social services or trustees of certain charities; answer A is therefore incorrect.

Regulated activity applies where the activity is intensive, frequent or takes place on 3 or more days in a 30-day period; answer B is therefore incorrect.

Duties and responsibilities under regulated activity will include:

- To undertake a regulated activity, a person must have been vetted by the scheme.
- It will be an offence for a barred person to undertake regulated activity for any length of time.
- Any employer taking on a person in a regulated activity will commit a criminal offence if they fail to check the status of an applicant, employee or volunteer.
- It will also be an offence for employers/providers to permit a barred person, or a person has not yet had a vetting and barring check, to work for any length of time (no matter how infrequent) in a regulated activity.
- It will be an offence for a barred person to undertake a regulated activity in a domestic circumstance.
- It will be an offence for a barred person to engage in or seek or offer to engage in a regulated activity for any length of time.

Crime, paras 1.10.3, 1.10.3.2

11 | Theft and Related Offences

QUESTIONS

Question 11.1

BROWNING was in a shop with RICHARDSON, who picked up a CD intending to steal it. RICHARDSON realised he was being watched by SATO, a store detective, and placed the CD in BROWNING'S pocket, without BROWNING knowing. BROWNING leaves the store still not realising that the CD is in his pocket, the alarm goes off but

BROWNING ignores it not believing he had set it off (no security guard is working). When he gets home he realises he has the CD, but as the CD was worth £3 and the bus fare is £5 to return it, BROWNING decides to keep it. He then writes to the store inviting them to come and get it.

May BROWNING have committed an offence of theft in these circumstances?

A Yes, when the alarm went off he should have returned to the store, this shows state of mind.

B Yes, when he keeps the CD only asking the store to collect it.

C No, he had no dishonest intent when he left the store, the point of appropriation.

D No, as he has reasonably written to the store telling them of the incident.

Question 11.2

DIBLEY went past a house where he knew a young lady lived. He climbed a ladder up to her window and peered in. She was lying naked on the bed, which was near the window. DIBLEY descended the ladder, took off all his clothes, except his socks, and climbed back up the ladder. As he reached the window, the young lady woke up and, thinking he was her boyfriend, invited him in. DIBLEY approached her on the bed hoping to have sexual intercourse with her. However, she then realised that he was not her boyfriend and asked DIBLEY to leave. Annoyed at the rejection he punched the young lady, breaking her jaw.

Considering the offences under s. 9(1) of the Theft Act 1968 (burglary) which of the following is correct?

A What would be vital is whether DIBLEY was inside or outside the room when invitation to enter was made.

B It is irrelevant whether DIBLEY was inside or outside the room when invitation to enter was made as grievous bodily harm is mentioned in both ss. 9(1)(a) and 9(1)(b) of the 1968 Act

C The vital point is what the intentions of DIBLEY were when he actually entered the building.

D As soon as the implied invitation to enter is withdrawn DIBLEY becomes a trespasser and commits this offence when he commits the assault.

Question 11.3

MCDOUGAL was walking past a post office, when he saw an elderly woman coming out. MCDOUGAL gently bumped into the lady and pickpocketed her purse intending to steal it. Realising what had happened the woman shouted 'help'. MCDOUGAL turned rounds and punched her in the face knocking her to the ground. He dropped the purse and ran off.

When, if at all, does MCDOUGAL commit the offence of robbery?

A When he bumps into to her to steal the purse.

B When he uses force by punching her to the face.

C He does not commit robbery as he dropped the purse; no theft has been committed.

D He does not commit robbery as at the time of the theft no actual force was used, only a bump.

Question 11.4

STEELE has had a dispute with his neighbour, PRATT. One night STEELE got home from the pub, having had too much to drink, and found paint had been poured over his car. He was convinced that PRATT was responsible and so forced his way into PRATT's house. STEELE intended to beat PRATT up, causing really serious injury; however, he discovered the house was empty.

In relation to the offence of burglary (under s. 9 of the Theft Act 1968), which of the following is correct?

A An offence under s. 9(1)(b) has been committed even though no grievous bodily harm was caused.

B An offence under s. 9(1)(a) has not been committed as no grievous bodily harm was caused.

C An offence under s. 9(1)(a) has been committed even though no grievous bodily harm was caused.

D An offence under s. 9(1)(a) has not been committed as no assault or theft was carried out.

Question 11.5

FISCHER and his family sold their house and bought a large camper van, which they kept permanently on a campsite. While they were out, GRINDLEY, tired from hitchhiking, broke the door lock to sleep inside the van. Having fallen asleep on a bunk bed, GRINDLEY was woken up by the sound of children. He ran from the van grabbing some cans of food on the way out.

Which of the following is correct in relation to GRINDLEY?

A He has *not* committed burglary as a camper van is a vehicle, never a 'building'.

B He has committed burglary, under s. 9(1)(b), as a camper van is a 'building' here.

C He has committed burglary, under s. 9(1)(a), as a camper van is a 'building' here.

D He has *not* committed burglary, as the camper van was not occupied when he entered.

Question 11.6

MORLANDER is in the rear garden of a large country house. He forces a ground floor window and enters, and when he enters his intention is to steal. As he is looking around for something to steal, he sees a samurai sword on display. The occupiers, who come in through the front door, disturb MORLANDER and he picks up the sword to frighten them. MORLANDER points the sword at the occupiers and threatens them with violence. Unafraid, the occupiers approach MORLANDER, who drops the sword and runs out of the open front door.

At what stage, if at all, does MORLANDER commit an offence of aggravated burglary?

A When he enters the house with intention to steal.

B When he picks up the sword with intention to threaten.

C When he points the sword at the occupiers with intention to threaten.

D No offence of aggravated burglary is committed in these circumstances.

Question 11.7

GRIFFITHS asked his colleague MORGAN if he could borrow her motor van to take his family on holiday for the weekend to West Wales. MORGAN agreed; however, GRIFFITHS had misled MORGAN, and actually takes the motor van to a pop festival with some friends. He returns it in good condition at the end of the weekend.

Has GRIFFITHS committed an offence (under s. 12 of the Theft Act 1968) of taking a vehicle without the owner's consent?

A Yes, he obtained MORGAN's permission by deception.

B Yes, but only if the journey was further than the agreed destination.

C No, his deception did not negate the consent he obtained.

D Yes, unless he could show he believed MORGAN would have consented.

Question 11.8

ELLIS and MCWHIRTER were in a supermarket car park when they saw a car with the keys in the ignition. They decided to take the vehicle and ELLIS got in the driver's seat; MCWHIRTER sat in the front passenger seat. While he was reversing out of the parking place, ELLIS struck KANG, a shopper who was walking past. Both ELLIS and MCWHIRTER got out of the car and ran off, leaving KANG behind with a bruised hip.

Has an offence been committed (under s. 12A of the Theft Act 1968) of aggravated vehicle-taking?

A No, the vehicle was not driven on a road.

B Yes, but only by ELLIS, the driver.

C Only if it can be shown that the vehicle was driven dangerously.

D Yes, by both ELLIS and MCWHIRTER.

Question 11.9

SEYMOUR was working for a company that was going through financial difficulties, and as a result, he was laid off. One Friday evening, SEYMOUR entered the company office through an insecure window. In order to cause financial hardship to the owners, he linked all the computers up to the Internet, intending that they should all stay on for the weekend.

Has SEYMOUR committed the offence of abstracting electricity by his actions?

A Yes, the offence is complete in these circumstances.

B Yes, but a charge of burglary would be more appropriate.

C No, because he has not abstracted or diverted electricity.

D No, using a telephone would not amount to using electricity.

Question 11.10

RENNIE and ELLIOT met one evening to discuss breaking into an electrical warehouse. It was agreed that RENNIE would break in and hand the goods to ELLIOT outside in his van. They were joined by SEDGMORE, who agreed to keep the goods in his house for a few weeks, and MALROW, who owned a second-hand store and would sell the goods. They agreed that the burglary would take place the following night.

Who, if anyone, has committed the offence of handling stolen goods in these circumstances?

A ELLIOT, SEDGMORE and MALROW only.
B All 4 have committed the offence.
C Only SEDGMORE and MALROW have committed the offence.
D None of these people has committed the offence.

Question 11.11

STUARTSON has been arrested for handling stolen goods and the officers dealing with the case are deciding what they would need to prove in order to secure a conviction in relation to 'stolen goods'.

In relation to this which of the following is correct?
A They only have to show that the goods were actually stolen.
B They would have to show that the goods were stolen by way of conviction of the 'thief'.
C They would have to show that the goods were actually stolen, and by whom they were stolen.
D They would have to show that the goods were actually stolen, and name the actual loser.

Question 11.12

LATIMER and BOWEN went for a meal in their favourite restaurant, one where they ate regularly. During the meal they consumed two bottles of wine each. For a laugh, at the end of the meal they both went to the toilet and climbed out of the window. They intended returning the next day to pay for the meal; however, the restaurant owner did not know this and called the police.

Have LATIMER and BOWEN committed an offence (under s. 3 of the Theft Act 1978) of making off without payment?
A Yes, but they would have a defence if they could show that they thought the owner would have consented in the circumstances.
B No, because they have not deceived the owner into thinking they would pay for the meals.
C No, they have not committed the offence in these circumstances as they intended returning to pay.
D Yes, they have committed the offence, regardless of their intention to pay, and would have no defence in the circumstances.

Question 11.13

GWYNN was at his friend PETERS' flat and he had with him a stolen credit card, which he had recently used to obtain goods by deception. GWYNN gave the card to EDDINGTON, so that EDDINGTON could use it the next day. GWYNN had no intention of using the card again.

Which of the following statements is true, in relation to s. 25 of the Theft Act 1968, regarding 'going equipped'?

A An offence has been committed by EDDINGTON only, as GWYNN did not intend using the card again.

B An offence has been committed by GWYNN and EDDINGTON in these circumstances.

C No offence has been committed by either EDDINGTON or GWYNN, as they were both in a dwelling.

D An offence has been committed by GWYNN; EDDINGTON commits no offence in these circumstances.

Question 11.14

EVANS fancied CATHCART, who worked with him. He asked her out during a Christmas party, but she refused as she was married. The following day, EVANS sent CATHCART an email, stating that, unless she had sex with him, he was going to phone her husband and tell him they were having an affair.

Has EVANS committed the offence of blackmail in these circumstances?

A Yes, if it can be shown that CATHCART was in fear of the consequences.

B No, as EVANS was not seeking to gain or cause loss.

C Yes, as EVANS has made unwarranted demands with menace.

D No, the offence is committed only where a person demands money or other property.

Question 11.15

PASCHKE is standing by a bus stop when his friend REGAN arrives in a motor vehicle and offers him a lift. Whilst the vehicle was stationary and switched off, PASCHKE notices that the ignition barrel of the vehicle has been damaged and suspects that the vehicle has been stolen. PASCHKE asks REGAN if the vehicle is stolen and REGAN says, 'What do you think?'. PASCHKE is still unsure whether the vehicle is stolen or not. REGAN goes to start the engine, but police officers arrive and arrest both

PASCHKE and REGAN as the vehicle was taken without consent, although this was not by PASCHKE.

Has PASCHKE committed the offence under s. 12(1) of the Theft Act 1968, of allowing himself to be carried?

A Yes, the fact he suspects the car to be stolen and his presence in it is enough; movement of the car is irrelevant.

B Yes, as the vehicle was actually taken without consent and PASCHKE suspects it was.

C No, as the vehicle did not actually move he cannot commit this offence; movement is essential.

D No, mere suspicion is not enough, PASCHKE must know the car is stolen; movement of the car is irrelevant.

Question 11.16

MUNRO commits a robbery and steals a mobile phone. He gives it to COMMONS, who works for a mobile telephone company, who alters the unique device identifier and sells the phone on to an unsuspecting buyer.

Considering the Mobile Telephones (Re-Programming) Act 2002, which of the following is true?

A This is an offence from the moment the phone is altered; there is no defence.

B This is an offence from the moment the phone is sold; there is no defence.

C This is an offence from the moment the phone is altered; there is a statutory defence however.

D This is an offence from the moment the phone is sold; there is a statutory defence however.

Question 11.17

MCIVOR visits his doctor in absolute agony due to a back injury. He demands an injection of a new wonder pain-killing drug, but as it is very expensive his doctor refuses and prescribes a strong pain-killer instead. Infuriated, MCIVOR pulls a knife from his pocket and threatens to kill the doctor unless he gets the new drug; in fear for his life, the doctor gives him the injection. MCIVOR apologises for his behaviour and leaves.

With respect to blackmail, which of the following is true?

A The offence is complete when the doctor gives MCIVOR the injection.

B The offence is complete when MCIVOR threatens the doctor.

C   This is not blackmail as MCIVOR has had no 'gain'.

D   This is not blackmail as the doctor has had no loss, the drug belonging to the NHS.

Question 11.18

NICHOLAS drove his van at the request of his friend to collect some copper wire, and he was surprised when he was directed to stop beside a large hedge. NICHOLAS was even more surprised when his friend started to load up his van with the heavy-duty copper wire that was hidden below this bush, but not suspecting wrongdoing he assisted. On arrival at a local scrap yard he was even more surprised to be arrested by police officers investigating the theft of copper wire from an electrical power substation next to the hedge. The police, however, have no evidence that NICHOLAS stole the wire, although he has numerous previous convictions for handling stolen goods. When questioned about the wire he said he had no knowledge that the goods were stolen, and that he 'asked no questions and was told no lies'.

In relation to a possible charge of handling stolen goods against NICHOLAS which of the following is correct?

A   He should be charged with both receiving or arranging to receive stolen goods and assisting or acting for the benefit of another.

B   He should be charged with either receiving or arranging to receive stolen goods and assisting or acting for the benefit of another, but not both.

C   He must be charged with receiving or arranging to receive stolen goods as it was obvious the goods were stolen.

D   He should not be charged with any handling offence as he had no knowledge that the goods were stolen.

Question 11.19

DOUGLAS worked in a petrol station owned by RANKIN. At the end of her shift one day she was told that her son had been in a car accident and was in hospital. DOUGLAS did not have a car and when she finished work, she took £10 from the till to pay for a taxi to take her to the hospital as she had no cash on her. In fact she had plenty of money in her bank account, but she didn't want to waste time by going to a cash point. DOUGLAS intended paying the money back the next day, thinking that RANKIN would not mind. RANKIN found that the till was short of money the next day and confronted DOUGLAS. RANKIN did mind that the money had been taken and contacted the police to report a theft.

Would DOUGLAS be able to claim a defence to the offence of theft in these circumstances?

A No, because RANKIN did not consent to the money being taken, and therefore it was theft.

B No, as she could have got her own money had she taken reasonable steps to get it.

C Yes, if she believed that RANKIN would have consented if he had known she was taking the money and the circumstances in which it was taken.

D Yes, if she believed that RANKIN would have consented if he had known she was taking the money.

Question 11.20

CRAWFORD obtains several thousand pounds in cash by stealing it from his elderly neighbour. CRAWFORD deposits the cash in his own account but transfers it electronically to the bank account held by his friend ELMS, who is initially unaware of the transfer. A few days later ELMS discovers the money in his account, and when he asks where it came from, CRAWFORD tells him the truth. ELMS agrees to keep it to assist CRAWFORD.

At what point, if any, does he commit an offence of dishonestly retaining a wrongful credit contrary to s. 24A of the Theft Act 1968?

A He commits an offence under s. 24A as soon as the money is transferred into his account.

B He commits an offence under s. 24A as soon as he becomes aware that the money was stolen.

C He commits an offence under s. 24A as soon as he becomes aware that the money was stolen and fails to have it cancelled.

D He does not commit an offence contrary to s. 24A but will commit an offence of handling stolen goods as he assists in the retention of the funds.

Question 11.21

MAGWICK was a landlord who refused to return to his tenant, HOLMES' deposit when the tenancy was terminated by MAGWICK. HOLMES believed he had been asked to leave without justification and that the deposit was being unfairly withheld. HOLMES and a friend went to MAGWICK's house and burst in when the door opened. HOLMES was hoping to take cash he thought that he was entitled to, however not finding any he took items of value instead. HOLMES claimed that he intended to keep the items until MAGWICK returned his deposit and if this failed he would sell the items and then use the money for a deposit on another flat, returning the money left over to the landlord. HOLMES would have taken that course of action as he knew he was entitled to cash but realised he had no right to take MAGWICK's items.

Is HOLMES guilty of robbery?

A Yes, he has used force to obtain items that do not belong to him.

B Yes, he has used force to obtain items that he had no rights to.

C No, he honestly believed he had legal right to deprive MAGWICK of the items.

D No, HOLMES did not apply the force himself in order to obtain the items.

ANSWERS

Answer 11.1

Answer **B** — A person commits theft if he or she dishonestly appropriates property belonging to another with the intention of permanently depriving the other of it (s. 1 of the Theft Act 1968).

As you probably know, for theft there has to be dishonesty, so when is BROWNING dishonest? When he leaves the shop the alarm goes off, however ignoring that shows no great dishonest mind; answer A is therefore incorrect.

Under s. 2(2) of the Theft Act 1968, if a person appropriates another's property, leaving money or details of where he or she can be contacted to make restitution will not of itself negate dishonesty (see *Boggeln* v *Williams* [1978] 1 WLR 873). The wording of s. 2(2) gives latitude to a court where the defendant was willing to pay for the property. The subsection says that such an appropriation may be dishonest, not that it will always be dishonest (as does this question); answer D is therefore incorrect.

So when does appropriating take place? When the rights of the owner are assumed; in this case where the CD is kept, not when the person leaves the shop; answer C is therefore incorrect.

Crime, para. 1.11.2.3

Answer 11.2

Answer **A** — First the question asks you to consider the offences under s. 9(1), so it is necessary to think of both 9(1)(a) and 9(1)(b). Despite the fact that s. 9(1)(a) and s. 9(1)(b) of the Theft Act 1968 create separate offences, there are a number of elements which are common to both and which can, therefore, be examined together. A 'building or part of a building' must be or have been 'entered' as 'a trespasser' in order for burglary to have been committed. The trespassory entry requirement demands a consideration not only of whether the entry was trespassory, but also whether the defendant knew that it was trespassory, or was reckless. The difference lies in s. 9(1)(a) with the need for an intention to commit certain offences and in s. 9(1)(b) with the need to do certain things in the building. Therefore in considering both offences intention at the point of entry is not vital; answer C is therefore incorrect.

However 'entry' is very relevant. In *R* v *Collins* [1973] QB 100 the defendant, having discovered that a woman was lying asleep and naked on her bed, stripped off his clothes and climbed up a ladder on to the window sill of the bedroom. At this moment the woman awoke and, mistakenly believing that the naked form at the window was her boyfriend, beckoned the defendant in. The defendant then got into her bed and it was only after the defendant had intercourse with her that the woman realised her error (this was when rape still formed part of s. 9 of the Theft Act). The difficulty of the case lay in determining whether the defendant had entered the building before or after an invitation to enter had been made. If he was already inside the room, having climbed through the window frame, and kneeling upon the inner sill (before any invitation had been made to him) he would already be guilty of burglary for he had already entered with intent to rape and the victim's subsequent consent could not alter that. If he was kneeling on the sill outside the window he would not have been guilty of burglary as the invitation to enter had been made while he was still outside the premises. So it is very relevant where DIBLEY was at the time entry was invited; answer B is therefore incorrect.

Even for s. 9(1)(b) the defendant must have entered the building or part of a building as a trespasser; it is not enough that he or she subsequently became a trespasser by exceeding a condition of entry; answer D is therefore incorrect.

So when asked to consider s. 9(1) in its entirety what is important are the elements mentioned in both 'building', 'entry' and 'trespasser'.

Crime, paras 1.11.4 (all sections), 1.11.5 (all sections)

Answer 11.3

Answer **A** — To commit robbery, a person must steal and, immediately before or at the time of doing so and in order to do so, use force on any person, or put or seek to put a person in fear of being subjected to force then and there.

The slightest use of force to accomplish a theft changes that theft into a robbery. An illustration can be found in the case of *R* v *Dawson* (1976) 64 Cr App R 170, where the defendant and two others surrounded their victim. One of the attackers 'nudged' the victim and while he was unbalanced another stole his wallet. In *Dawson*, the court declined to define 'force' any further than to say that juries would understand it readily enough. In line with general principles of *actus reus* (criminal conduct), the force used by the defendant must be used voluntarily. Therefore, the accidental use of force such as when a pickpocket, in the process of stealing a wallet from his victim on a train, is pushed into his victim by the train jolting on the railway line would not be a robbery; answer D is therefore incorrect.

However force used after the offence of theft does not make it robbery, that would be theft and assault. For robbery the force must be immediately before or at the time of the theft; answer B is therefore incorrect.

For robbery there must be theft, and this is theft as the property was acquired with the necessary intent. Long term acquisition is not required; answer C is therefore incorrect.

Crime, para. 1.11.3

Answer 11.4

Answer **C** — A person who enters a building as a trespasser *with intent to inflict* grievous bodily harm commits an offence under s. 9(1)(a) of the Theft Act 1968 (therefore answer B is incorrect). In proving an intention to commit grievous bodily harm under s. 9(1)(a), it is not necessary to prove that an assault was actually committed (*Metropolitan Police Commissioner* v *Wilson* [1984] AC 242) and thus answer D is incorrect.

An offence was not committed under s. 9(1)(b), as a person must be shown to have inflicted grievous bodily harm under that section (answer A is therefore incorrect).

Crime, paras 1.11.4.1, 1.11.4.5

Answer 11.5

Answer **B** — Something will qualify as a 'building' if it has some degree of permanence. In *B and S* v *Leathley* [1979] Crim LR 314, the Crown Court held that the defendants had committed burglary. They had stolen some meat from a freezer container in a farmyard, which was considered to be permanently in place.

The meaning of 'building' is extended by s. 9(3), and includes an inhabited vehicle or vessel, and applies to any such vehicle or vessel at times when the person having a habitation in it is *not in residence as well as at times when he or she is*. (This makes both answers A and D incorrect.)

Answer C is incorrect because of the intention of the person when he entered the building. GRINDLEY entered intending to sleep (not one of the prerequisites of s. 9(1)(a)). GRINDLEY did, however, steal property, having entered as a trespasser, which makes him guilty of burglary under s. 9(1)(b).

Crime, para. 1.11.4.2

Answer 11.6

Answer **D** — Aggravated burglary is defined at s. 10 of the 1968 Act as follows:

A person is guilty of aggravated burglary if he commits any burglary and at the time has with him any firearm or imitation firearm, any weapon of offence, or any explosive.

So, taking it logically, you must establish that the accused had any of the articles listed at the time he committed burglary, contrary either to s. 9(1)(a) or s. 9(1)(b). Certainly burglary is committed at the time MORLANDER entered with the requisite intent, but he had no weapons, therefore answer A is incorrect.

If the burglary is under s. 9(1)(b), the offender must have one of the above articles with him when he commits the theft or grievous bodily harm. It is at that point in time that aggravated burglary is committed (and not at the time of entry). *R* v *O'Leary* (1986) 82 Cr App R 341. MORLANDER commits no theft, as he leaves the sword behind him, and although an assault has probably taken place by threatening the occupiers with a sword, the injuries do not amount to grievous bodily harm; therefore answers B and C are incorrect. MORLANDER has committed many offences in the scenario, but aggravated burglary is not one of them.

Crime, para. 1.11.5

Answer 11.7

Answer **C** — An offence under s. 12 is committed by a person who takes a vehicle without the owner's consent or other lawful authority, for his own or another's use.

The issue of consent was dealt with in the case of *R* v *Peart* [1970] 2 QB 672. The defendant was convicted of the offence, after he falsely represented to the owner of a car that he needed it to drive from Bedlington to Alnwick to sign a contract. The owner let him have the vehicle, provided he returned it that day. As he had intended all along, Peart drove the car instead to Burnley in the evening.

The Court of Appeal subsequently quashed Peart's conviction, by following the decision in *Whittaker* v *Campbell* [1984] QB 318, where it was held that *there is no general principle of law that fraud vitiates consent.*

Consequently, even if consent is obtained by fraud, it is still consent (making answer A incorrect). The case of *Peart* shows that even though the journey taken was different from the one agreed, an offence is still not committed (making answer B incorrect).

Lastly, the defence provided under s. 12(6) would apply *where an offence has been committed.* Since an offence has not been committed in these circumstances, the defence would not apply (which is why answer D is incorrect).

Crime, para. 1.11.6

Answer 11.8

Answer **D** — First, a person must commit an offence under s. 12(1) of the Theft Act 1968 either by taking the vehicle, *or* by being carried in it. Then, under s. 12A, it must be proved that at any time after the vehicle was taken (whether by him or another) and before it was recovered:

- it was driven dangerously on a road or public place; *or*
- owing to the driving of the vehicle, an accident occurred whereby injury was caused to any person; *or*
- owing to the driving of the vehicle, an accident occurred whereby damage was caused to any property other than the vehicle; *or*
- damage was caused to the vehicle.

The Act does not specify that the accident involving an injury to a person should occur on a road (making answer A incorrect).

All that the prosecution has to prove is that *one* of the circumstances above occurred before the car was recovered (*Dawes* v *DPP* (1995) 1 Cr App R 65) (answer C is incorrect for this reason).

Answer B is incorrect because the offence may be committed by either the driver or the passenger, provided one of the circumstances apply.

Crime, paras 1.11.6, 1.11.7

Answer 11.9

Answer **A** — Under s. 13 of the Theft Act 1968, a person who dishonestly uses, without due authority, or dishonestly causes to be *wasted or diverted*, any electricity, shall be guilty of an offence.

As electricity is not 'property', a specific offence was created to deal with its dishonest use or waste. For this reason electricity cannot be 'stolen', and therefore its dishonest use or wastage cannot form an element of burglary (making answer B incorrect).

Diverting a domestic electrical supply so as to bypass the meter, or using another's telephone without authority (*Low* v *Blease* [1975] Crim LR 513) would be examples of this offence, as would unauthorised surfing on the Internet by an employee at work, provided in each case that dishonesty was present (making answers C and D incorrect).

Crime, para. 1.11.9

Answer 11.10

Answer **D** — Quite simply, there can be no offence under s. 22 of the Theft Act 1968, unless goods have been stolen (answers A and B are therefore incorrect). Even though two of the participants have arranged to receive stolen goods, they will not commit the offence until the burglary takes place (answer C is therefore also incorrect).

If the plan ever does come to fruition, RENNIE, as the person stealing the goods, would not commit the offence. It is debatable whether ELLIOT would do so, if he assisted with the burglary, as he might be guilty of that offence.

Crime, para. 1.11.10

Answer 11.11

Answer **A** — For goods to be handled they have to be stolen, if goods are not stolen there is no handling. Whether they are so stolen is a question of fact for a jury or magistrate(s). There is no need to prove that the thief, blackmailer, etc. has been convicted of the primary offence before prosecuting the alleged handler, neither is it always necessary to identify who that person was; answers B, C and D are therefore incorrect.

However, care needs to be taken if a defendant is to be accused of handling goods stolen from a specific person or place. If that is the case then ownership of the goods will become an integral part of the prosecution case and it will be necessary to provide evidence proving that aspect of the offence (*Iqbal* v *DPP* [2004] EWHC 2567 (Admin).

Crime, paras 1.11.10, 1.11.10.1

Answer 11.12

Answer **C** — This is a typical question where police officers would think practically and decide, 'I would arrest those, where it was necessary to do so'. Avoid this approach and answer questions purely as points of law.

A person commits an offence under s. 3 of the Theft Act 1978 if, knowing that payment on the spot for goods supplied or services received is required, he or she dishonestly makes off without paying *with intent to avoid payment*.

In the scenario, even though the couple have made off without paying, there is no offence if they intend to defer payment to a later date (even though morally their actions may be regarded as wrong!). (Answer D is therefore incorrect.)

There is no requirement that the person practised some deception to prove the offence; simply making off with the required intent is enough (which is why answer B is incorrect).

The defence in answer A has been made up and does not exist.

Crime, para. 1.11.14

Answer 11.13

Answer **D** — A person commits an offence under s. 25 of the Theft Act 1968 when, not at his place of abode, he has with him any article for use in the course of or in connection with any burglary, theft or cheat (cheat includes deception).

The offence is designed as a preventative measure and therefore cannot be committed by a deed done in the past. The offence will be committed by a person who has an article with him or her for use by *someone else* (*R v Ellames* [1974] 3 All ER 130).

Applying the Act to this scenario, GWYNN was not at his place of abode and had with him a credit card, which he intended EDDINGTON to use in the future in a cheat (offence committed, even though he had no intention of using it again, which is why answer A is incorrect).

The card was given to EDDINGTON and, although he intended using it, he *was* at his place of abode. Consequently, no offence is committed until EDDINGTON leaves his house, and therefore answer B is incorrect.

Answer C is incorrect because the offence may be committed by a person in a dwelling — provided it is not the place where he or she lives.

Crime, para. 1.11.13

Answer 11.14

Answer **B** — Blackmail is committed when a person, with a view to gain for himself or another, or with intent to cause loss to another, makes any unwarranted demands with menaces (s. 21 of the Theft Act 1968).

Under s. 34 of the Act, 'gain' and 'loss' mean to gain or lose in money or other property. It will not apply where a person is making demands for sexual favours. Consequently, answers A, C and D are incorrect.

Crime, para. 1.11.15

Answer 11.15

Answer **C** — On a charge of driving or allowing himself to be carried in or on a conveyance taken without authority, it must be proved that the accused knew that the conveyance had been taken without lawful authority (*R v Diggin* (1980) 72 Cr App R 204, *Boldizsar v Knight* [1980] Crim LR 653); therefore, answers A and B are incorrect. However, it seems that the accused need not be aware that the taker took the conveyance for his own or another's use.

It is also not enough for the prosecution to prove that the accused was in or on the conveyance. There must have been some movement of the conveyance (*R v Miller* [1976] Crim LR 417; also see *Diggin*). If a taker of a motor vehicle offers a person a lift and he gets into the seat next to the driver, the person is not allowing himself to be driven before the driver turns on the ignition switch (*Diggin*).

So answer D is almost correct. However, it is essential that a conveyance be moved in order for it to be taken, however small that movement may be, and this is the same even though the accused is only allowing himself to be carried. Answer D is therefore incorrect.

Crime, para. 1.11.6.3

Answer 11.16

Answer **C** — This offence was created to try to prevent the increasing criminal activity involving mobile handsets. The offence is committed where the unique identifier is either changed or interfered with, and is not reliant on a future sale of the phone; answers B and D are therefore incorrect. There is, however, a statutory defence, exclusive to manufacturers or those with written consent of the manufacturers; answer A is therefore incorrect.

Crime, para. 1.11.10.7

Answer 11.17

Answer **B** — The points to prove for an offence of blackmail are:

- with a view to gain;
- for self or another; *or*
- with intent to cause loss to another;
- made an unwarranted demand with menaces.

Using a knife to threaten to kill someone is most certainly an unwarranted demand ('unwarranted demand' is defined as an unreasonable or unfair demand) and menacing! 'Menaces' is loosely delineated as threat (including a veiled one) of any action detrimental or unpleasant to the person addressed. And the offence is complete at the time the demand is made, not when its desired consequences are brought about; answer A is therefore incorrect.

As the demand must be made with a view to the person's gain, has MCIVOR actually 'gained'? The gain must be in money or other property and can be temporary or permanent. In a case not mentioned in the manual, it was held that the drug was property and the injection involved 'gain' to the accused as he achieved pain relief. The fact that it was injected into him rather than being handed over did not mean that MCIVOR did not gain that property; answer C is incorrect. There does not have to be a loss, provided the demand is made with a view to gain; answer D is therefore incorrect.

Crime, para. 1.11.15.1

Answer 11.18

Answer **A** — Although generally speaking a charge should specify exactly what it is the person is actually accused of, and that where alternatives exist, to charge both would be bad for duplicity, handling stolen goods is a case in contrast.

In *R v Nicklin* [1977] 1 WLR 403 the accused was charged with handling stolen property by dishonestly receiving it, knowing or believing it to be stolen, contrary to s. 22(1) of the Theft Act 1968. The defendant pleaded not guilty to that charge but accepted that he had assisted in the removal of the stolen property (the circumstances mirror the scenario of this question). He was found guilty of handling stolen goods and dishonestly assisting in the removal or disposing of them for the benefit of (another) knowing or believing the same to have been stolen. He appealed (understandably) that he had been convicted of an offence with which he was not even charged!

His appeal was allowed and the conviction quashed, the Court of Appeal stated *per curiam* that a conviction of a particular type of handling can be upheld where the indictment simply alleges the offence of handling and the generalised form has led to no injustice or confusion; but the better practice is to particularise the form of handling for which the defendant is blamed. If there is any uncertainty about which form of handling two counts will generally cover every form; one count for the first limb of s. 22(1) of the Theft Act 1968, dishonestly receiving, and a second count for the second limb, dishonestly undertaking or assisting in the retention, removal, disposal or realisation or arranging to do those things.

It is not bad for duplicity to charge both strands of the offence therefore; answer B is therefore incorrect. In this scenario to charge only one strand would be wrong, following *Nicklin* a conviction would not be forthcoming; answer C is therefore incorrect.

You must show that the defendant knew or believed the goods to be stolen. Mere suspicion, however strong, will not be enough (*R v Griffiths* (1974) 60 Cr App R 14). Deliberate 'blindness' to the true identity of the goods would suffice but the distinction is a fine one in practice. It can be very difficult to prove knowledge or belief on the part of, say, a second-hand dealer who 'asks no questions'. Because there are practical difficulties in proving the required *mens rea*, s. 27(3) of the 1968 Act makes special provision to allow evidence of the defendant's previous convictions, or previous recent involvement with stolen goods, to be admitted; in these circumstances there would be more than enough evidence to charge the defendant, not to charge would be erroneous and therefore answer D is incorrect.

Crime, para. 1.11.10.4

Answer 11.19

Answer **C** — Under s. 2(1)(b) of the Theft Act 1968, a person's appropriation of property belonging to another is not to be regarded as dishonest if he/she appropriates the property in the belief that he or she would have the other's consent if the other knew of the appropriation *and* the circumstances of it. Therefore, the person appropriating the property must believe both elements, i.e. that the other person would have consented had he or she known of the appropriation and the circumstances of it. Answer D is therefore incorrect.

It is the belief of the person appropriating the property that is important, regardless of the belief of the owner. Therefore, even though RANKIN would state that he did not consent to the money being taken, if DOUGLAS can convince the court of the above two elements, she may have a defence. Answer A is therefore incorrect. This includes occasions where the defendant had access to other funds, which could have been obtained by taking reasonable steps as this directly relates to the circumstances under which the defendant took the money, i.e. urgency in attending at the hospital; answer B is therefore incorrect.

Crime, para. 1.11.2.1

Answer 11.20

Answer **C** — One consequence of the decision of the House of Lords in *R v Preddy* [1996] AC 815 is that, where a person dishonestly obtains a money transfer from another the sum thereby credited to the first person's account can no longer be categorised as stolen goods. This indeed was the view of the Law Commission when reviewing the impact of *Preddy*. Furthermore, even where a person, A, pays stolen bank notes directly into his account, the proceeds of a subsequent transfer from that account to an account held by another person B cannot be classed as stolen goods, because any credit balance thereby created in B's account is an entirely different chose ('thing in action') from the credit balance which previously represented the stolen money in A's account. B's credit balance admittedly represents the proceeds of A's original crime, but it has never done so in the hands of the original thief, and any argument that it does so in the hands of a handler of the stolen property (i.e. B) is circular, because that presupposes the very point it seeks to establish, namely that the funds in B's account are stolen goods! As they are not 'stolen goods' and therefore cannot be 'handled', answer D is therefore incorrect.

The Theft Act 1968, s. 24A addresses this problem in two ways.

First, s. 24A(2A) broadens the scope of s. 24A to cases in which the accused dishonestly retains a credit which he knows or correctly believes derives from an offence of:

> (2A) A credit to an account is wrongful to the extent that it derives from –
> (a) theft;
> (b) blackmail;
> (c) fraud (contrary to section 1 of the Fraud Act 2006); or
> (d) stolen goods.

If, for example, A pays stolen money into his account and transfers the funds from that account to an account owned by B, a wrongful credit has been made to B's account, and B may commit a s. 24A offence if he dishonestly retains it, knowing or believing it to be derived from one or other of those offences. In this scenario this is exactly what happened, and the s. 24A offence is complete only when the defendant dishonestly retained it; answers A and B are therefore incorrect.

Secondly s. 24A(8) provides that any money dishonestly withdrawn from an account to which a wrongful credit has been made can be classed once again as stolen goods.

It is curious that the proceeds of A's original theft can be classed as stolen goods when paid into A's own bank account, yet cease to be stolen goods when effectively 'transferred' to B's account, and yet revert to being stolen goods when dishonestly withdrawn as cash by B; but that is the law.

Any volunteers for a transfer to fraud investigation?

Crime, para. 1.11.16

Answer 11.21

Answer **B** — Section 8 of the Theft Act 1968 provides:

(1) A person is guilty of robbery if he steals, and immediately before or at the time of doing so, and in order to do so, he uses force on any person or puts or seeks to put any person in fear of being then and there subjected to force...

So there has to be a theft, with all the requirements (dishonesty, etc.) that go with s. 1 of the Theft Act 1968. In *R v Forrester* [1992] Crim LR 793 the landlord refused to return the defendant's deposit when the tenancy was terminated by the landlord. The defendant believed he had been asked to leave without justification and that the deposit was being unfairly withheld. The defendant and a friend went to the landlord's house and burst in when the door was opened. The friend held the landlord whilst the defendant seized some items. The defendant's defence was that he intended to keep the items until the landlord returned his deposit and if this failed he would sell the items and use the money for a deposit on another flat and would return the money left over to the landlord. The conviction for robbery was upheld by the Court of Appeal. It was held that he knew he had no right to the items themselves and so could not claim that he was not dishonest under s. 2(1)(a) Theft Act 1968. This may have been different had he actually taken cash, and not items, but he was not entitled to take the items; answer C is therefore incorrect. Note the difference between answers A and B, even if the items did not belong to him, the accused could take them provided the elements of s. 2(1)(a) of the Theft Act 1968 were met, i.e. he had a right in law to take them; answer A is therefore incorrect.

It is also immaterial who actually uses the force and to whom, provided there is force used on a person to 'steal' the offence of robbery is complete; answer D is therefore incorrect.

Crime, para. 1.11.3

12 | Fraud

STUDY PREPARATION

There is no doubt that offences where people deceive others are rising. It is becoming an increasingly complex area, and until recently the legislation was so widespread as to make it ineffective in dealing with the vast changes in how these offences were committed, even to the extent of being covered by two Acts of Parliament. There is no doubt fraud is a multimillion pound business.

The government has sought to address this by incorporating all fraud under one umbrella, the Fraud Act 2006. This act will now target fraudulent behaviour, not the consequences of that behaviour. The balance swings from 'was there a deception' to 'what was in the mind of the offender'.

In this chapter committing fraud by false representation, failing to disclose information and by abuse of a position of trust are examined. Also tested is possession of articles for use in fraud, and also the still complex forgery and counterfeiting legislation.

QUESTIONS

Question 12.1

PRYCE applied for a job with a computer company. He falsely stated in his application form that he was proficient in using several computer packages, which were required by the company in the job description that was sent out with the application form. At the time he made the application he knew that he was lying on the form, but was desperate for a job. He was later interviewed, but was unsuccessful and did not get the job.

Has PRYCE committed an offence (under s. 2 of the Fraud Act 2006) of fraud by false representation?

A Yes, even though he has not gained from his actions, he has received no actual payments.

B Yes, even though he only deceived the company into interviewing him by false representation.

C No, he was not given the opportunity to gain money by the company.

D No, because he has not made a financial gain.

Question 12.2

MORRIS, who is a child aged 14, was homeless and was sitting on a bench in the centre of his local town. He was sitting next to a bucket, which had 'SAVE THE CHILD' written on it. Believing he was collecting money for the charity 'Save the Children', several people placed money in the bucket. MORRIS, who was trying to get money for food and not for charity, did not say anything at any time. MORRIS was merely trying to collect money, he had no desire to deceive people. MORRIS told a police officer that he was not bothered whether people thought they were donating to a registered charity or not.

Has MORRIS committed an offence of fraud by false representation under s. 2 of the Fraud Act 2006?

A No, as the representation is not dishonest, and MORRIS does not realise his actions may be dishonest.

B No, he did not use any speech to make the false representation, and people donating made their own assumptions about the charity.

C Yes, but only if it can be shown that MORRIS's actions were dishonest by the ordinary standards of reasonable and honest people.

D Yes, as his sign is misleading, and he was reckless as to whether it was misleading or not.

Question 12.3

RAMAGE is a member of a gym to which she took PASSARO. At the gym there was a new person working in reception. RAMAGE showed her membership card to the receptionist, saying, 'She's a member, too, but she forgot her card'. PASSARO was not a member, but said nothing and was allowed entry, without paying the usual fee for guests. Both RAMAGE and PASSARO had agreed to do this before attending at the gym in order to secure free entry for PASSARO.

Who, if anyone, has committed an offence (under s. 2 of the Fraud Act 2006) of fraud by misrepresentation?

A Both have committed the offence in these circumstances.

B RAMAGE only; as PASSARO made no representation that she was a member.

C PASSARO only as RAMAGE herself made no 'gain', whereas PASSARO gained entry to the gym for free.

D Neither; as no actual 'gain' was made by either of them as they received no money or property.

Question 12.4

ANDERSON ordered some furniture from a second-hand shop. He paid a deposit and was due to pay the remainder on delivery, as that was part of his contract, which he had signed. When the furniture arrived, ANDERSON gave the delivery driver a cheque, aware that the bank would not honour it. However, he thought he would have money in the relevant account in a month's time, and would be able to pay the bill then.

Has ANDERSON committed an offence (under s. 3 of the Fraud Act 2006) of fraud by failure to disclose information?

A Yes, but only when or if he fails to pay for the furniture.

B Yes, he has caused a temporary loss to the company.

C No, as he does not intend to make a permanent default on the payment.

D No, as the shop suffers no loss, they only have to wait for the payment.

Question 12.5

YOSHIMI was a sales representative and was given a company mobile phone. According to company rules, employees had to pay for private telephone calls. At the end of each month, YOSHIMI received a copy of the mobile phone bill and was required to highlight any private calls made and pay for them by cheque or cash. YOSHIMI knew that the accounting department was always busy and the bills were never examined closely. As a result, YOSHIMI regularly made international calls to family in America, but never declared these as private calls and never paid for them.

Could YOSHIMI be found guilty of the offence of false accounting, under s. 17 of the Theft Act 1968?

A No, an offence under this section cannot be committed by an omission alone; there must be an act done by the accused.

B Yes, provided it can be shown that YOSHIMI intended to permanently deprive the company of the money owed.

C Yes, an offence under this section may be committed by an omission alone.

D No, an offence under this section cannot be committed unless it is shown that documents were falsified, defaced or destroyed.

Question 12.6

CHANNING is highly skilled in the forgery field, and produced a sophisticated set of plates from which he made a forged £20 note. Using a high specification laser copier, he photocopied a large quantity of these notes. Before releasing the notes, he spent some in local shops to test their quality.

Which elements of 'false instrument' would CHANNING be guilty of in these circumstances?

A Making and using a false instrument.

B Copying and making a false instrument.

C Using a false instrument only.

D He is not guilty of any false instrument offence.

Question 12.7

ALBRIGHT, who is 15 years old, wishes to watch his local football team play at home in the FA cup against West Ham United. However the tickets are too expensive for him and he decides he will climb a fence to watch the game. He does so and enjoys the game, however what he did not know was that for this special game anyone under 16 years of age was given free entry, on proof of age.

Which of the following is correct in relation to an offence under s. 11 of the Fraud Act 2006, obtaining services dishonestly?

A ALBRIGHT has committed an offence of obtaining services dishonestly as his intention was not to pay; the fact the game was free is irrelevant.

B ALBRIGHT has committed an offence of obtaining services dishonestly as he did not enter the ground properly, producing proof of age.

C ALBRIGHT has not obtained services dishonestly, the offence is not inchoate: it requires the actual obtaining of a service, watching football is not such a service.

D ALBRIGHT has not obtained services dishonestly, whatever his intentions, for his age the service was provided for free.

Question 12.8

ENGLISH is in possession of a pen as he walks down the High Street. He goes into the bank and obtains an application form for a credit card, which he fills out fraudulently. He obtains the card a few days later, and has it in his possession as he goes to a shop to buy goods he has no intention of paying for. He presents the card to the person on the cash till in the shop. From the moment he left his home with that pen in his pocket his sole intention was to obtain a credit card and then goods fraudulently.

In relation to an offence contrary to s. 6 of the Fraud Act 2006, possession of articles for use in fraud, which of the following is correct?

A The offence is complete when ENGLISH is in possession of the pen.

B The offence is complete when ENGLISH is in possession of the credit card application form.

C The offence is complete when ENGLISH is in possession of the credit card.

D The offence is complete when ENGLISH is in possession of the credit card, with intention to use it fraudulently.

Question 12.9

Officers from the fraud squad are investigating BARLEY, who works as a bank employee, following a complaint from her employer. BARLEY is suspected of having dishonestly obtained a transfer of £10,000, by a deception, from the bank account of a customer into her own account. The officers have been unable to identify the account from which the money was taken. The investigation has revealed that only £5,000 was credited to BARLEY's own account and that this sum of money was transferred out immediately, to an unknown account. The investigating officers have been unable to trace the remaining £5,000, which they believe was transferred to another account also.

In these circumstances has BARLEY committed an offence of fraud by abuse of position contrary to s. 4 of the Fraud Act 2006?

A Yes, but only if the investigating officers can prove that BARLEY unlawfully retained some or all of the money.

B Yes, there need be no consequences to the unlawful act and the offence is complete where no money was retained.

C No, because the amount credited to BARLEY's account is less than the amount debited from the customer's account.

D No, unless they can identify the account from which the £10,000 was taken.

Question 12.10

CIPLINSKI works for a leading commodities, financial futures and options broker. As such she is privy to sensitive information, although in work she cannot access any customer funds. Over the last month she has been transferring details of the broker's customer accounts from her work computer to her own laptop, with the intention of using the information to fraudulently transfer funds from their accounts to hers. She resigns from the brokers, and only when not employed by them does she try to transfer the money. Unfortunately for her she is found out and arrested by the police prior to any transfer of funds to her own account.

In relation to s. 4 of the Fraud Act 2006, fraud by abuse of position, at what point, if any, is the offence committed?

A When CIPLINSKI begins to transfer details to her own laptop.

B When CIPLINSKI accesses the information on her laptop with the intention of obtaining funds fraudulently.

C The offence cannot be committed as at the point when the transfer is arranged, CIPLINSKI is no longer in a position in which she was expected to safeguard, or not to act against, the financial interests of another person.

D The offence cannot be committed as CIPLINSKI was never in a position in which she was expected to safeguard, or not to act against, the financial interests of another person as she never had access to their funds in work.

Question 12.11

Section 2 of the Fraud Act 2006 creates an offence of fraud by false representation, and outlines when a representation is false.

In relation to s. 2 of the Fraud Act 2006, when would a representation be 'false'?

A A representation is false if it is completely untrue and the person making it knows this to be the case.

B A representation is false if it is completely untrue and the person making it knows this is or knows this might be the case.

C A representation is false if it is untrue or misleading and the person making it knows this to be the case.

D A representation is false if it is untrue or misleading and the person making it knows this is or knows this might be the case.

Question 12.12

GIVENS is a plumber who visits a house to give a quote on the job. He returns home and writes a letter to the householder asking for a £500 deposit to be sent to him. At the time he sent the letter GIVENS has no intentions of carrying out the work and only wishes to take the householder's money. The householder receives the letter, but does not send any money.

In relation to s. 2 of the Fraud Act 2006, fraud by false representation, which of the following is correct?

A The offence has been committed, and it was committed when the letter was posted.
B The offence has been committed, and it was committed when the letter was received by the householder.
C An offence has not been committed as the householder did not send any money.
D An offence has not been committed, but an attempt to commit the offence has been.

ANSWERS

Answer 12.1

Answer **B** — The offence of fraudulent misrepresentation is covered at s. 2 of the Fraud Act 2006.

The elements of the offence are that the defendant:

- made
- a false representation
- dishonestly
- knowing that the representation was or might be untrue or misleading
- with intent to make a gain for himself or another, to cause loss to another or to expose another to risk of loss.

A representation may be express or implied (s. 2(4)). It can be stated in words or communicated by conduct. There is no limitation on the way in which the representation must be expressed. It could be written, spoken, posted on a phishing website, spoken into a dictaphone or sent by email. A representation is defined as 'false' if it is untrue or misleading and the person making it knows that it is, or might be, untrue or misleading.

The representation must be made dishonestly. The current definition of dishonesty was established in *R* v *Ghosh* [1982] QB1053. That judgment sets a two-stage test. The first question is whether a defendant's behaviour would be regarded as dishonest by the ordinary standards of reasonable and honest people. If answered positively, the second question is whether the defendant was aware that his conduct was dishonest and would be regarded as dishonest by reasonable and honest people.

'Gain' and 'loss' are defined in s. 5 of the 2006 Act. Gain and loss extends only to gain and loss in money or other property (s. 5(2)(a)), whether temporary or permanent (s. 5(2)(b)) and means any property whether real or personal including things in action and other intangible property (s. 5(2)(b)).

The offence is entirely offender focused. It is complete as soon as the defendant makes a false representation, provided that it is made with the necessary dishonest intent. Even though no 'gain' has actually been achieved in this scenario the offence is still made out; answer A is therefore incorrect.

It differs from the deception offences in that it is immaterial whether or not any one is cognisant of the representation, deceived or any property actually gained or lost; answers C and D are therefore incorrect.

Crime, para. 1.12.3

Answer 12.2

Answer **A** — The elements of the offence under s. 2 of the Fraud Act 2006 are that the defendant:

- made
- a false representation
- dishonestly
- knowing that the representation was or might be untrue or misleading
- with intent to make a gain for himself or another, to cause loss to another or to expose another to risk of loss.

In this scenario the defendant certainly made a representation, i.e the sign and a representation may be express or implied (s. 2(4)). It can be stated in words or communicated by conduct, or written on a notice. There is no limitation on the way in which the representation must be expressed.

A representation is defined as 'false' if it is untrue or misleading and the person making it knows that it is, or *might be*, untrue or misleading. The sign itself does not actually say 'save the children' (if you missed this it is important you read the question carefully, in fact the sign says 'save the child') and therefore essentially the people donating 'mislead' themselves. Given his lack of intent to deceive this element of the offence is not made out, the words 'might be' do not import recklessness. Actual knowledge that the representation might be untrue is required — not awareness of a risk that it might be untrue; answer D is therefore incorrect. Had MORRIS actually intended that people misinterpret the sign then this would be a false misrepresentation, even though the sign was not spelt correctly; answer B is therefore incorrect.

The representation must also be made dishonestly. The *Ghosh* definition applies:

- Was what was done dishonest by the ordinary standards of reasonable and honest people?
- Must the defendant have realised that what he was doing was, by those standards, dishonest?

Both tests must be applied, and even though the first may be met the second is not, and again recklessness is not enough; answer C is therefore incorrect.

Crime, para. 1.12.3

Answer 12.3

Answer **A** — The elements of the offence under s. 2 of the Fraud Act 2006 are that the defendant:

- made
- a false representation
- dishonestly
- knowing that the representation was or might be untrue or misleading
- with intent to make a gain for himself or another, to cause loss to another or to expose another to risk of loss.

In the scenario RAMAGE makes a false statement about her friend's membership status, with the intention to deceive, knowing the statement to be untrue. PASSARO said nothing. However a representation may also be implied by conduct, or can be by omission. PASSARO failed to mention the fact she was not a member and her actions in walking past the receptionist as if she were a member (albeit on her friend's word) would be a false representation; answer B is therefore incorrect. The dishonesty would stem from the agreement PASSARO had with RAMAGE to dupe the gym.

It's not just a gain that makes this offence out, it also includes 'loss', that is, losing something that one might ordinarily have obtained, in this case the entry fee; answer D is therefore incorrect. So although RAMAGE made no gain, as she would have had free entry in any case she is compliant in an act that causes a loss to the gym; answer C is therefore incorrect.

Crime, para. 1.12.3

Answer 12.4

Answer **B** — This offence is covered by s. 3 of the Fraud Act 2006. The elements of the offence are that the defendant:

- failed to disclose information to another person when
- he was under a legal duty to disclose that information
- dishonestly

- intending, by that failure, to make a gain or cause a loss.

This offence is entirely offender focused. It is complete as soon as the defendant fails to disclose information provided he was under a legal duty to do so, and that it was done with the necessary dishonest intent. It differs from the deception offences in that it is immaterial whether or not any one is deceived or any property actually gained or lost.

Here ANDERSON failed to disclose that he did not have the funds to complete the contract as signed. A legal duty to disclose information can arise as a result of a contract between two parties or because of the existence of a particular type of professional relationship between them, and as such the burden fell. Here again the *Ghosh* test applies to dishonesty, certainly ANDERSON knew he was being dishonest as he knew the cheque would bounce, and there is no guarantee that funds will ever be available to him (although in the context of this offence this is entirely irrelevant).

'Gain' and 'loss' are defined in s. 5 of the 2006 Act. Gain and loss extends only to gain and loss in money or other property (s. 5(2)(a)), whether temporary or permanent (s. 5(2)(b)) and means any property whether real or personal including things in action and other intangible property (s. 5(2)(b)), so even a temporary loss is sufficient for the offence to be made out; answer A is therefore incorrect.

Permanently defaulting on payment is not required and where information that is subject to legal duty to be disclosed is not so disclosed then the offence is complete, provided there is dishonesty; answers C and D are therefore incorrect.

Crime, para. 1.12.4

Answer 12.5

Answer **C** — Section 17 of the Theft Act 1968 creates *two* offences: destroying, defacing, falsifying, etc. accounts and documents (s. 17(1)(a)); and using false or misleading accounts or documents in furnishing information (s. 17(1)(b)). An offence under s. 17 can be committed by omission as well as by an act. Failing to make an entry in an accounts book, altering a till receipt or supplying an auditor with records that are incomplete may, if accompanied by the other ingredients, amount to an offence. In *R v Shama* [1990] 1 WLR 661 the Court of Appeal upheld the conviction of a telephone operator who had failed even to start filling out standard forms provided by his employer for the recording of international calls. He was held to have falsified the forms by leaving them unmarked; answers A and D are therefore incorrect.

Unlike the offence of theft there is no requirement to prove an intention permanently to deprive — but there is a need to show dishonesty on behalf of the accused. Answer B is therefore incorrect.

Crime, para. 1.12.11.1

Answer 12.6

Answer **D** — Quite simply, offences classed as forgery include virtually every kind of document *except* bank notes. Therefore, as he has been involved in 'forging' bank notes, CHANNING cannot commit the offences of making and using a false instrument (answer A is incorrect), copying and making a false instrument (answer B is incorrect) and using a false instrument (answer C is incorrect). Offences relating to currency are dealt with by the Forgery and Counterfeiting Act 1981.

Crime, para. 1.12.11.4

Answer 12.7

Answer **D** — Section 11 of the 2006 Act makes it an offence for any person, by any dishonest act, to obtain services for which payment is required, with intent to avoid payment. The person must know that the services are made available on the basis that they are chargeable, or that they might be. It is not possible to commit the offence by omission alone and it can be committed only where the dishonest act was done with the intent not to pay for the services as expected. This offence replaces the offence of obtaining services by deception in s. 1 of the Theft Act 1978, though the new offence contains no deception element.

The offence is not inchoate: it requires the actual obtaining of the service. For example, data or software may be made available on the Internet to a certain category of person who has paid for access rights to that service. A person dishonestly using false credit card details or other false personal information to obtain the service would be committing an offence under this clause. However the section would also cover a situation where a person climbs over a wall and watches a football match without paying the entrance fee — such a person is not deceiving the provider of the service directly, but is obtaining a service, which is provided on the basis that people will pay for it; answer C is therefore incorrect.

However where services obtained are free, s. 11 cannot ever be charged, no matter the circumstances and intention of the defendant. In this scenario the services are free for those under 16, therefore anyone within that age range could not commit the offence. Proof of age is a restriction placed by the football administrators, not the law. For instance if ALBRIGHT had attempted formal entry and had been turned away because he had no proof of age with him, and had then climbed the fence he would still not be guilty of an offence under s. 11 of the 2006 Act; answers A and B are therefore incorrect.

Crime, para. 1.12.10

Answer 12.8

Answer **A** — Section 6 of the Fraud Act 2006 states:

(1) A person is guilty of an offence if he has in his possession or under his control any article for use in the course of or in connection with any fraud...

Section 6 makes it an offence for a person to possess or have under his control any article for use in the course of or in connection with any fraud. This wording draws on that of the existing law in s. 25 of the Theft Act 1968 and s. 24 of the Theft Act (Northern Ireland) 1969. (These provisions make it an offence for a person to 'go equipped' to commit a burglary, theft or cheat, although they apply only when the offender is not at his place of abode.) The intention is to attract the case law on s. 25, which has established that proof is required that the defendant had the article for the purpose or with the intention that it be used in the course of or in connection with the offence, and that a general intention to commit fraud will suffice.

It is any article that could be used in any of the fraud offences of the 2006 Act, and begins when the accused has the pen, together with the necessary intent; answers B, C and D are therefore incorrect.

Crime, para. 1.12.7

Answer 12.9

Answer **B** — The elements of the offence under s. 4 of the Fraud Act 2006 are that the defendant:

• occupies a position in which he was expected to safeguard, or not to act against, the financial interests of another person
• abused that position
• dishonestly

- intending by that abuse to make a gain/cause a loss
- the abuse may consist of an omission rather than an act.

Like the other two offences (contained in ss. 2 and 3 of the 2006 Act) s. 4 is entirely offender focused. It is complete once the defendant carries out the act that is the abuse of his position. It is immaterial whether or not he is successful in his enterprise and whether or not any gain or loss is actually made.

BARLEY clearly occupies a position of trust and abused that position by dishonestly transferring money to her own account, albeit fleetingly. For this offence there is no need to prove where the fraudulently obtained funds came from, nor that any of those funds were actually available to the defendant; the offence relates around the dishonest intentions of the defendant; answers A, C and D are therefore incorrect.

Crime, para. 1.12.5

Answer 12.10

Answer **A** — The elements of the offence under s. 4 of the Fraud Act 2006 are that the defendant:

- occupies a position in which he was expected to safeguard, or not to act against, the financial interests of another person
- abused that position
- dishonestly
- intending by that abuse to make a gain/cause a loss
- the abuse may consist of an omission rather than an act.

The point at which this offence is committed is when a person 'occupying a position' abuses it by transferring information that they intend making a gain or cause a loss. Although when CIPLINSKI actually attempts to access another person's funds she is no longer 'occupying a position' the offence was complete when she transferred the information from the work computer to her home one; answers B and C are therefore incorrect.

Even though at work she cannot access funds, she is still, as an employee of the brokers, responsible for not acting against the financial interests of the broker; answer D is therefore incorrect.

Crime, para. 1.12.5

Answer 12.11

Answer **D** — Section 2 of the Fraud Act 2006 states:

... (2) A representation is false if —
    (a) it is untrue or misleading, and
    (b) the person making it knows that it is, or might be, untrue or misleading.

A representation is false if it is untrue or misleading and the person making it knows this is or knows this might be the case. Therefore, an untrue statement made in the honest belief that it is in fact true, would not suffice. The words 'or might be' must involve a subjective belief on the part of the person making the representation.

So the representation does not have to be completely untrue, misleading is enough; answers A and B for that reason are untrue. The person making the statement need only believe that the statement may be untrue or misleading; for that reason answer C is therefore incorrect (as is answer A again)

Crime para 1.12.3

Answer 12.12

Answer **A** — Section 2 of the Fraud Act 2006 states:

(1) A person is in breach of this section if he —
    (a) dishonestly makes a false representation, and
    (b) intends, by making the representation —
        (i)   to make a gain for himself or another, or
        (ii) to cause loss to another or to expose another to the risk of loss.
(2) A representation is false if —
    (a) it is untrue or misleading, and
    (b) the person making it knows that it is, or might be, untrue or misleading.
(3) 'Representation' means any representation as to fact or law, including a representation as to the state of mind of —
    (a) the person making the representation, or
    (b) any other person.
(4) A representation may be express or implied...

There has certainly been a false representation, give me £500 for doing nothing!

Deception offences under the Theft Acts 1968 and 1978 required the 'target' of the deception to be deceived by the words or conduct of the defendant; if this element were not present there would only be an attempted deception. The Fraud Act

2006 removes this requirement so that where a defendant makes a false representation knowing that it is false or might be, the offence of fraud is complete; answers C and D are therefore incorrect.

The offence is complete the moment the false representation is made. The representation need never be heard nor communicated to the recipient and if carried out by post, would be complete when the letter is posted (*Treacy* v *DPP* [1971] AC 537); answer B is therefore incorrect.

Crime para 1.12.3

13 | Criminal Damage

STUDY PREPARATION

The definition of criminal damage needs attention in the first instance, and you will have to know the various components, such as lawful excuse, protection, recklessness, damage, property and belonging to another. In addition to these statutory issues there are many decided cases on each of these points.

It is important to learn the basic definition, before turning to the aggravated offences. Each one of these is similar to the other, with the defendant's intent being of key significance.

It is also worth paying attention to contamination of goods. Although the offences associated with the definition are reasonably long and complicated, this is an area that may receive considerable further attention in the current climate of terrorist threats.

QUESTIONS

Question 13.1

NEWLING runs a computer company specialising in software. Whilst waiting one day for a meeting with a potential client he drops the memory stick with a vital program on it on the floor. A rival sees the opportunity and stamps on the memory stick, breaking it completely. NEWLING was unable to give his presentation and did not get a contract.

In relation only to the program, has it been criminally damaged?

A Yes, as it is the intellectual property of NEWLING.
B Yes, as it is capable of being displayed it is real property.
C No, as it is not tangible property.
D Not unless it is the only copy of the programme.

Question 13.2

AUSTIN was in trouble with his business and wanted to burn some papers that the VAT people would find interesting. He takes his filing cabinet home and sets fire to the contents which are completely destroyed. However AUSTIN was unaware that his business partner had put several of his own important papers in the drawers that were also destroyed as both partners shared the filing cabinet.

Could AUSTIN be guilty of recklessly damaging the property of his partner?

A Yes but only if he was aware that there were other papers in the filing cabinet.

B Yes but only if he was aware that there may be other papers in the filing cabinet and still took the risk they would be damaged.

C No, if he simply believed that he was destroying his own property.

D No, unless it could be shown that he had checked the contents prior to setting fire to them.

Question 13.3

PHILLIPS is walking home from the pub and is feeling in a destructive mood. He takes a brick and throws it at a bus shelter, which he intends to destroy. Unfortunately for him there is no glass, just a strong synthetic material that is shatter proof. He throws the brick many times, but causes no damage at all to the shelter. Frustrated he sets fire to a bin full of litter at the next bus shelter he comes across on his route home. The fire damage caused to the shelter is also minimal, and the total bill for the damage is £200.

In these circumstances, which of the following is correct in relation to criminal damage and attempted criminal damage?

A He can be charged only with the second offence and can only be tried summarily, due to the value of the damage.

B He can be charged with both offences and can only be tried summarily, due to the value of the damage.

C He can be charged with both offences and may elect mode of trial.

D He can be charged with both offences and will be committed to the Crown Court.

Question 13.4

When proving an offence under s. 1(2) of the Criminal Damage Act 1971 (aggravated criminal damage), *mens rea* must be shown.

In which of the following circumstances is the offence made out?

A The person intended to cause criminal damage and intended to endanger a person's life.

B The person intended or was reckless as to whether damage would be caused, and intended or was reckless as to whether life would be endangered.

C The person intended or was reckless as to whether a person's life would be endangered.

D The person intended to cause criminal damage only, and was reckless as to whether a person's life would be endangered.

Question 13.5

Section 54 of the Anti-social Behaviour Act makes it an offence to sell aerosol paint to certain people.

To which of the following people would it be illegal to sell aerosol paint?

A Someone who is 16 years of age or under.

B Someone who is or appears to be 16 years of age or under.

C Someone who is under 16 years of age.

D Someone who is or appears to be under 16 years of age.

Question 13.6

Criminal damage under s. 2 of the Criminal Damage Act 1971 is an offence of intent.

When considering an offence under s. 2 (threats to destroy or damage property) what must the prosecution prove?

A That the accused intended that the victim would fear that the damage would be carried out immediately.

B That the accused intended to cause damage and intended to induce fear that damage would be carried out.

C That the accused intended that the victim would fear that the damage would be carried out.

D That the victim did in fact fear that the accused would carry out the threat to cause damage.

Question 13.7

FRANCIS and PRAFFITOUS are members of an extreme animal rights group. PRAFFITOUS applied for a job in a zoo, and they planned that if he was successful, he would damage customers' cars by placing sharp tacks under the tyres. FRANCIS bought 10 packets of tacks at a DIY store the day before PRAFFITOUS' interview, intending to give them to him if he got the job.

Has either person committed an offence under s. 3 of the Criminal Damage Act 1971 (having articles with intent to damage property)?

A Only FRANCIS; he has control of the articles, intending that PRAFFITOUS should use them to cause damage.

B Neither person, as FRANCIS does not intend to use the articles himself to cause criminal damage.

C Both people, because of their joint intent that PRAFFITOUS should use the articles to cause damage.

D Neither person, as the intent to commit damage is conditional on PRAFFITOUS being successful in his interview.

Question 13.8

DENNIS works in a butcher's shop. As a joke, on 1 April he came in early and sprinkled icing sugar on some meat on display. He then left a note for his boss, claiming to be from an animal rights group, saying they had sprinkled rat poison on the food. Unfortunately, before he was able to stop him, his boss threw the meat away.

Has DENNIS committed an offence under s. 38 of the Public Order Act 1986 (contamination of goods)?

A Yes, because he has caused economic loss to his employer.

B No, because he has not caused public alarm or anxiety.

C No, because he has not actually contaminated any goods.

D No, because he only intended his employer to treat it as a joke.

Question 13.9

Section 2 of the Criminal Damage Act 1971 makes it an offence, in certain circumstances, to threaten to damage or destroy your own property.

Which of the following is true in relation to this offence?

A It is an offence to threaten to damage your own property regardless of the circumstances.

B It is an offence to threaten to damage your own property, but only where there is danger to your own or any other person's life.

C It is an offence to threaten to damage your own property, but only where there is danger to any other person's life.

D It is an offence to threaten to damage your own property under *any* circumstances.

Question 13.10

PARLAND went to a local kebab shop following a night out with his friends. Having purchased a kebab he feared he had been overcharged and asked for a refund, which was refused. The owner of the kebab shop then asked him to leave or the police would be called. Grudgingly PARLAND went outside and walked away; after about 20 yards he kicked a parked car and was heard to say 'bloody immigrants' as he did so. The car was damaged. The owner of the kebab shop was in fact not an immigrant, having been born in England and the car did not belong to him.

Has PARLAND committed racially aggravated criminal damage?

A Yes, as the offence committed was aggravated by racism.

B Yes, as the hostility shown was based on the shop owner's membership or presumed membership of a racial or religious group.

C No, as the offence committed was not aggravated by racism, merely accompanied by it.

D No, as the victim was not the subject of the membership or presumed membership of a racial or religious group.

Question 13.11

FAWKES was arrested for an offence of being in charge of a motor vehicle whilst over the prescribed limit and following a reading that showed he was well over the prescribed limit he was placed in a cell and detained. FAWKES was angry that in his view he had not been properly given his rights, and so he put the blanket he had been given down the toilet and flushed it until the cell floor was flooded. As a result of his actions the cell had to be closed until it had been cleaned, and the blanket had to be sent to be cleaned and dried.

In relation to a possible charge of criminal damage in relation to FAWKES' actions, which of the following is correct?

A It would only be criminal damage to the blanket had the toilet contained urine or faeces when it was put down there.

B It would only be criminal damage to the cell as that had to be taken out of service and was out of commission.

C It would be criminal damage in relation to both as the blanket could not be used until it had been dried out and the flooded cell remained out of action until the water was cleared.

D It would not be criminal damage in either case as both would dry, and when dry they would return to their original state.

Question 13.12

MILBY has been charged with an offence of arson, contrary to s. 1(3) of the Criminal Damage Act 1971. It is alleged that MILBY set fire to a car belonging to a neighbour because of a long-standing dispute. The fire endangered no one, as it occurred in the middle of the night, away from any dwelling houses. The car was completely written off and the insurance company have placed its value as £3,500.

Which of the following statements is correct, in relation to where MILBY should be tried for this offence?

A Because the value of the damage was under £5,000, the case should be tried in the magistrates' court.

B Because it involved arson, the case should be tried in the Crown Court.

C Because no life was endangered, the case should be tried in the magistrates' court.

D Because the value of the damage was over £2,000, the case should be tried in the Crown Court.

Question 13.13

Constable SOUTER is on patrol when he comes across a car parked on the street. On looking in the car he sees a handbag on the passenger seat and also notices that the passenger door seems to be unlocked. The officer decides, for safe keeping, to remove the handbag from the car. When he pulls the car door handle it comes off in his hand, damaging it beyond repair. The owner of the car turns up and is furious the officer has damaged his car and states the door was locked and there was nothing in the bag in any case. The officer had honestly believed that the owner of the car would have wanted him to enter the car to protect his property.

Has the officer committed an offence of criminal damage, and if so would he have a 'lawful excuse'?

A Yes, he has committed the offence and would have a lawful excuse, as he was acting to 'protect' other property i.e. the handbag.

B Yes, he has committed the offence and would have a lawful excuse as he honestly believed the owner would have consented to his actions.

C Yes, he has committed the offence, but would have no lawful excuse; the owner would not have consented to his actions.

D No, he has not committed the offence as he does not have the required *mens rea*.

Question 13.14

COULTER is an animal lover and hates people who eat meat. She sends a letter to her local supermarket stating she intends to sprinkle rat poison over all their meat. Her intention is to cause harm to persons who eat meat. She then makes several stickers that state 'Don't eat dead animals' which she intends putting on the meat at the supermarket. However she is stopped by a police officer prior to arrival at the supermarket, who discover the stickers and the rat poison. In fact the supermarket has taken no action at all as a result of the letter she sent to them.

In relation to contamination of goods which of the following is correct?

A An offence is committed in relation to the letter only.

B An offence is committed in relation to the letter and the stickers.

C An offence is not committed as both the letter and the stickers related to future actions.

D An offence is not committed as the supermarket took no action.

ANSWERS

Answer 13.1

Answer **C** — Section 10 of the Criminal Damage Act 1971 describes 'property' as:

(1) In this Act 'property' means property of a tangible nature, whether real or personal, including money and —
   (a) including wild creatures which have been tamed or are ordinarily kept in captivity and any other wild creatures or their carcasses if, but only if, they have been reduced into possession . . . or are in the course of being reduced into possession; but
   (b) not including mushrooms growing wild on any land or flowers, fruit or foliage of a plant growing wild on any land.

Quite simply tangible means 'touchable' and you cannot touch a computer program or any other intellectual property; answers A and B are therefore incorrect. Even if the programme was the only copy it would not be criminal damage, although other offences may apply; answer D is therefore incorrect.

Crime, para. 1.13.2.3

Answer 13.2

Answer **B** — The m*ens rea* for criminal damage is satisfied by either intention or recklessness, and it is the latter, wider concept which has proved crucial.

The former concept of objective or 'Caldwell' recklessness (as set out in *Metropolitan Police Commissioner* v *Caldwell* [1982] AC 341) has now gone and the law has been restored to its former position by *R* v *G & R* [2003] 3 WLR 1060. In that case, the House of Lords decided that 'recklessness' in the context of criminal damage did not mean something different from the previous requirement of 'malicious damage' — namely that the defendant had foreseen the risk yet gone on to take it. Their Lordships held that a person acts recklessly for the purposes of s. 1(1) of the Criminal Damage Act 1971:

- with respect to a circumstance when he/she is aware of a risk that existed or would exist;
- with respect to a result or consequence when he/she is aware of a risk that it would occur and it is, in the circumstances known to him/her, unreasonable to take the risk.

So what did AUSTIN know? He knew that both he and his partner used the filing cabinet, the fact that he was unaware that papers other than his had been put in the cabinet is irrelevant, there had to have been a risk of that in a shared cabinet; answer A is therefore incorrect.

Even if he believes that he is destroying his own property yet is aware of a risk and still takes that risk he would be reckless; answer C is therefore incorrect. Checking to see if the papers were there takes recklessness out the equation, if they were his own papers –no offence; if his partners were there to his knowledge and he still set fire to them is deliberate, not reckless; answer D is therefore incorrect.

Crime, paras 1.13.2, 1.13.4

Answer 13.3

Answer **C** — Criminal damage is generally triable either way. However, where the value of the property alleged to have been destroyed or the value of the alleged damage is not more than £5,000 criminal damage (unless charged in the racially aggravated form) it is treated as if it were triable only summarily. This does not convert it into a summary offence for all purposes and thus there can still be an attempt to commit low value criminal damage even though only an attempt to commit an indictable offence is caught by s. 1(4) of the Criminal Attempts Act 1981 (*R v Bristol Justices, ex parte E* [1999] 1 WLR 390); answer A is therefore incorrect.

Even if the value involved is not more than £5,000, a count for criminal damage may be included in an indictment for another offence, and where that other offence is indictable, or triable either way, then simple criminal damage can still end up in the Crown Court.

In this case where the damage is caused by fire, it will be charged as arson under s. 1(3) of the Criminal Damage Act 1971, and this offence is triable either way, whatever the value of the damage; answer B is therefore incorrect.

The accused could be tried for both offences, and as one is triable either way the defendant could elect to be tried for both offences on indictment; answer D is therefore incorrect.

Crime, paras 1.13.2, 1.13.4

Answer 13.4

Answer **B** — A person is guilty of an offence under s. 1(2) of the Criminal Damage Act 1971, if they damage/destroy property intending *or* reckless as to whether damage is caused to their own property, or another's, *and* they intend *or* are reckless as to whether a person's life is endangered.

Either the elements of intent *or* recklessness must be proved in relation to both the damage and the endangerment to life for this offence to be made out. All four answers are fairly similar, but only answer B contains all the elements required to prove the offence. Consequently, answers A, C and D are incorrect.

Please note the change in the concept of recklessness brought about by the decision of the House of Lords in *R* v *G & R* [2003] 3 WLR 1060.

Crime, para. 1.13.3

Answer 13.5

Answer **C** — A person commits the offence by selling the aerosol to a person under 16 years of age. There is a defence courtesy of s. 4, for the person who reasonably believes the person was not under the age of 16 and took all reasonable steps to determine the purchaser's age. The section makes no mention of the apparent age of the purchaser; answers A, B and D are incorrect.

Crime, para. 1.13.7

Answer 13.6

Answer **C** — This is an offence of intention; that is, the key element is the *defendant's intention* that the person receiving the threat fears it would be carried out.

The s. 2 offence under the Criminal Damage Act 1971, which originates from the need to tackle protection racketeers, is very straightforward: there is no need to show that the other person actually feared or even believed that the threat would be carried out (making answer D incorrect).

Also, there is no need to show that the defendant intended to carry out the threat; nor does it matter whether the threat was even capable of being carried out (which is why answer B is incorrect).

Answers A and C are similar; however, C is correct because there is no requirement to show that the accused intended to cause fear of *immediate* damage.

Crime, para. 1.13.5

Answer 13.7

Answer **A** — Section 3 of the Criminal Damage Act 1971 states:

> A person who has anything in his custody or under his control, intending without lawful excuse to use it or cause or permit another to use it —
> (a) to destroy or damage any property belonging to some other person; or
> (b) to destroy or damage his own or the user's property in a way which he knows is likely to endanger the life of some other person;
> shall be guilty of an offence.

Answer B is incorrect, as a person may have control of articles which he or she intends to permit another to use. Answer C is incorrect, as PRAFFITOUS did not have the articles in his custody or control at any time.

Answer D is incorrect because a conditional intention to use an article if given circumstances arise will amount to an offence (*R* v *Buckingham* (1976) 63 Cr App R 159).

Crime, para. 1.13.6

Answer 13.8

Answer **D** — Under s. 38 of the Public Order Act 1986, it is necessary to prove that a person contaminated or interfered with goods, or made it appear that goods have been contaminated or interfered with, or threatened or claimed to have done so.

However, the person must have done so *with the intention* of causing public alarm or anxiety, or of causing injury to members of the public consuming or using the goods, or of causing economic loss to any person by reason of the goods being shunned by members of the public, or of causing economic loss to any person by reason of steps taken to avoid such alarm or anxiety, injury or loss.

Therefore, even though DENNIS in the circumstances may have contaminated goods, and even caused economic loss, he did not do so with the required intention and cannot be guilty of this offence. (Answer A is therefore incorrect.)

Had DENNIS been proved to have had the required intent, answers B and C would still be incorrect, because there is no need to prove a person actually caused public alarm/anxiety, and the offence may be committed without actually contaminating goods.

Crime, para. 1.13.8

Answer 13.9

Answer **C** — The Criminal Damage Act 1971, s. 2(b) states it is an offence for a person to threaten:

> (b) to destroy or damage his own property in a way which he knows is likely to endanger the life of that other or a third person;

So you can threaten to damage your own property, but it is only an offence where another's life is in danger. Consequently answers A, B and D are incorrect.

Crime, para. 1.13.5

Answer 13.10

Answer **D** — For simple criminal damage to be racially or religiously aggravated the circumstances as set out at s. 28(1)(a) of the Crime and Disorder Act 1998 apply, namely that the defendant demonstrates hostility towards the victim:

- at the time of, or
- immediately before or after

committing the offence, and that hostility is based on the victim's membership or presumed membership of a racial or religious group. The courts have shown that they are prepared to adopt a wide approach when interpreting this important legislation, however not wide enough to incorporate where the hostility is towards someone other than the actual victim of the offence. In this scenario the hostility was shown towards the kebab shop owner, however he was not the owner of the car and ultimately not the victim of criminal damage; answers A and B are therefore incorrect.

In *R* v *Rogers* [2005] EWCA Crim 2863 the Court of Appeal considered whether verbal abuse towards three Spanish women on the grounds of their being 'foreigners' constituted abuse towards a racial group under s. 28(4) of the Crime and Disorder Act 1998. The Court agreed it was, however it noted that the very wide meaning of racial group under s. 28(4) gives rise to a danger of aggravated offences being charged where mere 'vulgar abuse' had included racial epithets that did not truly indicate hostility to the race in question. Consequently, s. 28 should not be used unless the prosecuting authority is satisfied that the facts truly suggest that the offence was aggravated (rather than simply accompanied) by racism. This is a fine line, and police officers may have difficulty in distinguishing between the two; in this scenario had the car belonged to the shop owner would the defendant's actions have been seen to be aggravated by racism or merely accompanied by racism?

Thankfully on this occasion the distinction does not have to be made as the owner was not in fact the victim of the offence; and for this reason answer C is incorrect.

Crime, para. 1.13.2.1

Answer 13.11

Answer **C** — Although a key feature of the Criminal Damage Act 1971, strangely enough the terms 'destroy' or 'damage' are not defined. The courts have often been left to muse over what is and what is not 'damaged', and have taken an eclectic view when interpreting these terms. 'Destroying' property would suggest that it has been rendered useless, but there is no need to prove that 'damage' to property is in any way permanent or irreparable.

The Concise Oxford Dictionary explains damage as 'harm or injury impairing the value or usefulness of something ...'. In *Morphitis* v *Salmon* [1990] Crim LR 48, the transcript of Auld J's judgment reads:

> The authorities show that the term 'damage' for the purpose of this provision, should be widely interpreted so as to conclude not only permanent or temporary physical harm, but also permanent or temporary impairment of value or usefulness.

This view was endorsed in *R* v *Fiak* [2005] EWCA Crim 2381; in that case the defendant had been arrested and placed in a police cell which he flooded by stuffing a blanket down the cell lavatory and repeatedly flushing. The defendant argued that there was no evidence that the blanket or the cell had been 'damaged'; the water had been clean and both the blanket and the cell could be used again when dry. This argument of course assumes the absence of any possible contamination or infection from the lavatory itself, and the confident expectation that there would be none (how many police cell toilets would this apply to?). The Court of Appeal disagreed and held that, while the effect of the defendant's actions in relation to the blanket and the cell was remediable, the reality was that the blanket could not be used until it had been dried and the flooded cell was out of action until the water had been cleared. Therefore both had sustained damage for the purposes of the Act; answers A, B and D are therefore incorrect.

Crime, para. 1.13.2.2

Answer 13.12

Answer **B** — Section 1(3) of the Criminal Damage Act 1971 states that an offence committed under this section by destroying or damaging property by fire shall be charged as arson. The offence of criminal damage is triable either way, but if the value of the property destroyed or the damage done is less than £5,000, the offence is to be tried summarily (s. 22 of the Magistrates' Courts Act 1980). It follows that if the value of the damage is greater than £5,000, the offence is to be tried on indictment (this figure was previously £2,000).

However, if the damage in such a case was caused by fire (arson), s. 22 of the Magistrates' Courts Act 1980 will not apply, and the case must be tried on indictment and answers A and D are incorrect. This rule will apply even if the fire does not endanger life; therefore answer C is incorrect.

Crime, para. 1.13.2

Answer 13.13

Answer **D** — Simple damage is committed where:

> A person who without lawful excuse destroys or damages any property belonging to another intending to destroy or damage any such property or being reckless as to whether any such property would be destroyed or damaged shall be guilty of an offence (s. 1 of the Criminal Damage Act 1971).

The officer did not intend to damage the property nor was he reckless as to whether the property was damaged or not, there is no indication that there was a likelihood the door handle could be damaged. It was a simple 'accident'.

Not having the relevant *mens rea* means the officer does not need a lawful excuse. Both the excuses relate to damage that was caused deliberately, and in this case that was not so. To use the 'excuses' the person would have to believe that either he was damaging property with consent, or that such consent would have been forthcoming or that he was damaging property to protect other property. As this was not the case answers A, B and C are therefore incorrect.

Crime, paras 1.13.2.6, 1.13.2.7

Answer 13.14

Answer **A** — Section 38 of the Public Order Act 1986 creates two offences. The first involves the contamination of, interference with or placing of goods with the intentions set out at s. 38(1)(a)–(d).

(a) of causing public alarm or anxiety, or

(b) of causing injury to members of the public consuming or using the goods, or

(c) of causing economic loss to any person by reason of the goods being shunned by members of the public, or

(d) of causing economic loss to any person by reason of steps taken to avoid any such alarm or anxiety, injury or loss,

This is a crime of 'specific' intent and the particular intention of the defendant must be proved.

Section 38(2) involves the making of threats to do, *or* the claiming *to have done* any of the acts in s. 38(1), with any of the intentions set out at s. 38(1)(a), (c) or (d). It is difficult to see how a threat or claim made with the intention of causing injury to the public (s. 38(1)(b)) would not also amount to an intention to cause them alarm or anxiety. In this case clearly her intention is to alarm people so much they stop eating meat.

The offence is complete when the threat is issued with the necessary intent, and being a crime of specific intent it does not require any action from the person threatened. It is immaterial that no action has yet been taken, nor that the shop ignored the letter; answers C and D are therefore incorrect.

Under s. 38(3) of the 1986 Act:

It is an offence for a person to be in possession of any of the following articles with a view to the commission of an offence under subsection (1) —

(a) materials to be used for contaminating or interfering with goods or making it appear that goods have been contaminated or interfered with, or

(b) goods which have been contaminated or interfered with, or which appear to have been contaminated or interfered with.

Being in possession of the poison would fit the criteria laid out here, however do the stickers make it appear that goods have been contaminated? The answer is no, so the stickers themselves do not constitute an offence under this section. Had the stickers said 'contaminated meat–danger!' then this would have been enough; answer B is therefore incorrect.

Crime, para. 1.13.8

14 Offences Against the Administration of Justice and Public Interest

STUDY PREPARATION

This chapter tests your knowledge of those offences which exist to deter people from interfering with the proper course of justice. Included in this chapter are questions relating to perjury, false statements, contempt of court and corruption. The common law offence of perverting the course of justice is included, as are the statutory offences of intimidating witnesses and jurors. Particular crimes relating to those who assist offenders by protecting or hiding them are tested, as are those relating to wasting police time — an area that may also come into greater use as pressures on police resources intensify.

QUESTIONS

Question 14.1

SPENCER is giving evidence in court in his own defence. He is not religious and has taken the affirmation instead of swearing on the Bible. The evidence he gives is that he was not at the scene of the offence, stating he was elsewhere. This is in fact untrue and SPENCER knows it.

Has SPENCER committed perjury?

A No, perjury cannot be committed by a defendant.

B No, perjury can only be committed by a 'sworn' witness.

C Yes, provided it is shown he intended to mislead the court.

D Yes, he has given false testimony and knows it to be false.

Question 14.2

BERRY has committed a summary offence. Constable WEST is making inquiries into the whereabouts of BERRY and goes to BERRY's sister's house to see if he is there. BERRY is in fact in the house, and his sister knows he is. BERRY has told her that he committed the offence. Constable WEST asks the sister if she has seen BERRY. She says she hasn't and that he has gone to his cousin's home in Manchester. Having no reason to disbelieve her, the officer leaves, intending to pursue the matter with Greater Manchester Police.

Which of the following statements is true?

A The sister has committed an offence of assisting an offender.

B The sister has committed an offence of harbouring an offender.

C The sister has not committed an offence of assisting an offender.

D The sister has committed no offence.

Question 14.3

HATELEY is giving evidence in Crown Court and is being asked about a particular date when he saw the accused taking pictures of the premises he is accused of robbing. HATELEY tells the court that he saw the male on 5 July; in fact HATELEY cannot remember when he saw the accused exactly. He remembers that he did see him and that is was in early July, however to make himself sound convincing he makes up that it was 5 July, even though he believes that may be untrue. In reality it may well have been 5 July, although there is no way of knowing whether it was or not.

In these circumstances has HATELY committed perjury?

A Yes, he has made a statement he believes not to be true.

B Yes, he has made a statement he knows to be false.

C No, it is not a material fact as it does not relate to the actual committing of the offence.

D No, there is a chance the statement could be true i.e. if it was actually the 5th of July he saw him.

Question 14.4

TORJESON makes a mobile telephone call to his neighbour stating that a child has just fallen into the river and been swept downstream. His neighbour calls the police and a search commences. Several officers are involved, and the force air support unit is called in to assist. Later TORJESON admits he made the incident up as he had received a speeding ticket last week. In total 25 police hours were wasted and the cost came to £21,000.

Which of the following statements is true?

A TORJESON is guilty of wasting police time as the limit of 21 hours has been passed.

B TORJESON is guilty of wasting police time as he falsely raised fears for the safety of a person.

C TORJESON is not guilty of wasting police time as he did not contact the police himself.

D TORJESON is not guilty of wasting police time as the cost did not exceed £25,000.

Question 14.5

MILLIGAN has been sold laminate flooring, which is defective, and has issued a county court claim against ACME Co. Ltd, who supplied the goods. FRANKS is an expert laminate floor fitter and intends to give evidence on MILLIGAN's behalf at court. In order to prevent this, ACME's managing director have written a letter to FRANKS warning him that he will lose business if he gives evidence against the company.

Does this letter amount to intimidation of a witness?

A Yes, provided there was intention to intimidate FRANKS.

B Yes, provided the company were reckless as to whether FRANKS would be intimidated.

C No, as the threat was not made in person.

D No, intimidating witnesses applies only to criminal court cases, not county court cases.

Question 14.6

SUMMERS is an accredited Police Community Support Officer (PCSO) and is dealing with ARTHURS for a fixed penalty offence. He requires ARTHURS to provide his name and address. ARTHURS refuses and SUMMERS exercises his power of detention as provided by sch. 4 to the Police Reform Act 2002. ARTHURS is less than impressed at this, and pushes the PCSO over and makes good his escape.

Consider the offence at common law of escaping. Which of the following is correct?

A ARTHURS has committed this offence; the offence is complete.

B ARTHURS has committed this offence provided he remains at liberty for at least 24 hours.

C ARTHURS has not committed this offence, as it relates to escaping from prisons, etc.

D ARTHURS has not committed this offence, and it relates to lawful custody, i.e. by a police officer.

Question 14.7

CHILCOTT picks up a glass bottle and uses it to assault SCRIVENS. He then runs out of the hotel bar where the assault took place and bumps into a member of the hotel staff, who knows who CHILCOTT is. Thinking he will identify him he tells the member of staff to 'keep your nose out if your missus wants to keep her good looks'. The member of staff is intimidated by this.

Has CHILCOTT committed the offence of intimidating a witness in these circumstances?

A Yes, as he has intimidated a potential witness to an offence.

B Yes, even though a police investigation as such has not commenced.

C No, as he has not directly threatened the potential witness.

D No, as an investigation was not being carried out at the time of the intimidation.

Question 14.8

Constable EVANS has written a statement regarding the arrest of an offender that he witnessed. The officer has stated that he saw the accused in possession of the drugs found on him by his sergeant. In fact the constable did not actually see the accused with the drugs on him, the sergeant told him that he had taken the drugs from him and he believed that to be true. The accused had pleaded guilty and both officers' statements have been read out in court, neither officer was present when this happened.

In relation to this which of the following is correct?

A The constable has committed perjury as he has made a statement which he knows to be false or does not believe to be true.

B The constable has made a false statement in criminal proceedings as he has made a statement which he knows to be false or does not believe to be true.

C The officer has not committed perjury as he made a statement he thought was true, the fact it wasn't is irrelevant.

D The officer has not made a false statement in criminal proceedings as he made a statement he thought was true, the fact it wasn't is irrelevant.

Question 14.9

CLEASE was a witness in a trial at Crown Court. Two days before the trial he was approached by the defendant, ALDUESCUE who pleaded with him to lie in court. When CLEASE refused, ALDUESCUE became aggressive and threatened CLEASE. CLEASE stated that he found the actions of ALDUESCUE to have been intimidating, but that he himself did not feel intimidated, and he went on to give truthful evidence in court.

Has an offence of intimidating a witness been committed contrary to s. 51 of the Criminal Justice and Public Order Act 1994?

A No, as CLEASE went on to give evidence in court.

B No, as CLEASE was not actually intimidated.

C Yes, but only because ALDUESCUE asked CLEASE to lie.

D Yes, as ALDUESCUE has committed an act which intimidates.

Question 14.10

HARKANNIN attended a police station and made an allegation of rape against a taxi driver, whom she stated had driven her home the previous evening. HARKANNIN said that she did not know the identity of the person who raped her and could not describe the taxi or the driver as she had been extremely intoxicated at the time. The police spent the next 2 days investigating the incident, but HARKANNIN later told them that she had made up the story because she had been late going home that night and she had a jealous boyfriend.

Would HARKANNIN's actions amount to an offence against the administration of
justice and public interest in these circumstances?

A No, because a course of justice had not commenced before HARKANNIN made the allegation.

B No, because HARKANNIN did not identify any individual who may have been arrested or inconvenienced by her statement.

C Yes, HARKANNIN's conduct could amount to perverting the course of justice, as there were possible consequences of detention, arrest, charge or prosecution.

D Yes, this could amount to an offence of wasting police time as over 24 hours police time had been used, but it could never be perverting the course of justice.

Question 14.11

LEDERER has been convicted of theft at Crown Court and given a custodial sentence. A private security company is responsible for transporting detainees to the local prison. Whilst en route to the prison BRANDRICK rams the prison van with his Transit van and then overpowers the guards; subsequently he assists LEDERER to escape by unlocking his cell on the prison van.

In relation to the offence of assisting escape contrary to s. 39 of the Prison Act 1952, which of the following is true in respect of BRANDRICK's actions?

A He commits the offence when he rams the prison van with the intention of assisting the escape.

B He commits the offence only where he physically assisted the escape by unlocking the cell.

C He does not commit the offence as it relates only to escape from police or prison transport, not from a private security company.

D He does not commit this offence as it does not relate to prisoners in transit to or from prison.

Question 14.12

OTSUKI is a well known local car thief. Whilst out driving a stolen car he kills a pedestrian, and he is circulated as wanted for an offence of causing death by dangerous driving. OTSUKI asks his friend to help him avoid arrest, telling him there is a warrant for non appearance at court out for him. His friend agrees to hide him for a few days, and does so.

Has there been an offence of assisting an offender in these circumstances?

A Yes, provided the friend's action delayed the arrest of OTSUKI.

B Yes, but only because the offence he is wanted for is indictable.

C No, as the friend did not realise that OTSUKI was wanted for an offence.

D No, as the friend did not directly lie to the police about OTSUKI's whereabouts.

Question 14.13

DALISH has his motorbike stolen and reported it to the police. A short time later he received information that a local youth was riding round on the bike, DALISH went to see the youth. When he attended at the house he saw the motorbike in the front garden, undamaged. The father of the youth who stole the bike offers to give DALISH some free parts for the bike if he doesn't report it to the police and

DALISH accepts the money and only tells the police that he has found his motorbike and it was undamaged.

Has DALISH committed an offence of concealing a relevant offence contrary to s. 5 of the Criminal Law Act 1967?

A Yes, as he has agreed to accept money for his silence.

B Yes, as he has agreed to accept money for his silence which goes beyond reasonable compensation.

C No, as the agreement he reached was not with the person who stole the motorbike

D No, as free parts for the bike would be seen as reasonable consideration.

ANSWERS

Answer 14.1

Answer **D** — Section 1(1) of the Perjury Act 1911 states:

> If any person lawfully sworn as a witness or as an interpreter in a judicial proceeding wilfully makes a statement material in that proceeding, which he knows to be false or does not believe to be true, he shall be guilty of perjury...

'Any person' includes the defendant and therefore answer A is incorrect. There is no requirement to show intention to mislead the court; simply making the statement deliberately is enough, and therefore answer C is incorrect. It is possible for a witness or interpreter to make a solemn affirmation in place of the oath, whether or not the taking of an oath would be contrary to his or her religious beliefs, and s. 15(2) of the Perjury Act 1911 provides that references therein to 'oaths' and 'swearing' embrace affirmations. The affirming witness is therefore equally subject to the Perjury Act 1911 and answer B is also incorrect.

Crime, para. 1.14.2

Answer 14.2

Answer **C** — The offence of assisting offenders applies only where a relevant offence has been committed. A 'relevant offence' means —

(a) an offence for which the sentence is fixed by law,

(b) an offence for which a person of 18 years or over (not previously convicted) may be sentenced to imprisonment for a term of five years (or might be so sentenced but for the restrictions imposed by section 33 of the Magistrates' Courts Act 1980).

The offence committed here is summary only and therefore answer A is incorrect.

The Serious Organised Crime and Police Act 2005, sch. 7, part 3 contains amendments consequential on the repeal of the definitions and concepts of an 'arrestable offence' and a 'serious arrestable offence'. In general, this will mean that police powers which were available in cases involving 'serious arrestable offences' and 'arrestable offences' will now only be available in cases involving indictable only or triable either way offences.

Harbouring offenders applies to people who have escaped from a prison or other institutions, and therefore answer B is incorrect. The sister has almost certainly committed an offence of perverting the course of public justice and, arguably, wasting police time, under s. 5(2) of the Criminal Law Act 1967; answer D is therefore incorrect.

Crime, paras 1.14.7, 1.14.9

Answer 14.3

Answer **A** — Section 1 of the Perjury Act 1911 states:

(1) If any person lawfully sworn as a witness or as an interpreter in a judicial proceeding wilfully makes a statement material in that proceeding, which he knows to be false or does not believe to be true, he shall be guilty of perjury...

(2) The expression 'judicial proceeding' includes a proceeding before any court, tribunal, or person having by law power to hear, receive, and examine evidence on oath.

(3) Where a statement made for the purposes of a judicial proceeding is not made before the tribunal itself, but is made on oath before a person authorised by law to administer an oath to the person who makes the statement, and to record or authenticate the statement, it shall, for the purposes of this section, be treated as having been made in a judicial proceeding.

On a literal interpretation of section 1 of the Perjury Act 1911, it would seem that a person could be convicted of perjury as a result of a statement which he did not believe to be true, but which was in fact true after all; answer D is therefore incorrect. After all it does not allude to the fact that the statement actually does have to be false!

However in this scenario HATELY does not believe the statement to be false, only that it may not be true, answer B is therefore incorrect.

A 'statement material in that proceeding' means that the content of the evidence tendered in that case must have some importance to it and not just be of passing relevance. Clearly being caught photographing a premises prior to robbing it will be of more than just 'passing relevance'; answer C is therefore incorrect.

Crime, para. 1.14.2

Answer 14.4

Answer **B** — The definition of this offence (Criminal Law Act 1967, s. 5(2)) includes the phrase 'making to any person a false report' and therefore answer C is incorrect. Contrary to popular belief, there is no time limit for this offence, and answer A is also incorrect. Likewise, there is no monetary value placed on this offence and therefore answer D is incorrect.

Crime, para. 1.14.10

Answer 14.5

Answer **A** — Section 39 of the Criminal Justice and Police Act 2001 extended the offences of intimidation of witness offences outlined in s. 51 of the Criminal Justice and Public Order Act 1994 to proceedings in civil cases. The 1994 Act applies to the investigation or trial of those in criminal proceedings. Answer D is therefore incorrect. The new offence is very similar to the 1994 Act offence and is an offence of specific intent, so recklessness will not suffice (answer B is therefore incorrect). The offence includes doing any act, provided it was with the intention of intimidating a witness and provided the defendant knew the person might be a witness. This would include writing letters, making phone calls, etc., and is not limited to personal threats (answer C is also incorrect).

Crime, para. 1.14.5.2

Answer 14.6

Answer **A** — This offence applies to persons in lawful custody, anywhere. It is not restricted to custody units, prison, etc. Answer C is therefore incorrect. Whether a person is 'in custody' or not is a question of fact and the word 'custody' is to be given its ordinary meaning (*E* v *DPP* [2002] Crime LR 737). This could be shown by providing evidence that the person's liberty was restricted (as it is in the question), and that it was lawful (sch. 4 to the 2002 Act provides this). This custody is not restricted to sworn police officers and would include police community support officers (PCSOs), Investigating Officers or Escort Officers (who are given powers by the 2002 Act); answer D is therefore incorrect. The offence of escaping is completed immediately that liberty is obtained and is not subject to time restrictions on such liberty; therefore, answer B is incorrect.

Crime, para. 1.14.9

Answer 14.7

Answer **D** — The offence under s. 51 of the Criminal Justice and Public Order Act 1994 is designed to protect witnesses, jurors and others involved in the judicial process. It includes threats to a person other than the victim; answer C is therefore incorrect.

This is an offence of 'specific intent' or perhaps even multiple intent as it must be shown that the act was done with the intentions set out in s. 51(1)(a) and (c). It must also be shown that the defendant knew or believed the other person to be assisting in the investigation of an offence or that he or she was going to testify/appear on the jury in proceedings for an offence.

In this scenario CHILCOTT believed that the member of staff would identify him, and as such would be a witness in court against him, however the prosecution must present evidence that an investigation was in fact being carried out at the time of the alleged offence (*R* v *Singh* [2000] 1 Cr App R 31). It was not, so CHILCOTT cannot have committed this offence (a criminal attempt may however be committed on the basis of a mistaken belief); answers A and B are therefore incorrect.

Crime, para. 1.14.5.1

Answer 14.8

Answer **D** — Perjury is committed by persons giving evidence that is false or they do not believe it to be true when sworn as witnesses at court; making a false statement relates to a written statement being tendered in evidence (the bit at the top of an MG11). In this scenario perjury could never be committed as neither officer was a sworn witness; answers A and C are therefore incorrect.

Like perjury making a false statement in criminal proceedings contrary to s. 89 of the Criminal Justice Act 1967 is concerned with someone who wilfully makes a statement material in those proceedings which he knows to be false or does not believe to be true. In the scenario the officer makes a statement he believes to be true, and that is the important factor, his belief. The fact he is incorrect is immaterial, had he not believed the sergeant and still made the statement however he would have been liable; answer B is therefore incorrect.

Crime, para. 1.14.3

Answer 14.9

Answer **D** — Section 51 of the Criminal Justice and Public Order Act 1994 states:

(1) A person commits an offence if —

(a) he does an act which intimidates, and is intended to intimidate, another person ('the victim')...

In a decision that seems to contradict the specific wording above the Court of Appeal held, *inter alia*, that intimidation does not have to be successful, in that the victim does not actually have to be deterred from giving evidence or put in fear. Answers A and B are therefore incorrect. Whilst it will be material evidence if the victim was neither deterred from giving evidence nor put in fear, a person may intimidate another person without the victim being intimidated (*R v Patrascu* [2004] EWCA Crim 2417). Note that this section extends well beyond simply asking a person to lie, and can include other ways of obstructing justice through witness intimidation. Answer C is therefore incorrect.

Crime, para. 1.14.5.1

Answer 14.10

Answer **C** — It is an offence at common law to do an act tending and intended to pervert the course of public justice. 'The course of public justice' includes the process of criminal investigation (see *R v Rowell* (1977) 65 Cr App R 174) — it is not necessary that an investigation has commenced *before* the person makes a false complaint, such as the one above. Answer A is therefore incorrect.

The conduct referred to in the scenario *may* amount to an offence of wasting police time (contrary to s. 5 of the Criminal Law Act 1967), although contrary to popular belief there is no minimum number of hours which must be wasted before a prosecution can be brought for this offence. However it has also been held to amount to perverting the course of justice (see *R v Goodwin* (1989) 11 Cr App R (S) 194, where a false allegation of rape was made to the police). Answer D is therefore incorrect.

Where a person makes a false allegation to the police justifying a criminal investigation with the possible consequences of detention, arrest, charge or prosecution, and that person intends that the allegation be taken seriously, the offence of perverting the course of justice is *prima facie* made out. This will be the case *whether or not the allegation is capable of identifying specific individuals*, (see *R v Cotter* [2002] 2 Cr App R 29, a case involving the boyfriend of a well-known black Olympic athlete who falsely claimed to have been attacked as part of a racist campaign). Answer B is therefore incorrect.

Crime, para. 1.14.4

Answer 14.11

Answer **D** — Section 39 of the Prison Act 1952 states:

Any person who aids any prisoner in escaping or attempting to escape from a prison or who, with intent to facilitate the escape of any prisoner, sends anything (by post or otherwise) into a prison or to a prisoner or places any thing anywhere outside a prison with a view to its coming into the possession of a prisoner, shall be guilty of [an offence].

The wording of the section seems to indicate that it only relates to 'escaping' from a prison, and this was verified by the Court of Appeal in *R v Moss and Harte* (1986) 82 Cr App R 116 where it was held that the offence under s. 39 of the 1952 Act does not apply to a prisoner who escapes while in transit to or from prison; answers A, B and C are therefore incorrect.

Crime, para. 1.14.9

Answer 14.12

Answer **C** — For there to be an offence under s. 4 of the Criminal Law Act 1967 (assisting offenders) there must first have been a relevant offence committed by someone. That relevant offence must, in the case of the above offence, have been committed by the 'assisted' person, in this case causing death by dangerous driving.

The defendant can commit the offence before the person he or she has assisted is convicted of committing the relevant offence.

It must be shown that the defendant knew or believed the person to be guilty of that, *or some other* relevant offence. Therefore, if the defendant believed that the 'assisted' person had committed a robbery when in fact he or she had committed a theft, that mistaken part of the defendant's belief will not prevent a conviction for this offence. The relevant offences are:

(a) an offence for which the sentence is fixed by law,
(b) an offence for which a person of 18 years or over (not previously convicted) may be sentenced to imprisonment for a term of five years (or might be so sentenced but for the restrictions imposed by section 33 of the Magistrates' Courts Act 1980).

As the friend believed the 'assisted' person is only guilty of failing to appear in court, and this is not a relevant offence, then they do not commit an offence contrary to s. 4 of the 1967 Act., also note that relevant offence has a broader meaning than indictable offence; answers A and B are therefore incorrect.

This offence must involve some positive act by the defendant; simply doing or saying nothing will not suffice. In this case the positive act of hiding the accused would be enough; answer D is therefore incorrect.

Crime, para. 1.14.7

Answer 14.13

Answer **B** — Section 5 of the Criminal Law Act 1967 states:

(1) Where a person has committed a relevant offence, any other person who, knowing or believing that the offence or some other relevant offence has been committed, and that he has information which might be of material assistance in securing the prosecution or conviction of an offender for it, accepts or agrees to accept for not disclosing that information any consideration other than the making good of loss or injury caused by the offence, or the making of reasonable compensation for that loss or injury, shall be liable...

The main focus of this offence is:

- the acceptance of, or agreement to accept 'consideration' (i.e. anything of value);
- beyond reasonable compensation for loss/injury caused by the relevant offence;
- in exchange for not disclosing material information.

In this scenario all 3 points are present so the offence is complete.

The legislation does not state that the agreement has to be with the person who committed the offence, only that one was committed; answer C is therefore incorrect. Had any part on the motorbike been broken or damaged, then the replacement part may well have been reasonable compensation, however as this is not the case answer D is therefore incorrect.

There has to be more than just an agreement of silence for the 'consideration', it must go beyond any consideration other than the making good of loss or injury caused by the offence, or the making of reasonable compensation for that loss or injury; answer A is therefore incorrect.

Crime, para. 1.14.8

15 Offences Arising from Immigration, Asylum and People Exploitation

STUDY PREPARATION

This chapter deals with one of the most contentious policing issues of modern times, that of illegal entry to the United Kingdom. The events of 11 September 2001 prompted swift and considerable changes to immigration offences throughout the world. Immigration, asylum and exploitation of people has become an increasingly significant area of criminal activity in Wales and England, and central government has been swift to react with legislative changes to deal with the escalating problem. The unlawful exploitation of vulnerable people has, as it should be, been a priority; legislation dealing with that is tested here.

QUESTIONS

Question 15.1

HASSANI is originally from Pakistan, but is now a British citizen. His brother (who is not a British citizen) wishes to come to Britain on a permanent basis, but has falsely filled out an entry application stating he is coming on holiday. HASSANI has signed this form to say that his brother will stay with him on holiday for two weeks. HASSANI knows this to be false.

Who, if either, commits an offence under s. 24A of the Immigration Act 1971?

A The offence only applies to British citizens, so only HASSANI commits it.

B Both HASSANI and his brother, as the offender's nationality is of no relevance.

C The offence is aimed specifically at non-British citizens, so the offence is committed only by the brother.

D Neither, this offence applies only to applications for citizenship.

Question 15.2

It is an offence under s. 36 of the Criminal Justice Act 1925 to make an untrue statement to procure a passport.

In relation to this offence, which of the following is true in relation to the person making that statement?

A That he makes the statement believing it not to be true.

B That he makes the statement knowing or believing it not to be true.

C That he makes the statement and is reckless as to whether it is true or not.

D That the statement is to his knowledge untrue.

Question 15.3

Under s. 2 of the Asylum and Immigration (Treatment of Claimants etc.) Act 2004, a person will commit an offence if, when at a leave or asylum interview, he or she does not have with him or her a passport or other document establishing his or her nationality or citizenship. Section 2(3) of the Act provides a time period, during which a person may produce the passport or document, to avoid prosecution for the offence.

In relation to this period, when must the passport or document be produced?

A Within 3 days to the Secretary of State.

B Within 3 days to an immigration officer or to the Secretary of State.

C Within 7 days to the Secretary of State.

D Within 7 days to an immigration officer or to the Secretary of State.

Question 15.4

ELBEGDORJ owns a warehouse which processes fresh fish and shellfish. The product is caught locally and then sold on to small businesses in a local coastal town. ELBEGDORJ has formed a relationship with SOWDEN, who supplies workers to the warehouse during the summer months, when business increases due to tourism. ELBEGDORJ is aware that SOWDEN does not have a licence to procure the workers' services, but being grateful for the extra help, asks no questions.

ELBEGDORJ pays the workers a minimum wage, but does not pay MOORE for supplying them.

Would ELBEGDORJ be guilty of an offence under the Gangmasters (Licensing) Act 2004?

A No, because the workers are not gathering produce.

B No, only MOORE commits an offence, by supplying the workers.

C No, because the workers are paid for their services.

D Yes, ELBEGDORJ commits an offence by entering into an arrangement with MOORE.

Question 15.5

The Gangmasters (Licensing) Act 2004 regulates certain aspects of unlawful exploitation of vulnerable groups of people within England and Wales, in relation to work that they are expected to do.

Which of the below is *specifically* listed in the definition of 'work', contained in s. 3 of the Act?

A Working in restaurants or takeaways.

B Prostitution.

C Agricultural work.

D Manual labour on building sites, etc.

Question 15.6

It is an offence under s. 4 of the Asylum and Immigration (Treatment of Claimants etc.) Act 2004 to traffic people for exploitation.

The definition of exploitation can be found in s. 4(4) of the Act. Which of the following is *specifically* listed in the definition?

A Exploiting a person for the purposes of organ transplants.

B Exploiting a person for the purpose of prostitution.

C Exploiting a person for the purpose of enforced marriage.

D Exploiting a person for the purpose of child pornography.

Question 15.7

UREN is a transport manager for a haulage company, which operates in the UK and Europe. UREN is aware that several of his drivers transport illegal immigrants into the UK. However, because his role includes allocating workloads, he is often asked by drivers to swap routes at the last minute. UREN suspects that the drivers request these changes to allow them to pick up people, but he turns a blind eye and generally accedes to their requests. UREN is not involved in any of the arrangements, but he believes that most of the people transported may be exploited by being used as cheap labour.

Would UREN be guilty of an offence under s. 4 of the Asylum and Immigration (Treatment of Claimants etc.) Act 2004 (trafficking people for exploitation)?

A Yes, but only if it can be shown that he holds more than a mere belief that the people will be exploited.

B No, because he does not arrange to transport the people.

C Yes, he would be guilty of the offence in these circumstances alone.

D No, because he is not directly involved in the exploitation of people.

Question 15.8

ALBERTS and SMYTHE were both British citizens and were taking an extended holiday in Spain, staying on SMYTHE's yacht. ALBERTS met and fell in love with ALLONSO, a Spanish citizen, and they decided they could not be apart when ALBERTS was due to return to Britain. ALLONSO was deported from the UK some 2 years previously but has not told either ALBERTS or SMYTHE and she persuades ALBERTS to take her back to the UK on the yacht and thereby avoid immigration. ALBERTS believes that as ALLONSO is an EU member state national there would be no problem in ALLONSO arriving in this manner, and SMYTHE agrees to the use of his yacht for this purpose. ALBERTS unfortunately does not have good sea legs and has to fly back to the UK. SMYTHE and ALLONSO arrive at Brixham in Devon on the yacht and are met there by ALBERTS after they had disembarked from the yacht.

Which of the following statements is correct, in respect of the offence of assisting entry to the United Kingdom in breach of a deportation order contrary to s. 25B of the Immigration Act 1971?

A Only SMYTHE commits the offence, as the person who actually brought ALLONSO into the country.

B Only ALBERTS commits the offence, as it was his scheme to bring ALLONSO to the UK by this method.

C Both ALBERTS and SMYTHE commit the offence as they colluded together to assist ALLONSO's arrival.

D Neither ALBERTS nor SMYTHE commit the offence in these circumstances.

Question 15.9

SHIRAZI is an Iraqi national who wishes to enter Britain, and gets as far as France. There he meets other persons who also wish to gain illegal entry into Britain. SHIRAZI is introduced to DOWLING, a French national, who agrees to help SHIRAZI and gives him a false passport and arranges for him to be smuggled in, in the back of a lorry.

Considering the offence of assisting unlawful immigration to member states (contrary to s. 25 of the Immigration Act 1971), which of the following is correct?

A DOWLING commits the offence only because he gave SHIRAZI a false passport.

B DOWLING commits the offence when he gives SHIRAZI a false passport, and also when he arranges transportation.

C DOWLING does not commit the offence because he was outside the United Kingdom when he helped SHIRAZI.

D DOWLING does not commit the offence because he himself is not a British citizen.

Question 15.10

OSTANI is an asylum seeker and has been issued with a registration card by the Secretary of State. OSTANI notices after a few weeks that his date of birth on the card is incorrect. Not wishing to make a fuss he changes the last number of his date of birth himself.

Has OSTANI committed an offence of misuse of a registration card contrary to s. 26A of the Immigration Act 1971?

A Yes, it is an offence to alter any detail contained on a registration card.

B Yes, although the holder can amend some details it is an offence to alter any personal details on a registration card.

C No, there was no intention to deceive and this is required for the offence to be committed.

D No, as the change was merely as the result of a mistake by the card issuer no offence is committed.

Question 15.11

TIMPKINS is thinking of setting up a company to assist asylum seekers to enter the UK. For this service they intend charging a small fee to cover their administration costs. He is concerned that they do not commit an offence contrary to s. 25A of the Immigration Act 1971.

How can he ensure the company will not be caught by the above legislation?

A It is automatically exempt as such companies are not restricted.

B It must register with the National Immigration Service as a service provider.

C It must make no charge for the service it provides.

D It will be caught by the legislation as assisting asylum seekers is illegal.

ANSWERS

Answer 15.1

Answer **C** — Section 24A of the Immigration Act 1971 is aimed at the actions of non-British citizens only, so as a British citizen, HASSANI can never commit this offence (answers A and B are incorrect). It applies to any application to obtain or seek to obtain leave to enter the UK in any circumstances, including holidays, and therefore answer D is incorrect. HASSANI's brother commits the offence as he uses means which include deception to achieve his leave to enter.

Crime, para. 1.15.2.4

Answer 15.2

Answer **D** — The offence is made out where the person who makes the statement does so in the knowledge that it is untrue. His beliefs and actions in relation to checking the veracity of the statement are of no consequence. What is important is that he knows the statement he made is untrue. Answers A, B and C are therefore incorrect.

Crime, para. 1.15.5

Answer 15.3

Answer **B** — The passport or document must be provided to an immigration officer or to the Secretary of State within a period of *3* days, beginning with the date of that interview. Answers A, C and D are therefore incorrect.

Crime, para. 1.15.5

Answer 15.4

Answer **D** — An unlicensed gangmaster is a person who illegally supplies people to conduct the work listed in s. 3 of the Gangmasters (Licensing) Act 2004. The work listed in this section is essentially agricultural work, gathering shellfish *and includes* processing or packaging any produce derived from agricultural work, shellfish, fish or products derived from shellfish or fish. Answer A is therefore incorrect.

Section 6 of the Act makes provision for licences to be issued by the Gangmasters Licensing Authority (GLA) to suitable persons. It is an offence to act as a gangmaster without a licence (see s. 12(1)). It is a further summary offence to enter into an arrangement with a gangmaster where, in supplying the workers or services, the gangmaster contravenes s. 6 (s. 13(1)). Answer B is therefore incorrect. Lastly, it is irrelevant that the workers were paid for their services — the offence is complete when ELBEGDORJ enters into an arrangement with MOORE. Answer C is therefore incorrect.

Crime, para. 1.15.3.4

Answer 15.5

Answer **C** — The deaths of 23 illegal immigrants in Morecambe Bay in February 2004 drew attention to unlawful exploitation of vulnerable groups of people within England and Wales. On that occasion, the illegal workers were gathering shellfish. The definition of a gangmaster is very wide. In summary a gangmaster is a person who supplies a worker to do work to which the 2004 Act applies for another person (s. 3 of the Gangmasters (Licensing) Act 2004). The work listed in this section is essentially agricultural work, gathering shellfish and includes processing or packaging any produce derived from agricultural work, shellfish, fish or products derived from shellfish or fish. Answers A, B and D are therefore incorrect.

Crime, para. 1.15.3.4

Answer 15.6

Answer **A** — The definition of exploitation under s. 4(4) is fairly wide and includes where a person is:

- a victim of behaviour that contravenes Article 4 of the European Convention on Human Rights (slavery and forced labour);
- encouraged, required or expected to do anything as a result of which they (or another person) would commit an offence under the Human Organ Transplants Act 1989;
- subjected to force, threats or deception designed to induce them to provide services, provide another person with benefits or enable another person to acquire benefits of any kind;
- requested or induced to undertake *any activity* having been chosen on the grounds they are mentally or physically ill or disabled, young or have a family relationship with a person and a person without the illness, disability, youth or family relationship would be likely to refuse the request or resist the inducement.

Of the choices in this question, only exploiting a person for the purposes of organ transplants appears specifically in the list. Therefore answers B, C and D are incorrect. However, any of the other scenarios may fall within the offence, depending on the circumstances.

Crime, para. 1.15.3.3

Answer 15.7

Answer **C** — An offence is committed under s. 4(1) of the Asylum and Immigration (Treatment of Claimants etc.) Act 2004, when a person arranges *or* facilitates the arrival in the UK of an individual (the 'passenger'). The dictionary definition of 'facilitate' includes to 'smooth the progress of', 'make easy', or 'make possible'. Even though UREN is not directly involved in the arrangements, he could certainly be accused of facilitating the arrival of the passengers. Answer B is therefore incorrect.

Section 4(1) continues that the person will be guilty of the offence, if he or she:

(a) intends to exploit the passenger in the UK or elsewhere, or
(b) believes another person is likely to exploit the passenger in the UK or elsewhere.

Therefore, even though UREN is not directly involved in the exploitation of the passengers, he commits the offence because of his belief that they will be exploited (and answer D is incorrect). Answer A is incorrect because the prosecution would have to show a *belief* by the accused and no more. The definition of 'exploitation' under s. 4(4) includes where a person is victim of Art. 4 of the Human Rights Convention — slavery and forced labour.

It should be noted that there are further offences contained in s. 4, namely, arranging or facilitating the travel within the UK of a passenger, with the same intent (s. 4(2)), and arranging or facilitating the *departure* from UK of above person with the same intent (s. 4(3)).

Crime, para. 1.15.3.3

Answer 15.8

Answer **D** — An offence of assisting entry to the United Kingdom in breach of a deportation order contrary to the Immigration Act 1971, s. 25B is committed *inter alia* where the defendant does an act which assists the individual to arrive in, enter or remain in the United Kingdom, and that person is subject to a deportation order.

The defendant must have known or had reasonable cause for believing that their act facilitated assisting the entry in breach of that deportation order, therefore they must have known/had reasonable cause to believe that there was such an order in existence. As in the scenario neither man knew of the deportation order they commit no offence; answers A, B and C are therefore incorrect.

It should be noted that ALLONSO, however, may be guilty of an offence under s. 24(1)(a) of the 1971 Act, of being a person who is not a British citizen who knowingly enters the UK in breach of a deportation order or without leave.

Crime, para. 1.15.3.1

Answer 15.9

Answer **D** — Section 25 of the Immigration Act 1971 is a very broadly worded offence, which requires that the defendant facilitated the commission of any breach of immigration law by someone who is not an EU citizen. This would include actions clearly facilitating the entry, such as furnishing the person with a false passport, but also less apparent help, such as organising transport into the UK; answer A is therefore incorrect.

Although this offence can be committed outside the United Kingdom, it can only be committed by British citizens and others with relevant forms of British citizenship. As DOWLING is not a British citizen he will not commit this offence; answers A, B and C are therefore incorrect.

Hands up all those who missed where it said that he was a French national!

Crime, para. 1.15.3.1

Answer 15.10

Answer **C** — Section 26A of the Immigration Act 1971 states:

(3) A person commits an offence if he —
   (a) makes a false registration card,
   (b) alters a registration card with intent to deceive or to enable another to deceive
   . . .

A registration card here is a document which:

- carries information about a person (whether or not wholly or partly electronically); and
- is issued by the Secretary of State to the person wholly or partly in connection with a claim for asylum (whether or not made by that person) (s. 26A(1)).

These offences require different degrees of intent and the wording of each needs to be considered carefully and they are similar to the more general offences of forgery. In this scenario although he altered the card there was no intent to deceive or to enable another to deceive and therefore there is no offence; answers A, B and D are therefore incorrect.

Crime, para. 1.15.4

Answer 15.11

Answer **C** — Section 25A of the Immigration Act 1971 states:

(1) A person commits an offence if —
  (a) he knowingly and for gain facilitates the arrival in the United Kingdom of an individual, and
  (b) he knows or has reasonable cause to believe that the individual is an asylum-seeker.

In order to prove this particular offence it must be shown that the defendant acted in the knowledge that he or she was facilitating the arrival in the United Kingdom of a person whom he or she knew was (or had reasonable cause to believe to be) an asylum-seeker *and* that, in so doing, he or she acted 'for gain'.

'Asylum-seeker' means a person who intends to claim that to remove him or her from, or require him or her to leave, the United Kingdom would be contrary to the United Kingdom's obligations under the Refugee Convention or the Human Rights Convention (in each case as defined under s. 167(1) of the Immigration and Asylum Act 1999) (s. 25 A(2)).

The above offence does not apply to anything done by a person acting on behalf of an organisation which aims to assist asylum-seekers and *does not charge for its services* (s. 25A(3)).

So a company can set up to help asylum-seekers, and they will not commit an offence provided they do not charge for the service. They need not register either with NIS; answers A, B and D are therefore incorrect.

Crime, para. 1.15.3.1

Question Checklist

The checklist below is designed to help you keep track of your progress when answering the multiple-choice questions. If you fill this in after one attempt at each question, you will be able to check how many you have got right and which questions you need to revisit a second time. Also available on-line, to download visit: www.blackstonespolicemanuals.com.

	First attempt Correct (✓)	Second attempt Correct (✓)
1 State of Mind		
1.1		
1.2		
1.3		
1.4		
1.5		
1.6		
1.7		
1.8		
1.9		
2 Criminal Conduct		
2.1		
2.2		
2.3		
2.4		
2.5		
2.6		
2.7		
2.8		
2.9		
2.10		
2.11		

	First attempt Correct (✓)	Second attempt Correct (✓)
2.12		
2.13		
3 Incomplete Offences and Police Investigations		
3.1		
3.2		
3.3		
3.4		
3.5		
3.6		
3.7		
3.8		
3.9		
3.10		
3.11		
3.12		
3.13		
4 General Defences		
4.1		
4.2		
4.3		
4.4		

	First attempt Correct (✓)	Second attempt Correct (✓)
4.5		
4.6		
4.7		
4.8		
4.9		
4.10		
4.11		
4.12		
4.13		
4.14		
4.15		

5 Homicide

5.1		
5.2		
5.3		
5.4		
5.5		
5.6		
5.7		
5.8		
5.9		
5.10		
5.11		
5.12		

6 Misuse of Drugs

6.1		
6.2		
6.3		
6.4		
6.5		
6.6		
6.7		
6.8		
6.9		
6.10		
6.11		
6.12		
6.13		

	First attempt Correct (✓)	Second attempt Correct (✓)
6.14		
6.15		
6.16		
6.17		
6.18		
6.19		

7 Offences Against the Person

7.1		
7.2		
7.3		
7.4		
7.5		
7.6		
7.7		
7.8		
7.9		
7.10		
7.11		
7.12		
7.13		
7.14		
7.15		
7.16		
7.17		

8 Miscellaneous Offences Against the Person

8.1		
8.2		
8.3		
8.4		
8.5		
8.6		

9 Sexual Offences

9.1		
9.2		
9.3		
9.4		
9.5		

	First attempt Correct (✓)	Second attempt Correct (✓)
9.6		
9.7		
9.8		
9.9		
9.10		
9.11		
9.12		
9.13		
9.14		
9.15		
9.16		
9.17		
9.18		
9.19		
9.20		
9.21		
9.22		
9.23		
9.24		
9.25		
9.26		
9.27		
9.28		
9.29		
9.30		
9.31		
9.32		

10 Child Protection

	First attempt Correct (✓)	Second attempt Correct (✓)
10.1		
10.2		
10.3		
10.4		
10.5		
10.6		
10.7		
10.8		
10.9		
10.10		
10.11		

	First attempt Correct (✓)	Second attempt Correct (✓)
10.12		
10.13		

11 Theft and Related Offences

	First attempt Correct (✓)	Second attempt Correct (✓)
11.1		
11.2		
11.3		
11.4		
11.5		
11.6		
11.7		
11.8		
11.9		
11.10		
11.11		
11.12		
11.13		
11.14		
11.15		
11.16		
11.17		
11.18		
11.19		
11.20		
11.21		

12 Fraud

	First attempt Correct (✓)	Second attempt Correct (✓)
12.1		
12.2		
12.3		
12.4		
12.5		
12.6		
12.7		
12.8		
12.9		
12.10		
12.11		
12.12		

	First attempt Correct (✓)	Second attempt Correct (✓)
13 Criminal Damage		
13.1		
13.2		
13.3		
13.4		
13.5		
13.6		
13.7		
13.8		
13.9		
13.10		
13.11		
13.12		
13.13		
13.14		
14 Offences Against the Administration of Justice and Public Interest		
14.1		
14.2		
14.3		
14.4		
14.5		

	First attempt Correct (✓)	Second attempt Correct (✓)
14.6		
14.7		
14.8		
14.9		
14.10		
14.11		
14.12		
14.13		
15 Offences Arising from Immigration, Asylum and People Exploitation		
15.1		
15.2		
15.3		
15.4		
15.5		
15.6		
15.7		
15.8		
15.9		
15.10		
15.11		

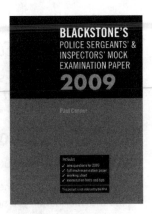